HOW TO RETIRE RICH

ALSO BY JAMES O'SHAUGHNESSY

What Works on Wall Street

Invest Like the Best

HOW TO

RETIRE

RICH

TIME-TESTED STRATEGIES
TO BEAT THE MARKET
AND RETIRE IN STYLE

JAMES O'SHAUGHNESSY

BROADWAY BOOKS • NEW YORK

BROADWAY

A hardcover edition of this book was published in 1998 by Broadway Books.

HOW TO RETIRE RICH. Copyright © 1998 by James O'Shaughnessy. All rights reserved. Printed in the United States of America. No part of this book may be reproduced or transmitted in any form or by any means, electronic or mechanical, including photocopying, recording, or by any information storage and retrieval system, without written permission from the publisher. For information, address Broadway Books, a division of Bantam Doubleday Dell Publishing Group, Inc., 1540 Broadway, New York, NY 10036.

Broadway Books titles may be purchased for business or promotional use or for special sales. For information, please write to: Special Markets Department, Bantam Doubleday Dell Publishing Group, Inc., 1540 Broadway, New York, NY 10036.

BROADWAY BOOKS and its logo, a letter B bisected on the diagonal, are trademarks of Broadway Books, a division of Bantam Doubleday Dell Publishing Group, Inc.

First trade paperback edition published 1999.

Designed by Debbie Glasserman

The Library of Congress has catalogued the hardcover edition as:
O'Shaughnessy, James P.
How to retire rich : time-tested strategies to beat the market and retire in style / by James O'Shaughnessy.
p.   cm.
Includes index.
ISBN 0-7679-0072-3 (hardcover)
1. Retirement income—United States—Planning.   2. Finance, Personal—United States—Planning.   3. Individual retirement accounts—United States.   4. Saving and investment—United States.
5. Mutual funds—United States.   I. Title.
HD7125.08   1998
332.024′01—dc21   97-28937
CIP

ISBN 0-7679-0073-1

99   00   01   02   03   10   9   8   7   6   5   4   3   2   1

For Melissa, my love

CONTENTS

ACKNOWLEDGMENTS

This is my third book, and I find that with each book I write, more and more people contribute to the endeavor. I had been thinking about the savings crisis in this country for several months before my agent, Wesley Neff, convinced me to write a book addressing the subject. Wes has been extremely supportive, and I owe him much gratitude for his help and friendship. Thanks also to the fine people at Broadway Books, from publisher Bill Shinker to my editor Suzanne Oaks. Everyone pitched in with great spirit and enthusiasm, and I'm truly impressed by their organization.

I also owe everyone at O'Shaughnessy Capital Management many thanks for their support and advice. Dan Kraninger was very helpful with every aspect of the book, and assisted me in fleshing out the mutual fund chapter while driving between speeches in Florida. Chris Loveless and Scott Stickler were great resources as well. I'm grateful for Chris's expertise on 401(k) plans and for Scott's advice on on-line brokers and the mechanics of trading. Thanks also to Cheryl Clifford, Jennifer Donofrio, and Susan Turturino, who, in addition to always being there to chat with me when I suffered writer's block, were very helpful in describing their vision of what a rich retirement means.

Yet I really owe the greatest gratitude to my wife, Melissa. In addition to loving her dearly, I relied on her extensively while writing this book. It would never have been completed without her unbelievable effort. While serving as my primary editor, she was really my coauthor. From beginning to end, she assisted me with every aspect of the project, editing every line in the book and helping me rephrase my ideas so that they were easier to grasp. She threw her heart and soul into making sure that the finished work was clear, concise, and meaningful. Missy spent weekends and countless late night hours pouring over each page of the manuscript, invariably making it better. As Mark Twain said, "The difference between the *almost* right word and the *right* word is really a large matter—it's the difference between the lightning bug and the lightning." Missy changed my lightning bugs into lightning, and for this I am forever grateful.

CHAPTER ONE

WHAT IS RICH?

What is rich? Many people fantasize about the lifestyles of celebrities and moguls—about what it must be like to live in a mansion, travel in a private airplane, and have other people pay your bills, walk your dog, or take care of your children. For most of us, however, that notion of rich is pure fantasy and not even the kind of life we strive for.

So, then, for most of us, what really is *rich?* Some might argue that rich is an absolute sum—say, $2 million, or $8 million, or $20 million. The number is different for everybody. I might envy my neighbor who drives a shiny new Mercedes, yet he might be envious of that beautiful house down the street that he drives by every day but could never afford.

For most people, being rich means never having to worry about money. It means living comfortably, getting the children through college, and helping them out with a down payment on a car or house. It means not worrying about where the next paycheck is coming from or how to pay for that gift for a dear friend or new granddaughter. For most people, to be truly rich is to be financially unconstrained and to have the ability to live life in a manner that suits you when it suits them.

What we perceive as rich will naturally change over the course of our lives. Someone who is 32 years old most likely has a very different idea about what rich means than a person who is 55.

At 32, rich might mean paying off all those college loans and credit card balances and having enough left to put a down payment on a new home. At 55, rich might mean having the time and money to golf, travel, and know that a comfortable retirement is not far off.

Some of us want to pass money on to our heirs, while others prefer to give our money away while we're still alive. For some, living in a modest, rented condominium but having the freedom to go anywhere in the world at a moment's notice is truly rich. Others want a beautiful home and land to sink their roots into and say, "It's mine, I own it, and no one can take it away from me."

Despite these differences, it seems that to be rich is to be free. It means having the freedom to do what you want when you want to do it.

For many, to be rich means to be free of debt and the worries debt can cause. It means having the freedom to travel, relax, be with friends, or just plain goof off.

When Elizabeth I of England was dying, she was asked what she wanted most before she died. She replied that she would give all the wealth in her kingdom for one more minute of life. Being rich means having time, the most precious commodity in the world. Being rich lets you spend time with friends and loved ones, enjoy your hobbies and avocations, and do what you want without being limited by your finances.

My goal is to teach you how to invest your money so that you can retire rich. To not worry about money as you approach your later years, to be able to play those 18 holes of golf, spend extra time and money on your children and grandchildren—these things add up to a rich retirement.

If you want to retire well or early, you're going to *need* to be rich. According to many retirement planners, just to maintain the lifestyle you have right now, your investments should generate about 80 percent of your current salary. With diligence on your part and the strategies described in this book, you can retire rich—whatever that means to you.

SAVING FOR RETIREMENT

Over the last 50 years, the way people saved for a comfortable retirement was straightforward. The model was basically a stool with three legs: Social Security, corporate pension plans, and personal savings.

But the model isn't so simple anymore. The future of Social Security is continually in question. Pension plans that paid out a guaranteed sum are rapidly being replaced by 401(k) plans that have no such guarantee. As a result, the importance of that third leg on the stool—personal savings—has never been greater, and it's becoming essential for all of us to be able to make informed, intelligent investment decisions that will maximize the return on our savings.

THE WOES OF SOCIAL SECURITY

Until recently, Social Security was the foundation of just about everyone's retirement benefits. Created by the U.S. government in 1935, it constituted a wonderful retirement plan intended to provide a living income for people over the age of 65. Offering it was essentially the government's way of saying, "Congratulations, you old coot, you beat the actuarial tables!" However, the fundamental problem with Social Security is that, when it was enacted, the average human life expectancy was 65 years! Life expectancies have lengthened considerably since Social Security was introduced. If we enacted a similar law today, we would promise retirement benefits to only those over 80 or 85!

With medical advances proceeding at an unprecedented pace, our lives are bound to be even longer. The average American retiree can currently expect to live at least 18 years in retirement. Imagine how long the golden years will be 25 or 50 years from now! This trend has exerted tremendous pressure on the Social Security system, since it was never intended to support so many for so long.

What's more, back in the 1930s and 1940s, 16 workers contributed to Social Security for each person drawing benefits. Today, only about 3 workers support each Social Security recipient. And 40 years from now, a mere 2 workers will contribute to Social Security for each retiree. Obviously, these demographic trends have strained the Social Security system even more.

Will Baby Boomers Make Social Security Go Bust?

The first wave of the 76 million baby boomers just turned 50, and they have only 15 years to go until they reach the traditional retirement age of 65. For the most part, they have overspent and undersaved. The Social Security Administration is obviously going to have a very difficult time maintaining the payment schedules that baby boomers will require. Indeed, according to a recent poll, more Americans under the age of 35 believe in UFOs than expect to collect Social Security!

The cost of Social Security is projected to rise from 11 percent to 17–22 percent of an American worker's payroll by the year 2040. And that figure does not include Medicare, an even larger government expenditure! Our government has set no funds aside for the trillions of dollars promised for Social Security and Medicare benefits. Something has got to give. As the famous economist Herbert Stein says, "Unsustainable trends tend not to sustain themselves."

Even the experts are deeply concerned about Social Security's fate. Haeworth Benson, chief actuary for the Social Security Administration in the mid-1970s, says that the Social Security system will not be viable in its present form when the first group of baby boomers retire in about 2010. But the problems will start even earlier than that. Look in the Social Security's so-called trust fund in 2002 and all you'll find is an IOU for close to $3 trillion! The money has already been spent, and there aren't many ways to recover it. The government will have to cut spending by $3 trillion, raise taxes by $3 trillion, or convert the IOU into long-term government bonds, which would increase the national debt by 35 percent. Ouch!

Most baby boomers heading toward retirement had better prepare themselves for means testing of retirement benefits. In other words, the richer you are, the less you'll get. Most of us should also plan on paying larger taxes on the benefits we receive and on receiving any benefits from the government at a later age than the original 65 cutoff. The hope that Social Security will provide a reasonable income is disappearing fast. Indeed, the amount of Social Security that higher-income retirees can expect to receive falls to a very modest sum. People with earnings in the top Social Security tax bracket—currently about $60,000 a year—can expect to receive only about 24 percent of their pay that was subject to Social Security tax. To add insult to injury, up to 85 percent of the Social Security benefits received by higher-income retirees may be subject to federal income tax.

The news is somewhat better for moderate- and lower-income people. For them, Social Security will probably continue to replace a greater percentage of their income. A person with a non-working spouse and earning $44,000 a year can expect Social Security to replace 46 percent of his or her income.

Thus, those of us who aspire to a rich retirement shouldn't count on the largesse of Social Security. (You can find out your projected annual benefits by calling the Social Security Administration at 800-772-1213. Request a report showing the approximate size of your benefits based on your past and projected future income.)

IN WITH 401(K) PLANS, OUT WITH TRADITIONAL PENSION PLANS

While doubts cloud the future of Social Security, a revolution is occurring in the way private corporations provide pensions for their employees. In the past, workers spent the lion's share of their working life with the same company. That company usually had a traditional, defined benefit plan that paid pensioners a fixed monthly income throughout their retirement. The sum paid out was generally based on a person's final salary and the number of years he or she had been with the company.

The use of defined benefit plans has declined dramatically over the last decade, for several reasons. First, workers are changing jobs much more often than they used to, and they want their pensions to be portable. Also, corporations have done a great deal of restructuring, and they are increasingly reluctant to be responsible for all the investment decisions, costs, and regulations associated with defined benefit plans. Indeed, the number of traditional defined benefit plans paying premiums to the Pension Benefit Guaranty Corporation (a government agency that insures corporate pensions) fell from 105,000 in 1988 to 58,000 in 1995. That is a decline of almost 50 percent!

In addition, traditional plans are not as reliable as they used to be. The percentage of large corporations with fully funded defined benefit plans declined sharply in 1995. This means that many companies have less money in the till than they have committed to pay out to retired workers in the near future. Sounds a little like what the government has done with Social Security, doesn't it?!

Many defined benefit pension plans have been replaced by defined contribution plans—commonly, 401(k) plans—which offer no guaranteed return on your money and no guaranteed sum when you retire. One of the biggest advantages of 401(k) plans is that they are portable, enabling you to take your pension with you if you change jobs.

With a 401(k) plan, it is up to you, not your employer, to make investment decisions. As a result, 401(k)s offer advantages for the well-informed investor. They allow you to set a significant portion of your salary away before taxes, which is like getting an instant return on every dollar saved equal to your tax rate. For example, if your income is taxed 30 percent, you'll instantly make

30 percent on the money you save because the government doesn't get its paws on your money. Second, many employers will match your 401(k) contribution, within limits. Whenever possible, take full advantage of this bonus. It's the easiest way to save money there is.

The popular 401(k) plan of today is here to stay, and in chapter 5 I'll show you how to make the most of yours. It can be an essential tool to help you prepare for a comfortable retirement.

Personal Savings: Your Ticket to Rich

You can't count on Social Security. Pension funds are not always reliable. Your 401(k) is a great tool but may get you only so far. So what's left to make you rich? Personal savings. If you adopt the sensible, easy-to-follow plans detailed in the following chapters, you can retire rich.

By looking at 45 years' worth of stock market data, I uncovered revolutionary strategies that can, when implemented properly, make a huge difference in your net worth as you save for your retirement. (For the sake of tax savings and simplicity, I recommend using an IRA [Individual Retirement Account] for your personal savings, at least for the first $2,000 a year that you save.)

SAVE, SAVE, AND SAVE SOME MORE

Your success comes down to how much you save and how much you spend. The sooner you start saving, the richer you'll be when you retire. *Every dollar you save today will have a powerful impact on your retirement.* Let's say you're 38 years old. If you use my most aggressive strategy, called Reasonable Runaways, and receive the same return the strategy has generated over the last 45 years, each dollar you save today will be worth $138 when you're 65! (Reasonable Runaways and my other strategies are explained in chapter 3.)

Take a dollar bill out of your pocket and imagine how little it means to you now. But how much will $138 mean to you when you're 65? A lot more, I'll bet. Do you have $10 lying on your bureau? Instead of grabbing it to pay for video rentals, invest it in the Reasonable Runaways strategy. It will likely be worth about $1,387 when you hit 65. Thinking of buying that $100 watch you saw at the mall on Saturday? That $100 invested in Reasonable Runaways could be worth $13,870 when you retire. Never underestimate the power of saving and investing your money.

A March 31, 1997, article in the *Wall Street Journal* drives home the importance of saving for retirement. The story focuses on the woes of William M. Walters, who at the age of 73 is forced to go back to work to support himself and his wife. Despite being employed during his entire adult life, he never had a pension plan and never got around to saving for his retirement. Social Security pays Mr. Walters and his wife just $16,000 a year, so he recently took a job stocking and delivering food for the Chattanooga, Tennessee, School System. The $640 a month he earns there helps make ends meet, but the job is backbreaking labor and prevents Mr. Walters from staying home to care for his ailing wife.

Unfortunately, Mr. Walters is not alone. The number of elderly day laborers in this country has doubled in the last five years. People who never found the time to save money for their retirement are forced to go back to work, sometimes just to put food on the table.

Never forget that the money you save and invest wisely *now* can have a huge impact on the quality of your life in the future. Mr. Walters's life certainly would be much easier now had he saved some money when he was younger. Had he managed to save just $1,000 when he was 43 and invested it in Reasonable Runaways, he would now have about $128,000. That would generate more than enough income for him to cover his expenses, and he wouldn't have to have a job at all.

START SAVING NOW

One of the best things you can do is to start saving *now*. I can't overstate the importance of this. Let me give you an example. Katie and Stacy are 25-year-old twin sisters. They've both just read *How to Retire Rich* and are very excited about the prospect of retiring rich. Katie starts saving her money right away, putting $2,000 a year into her IRA and investing it in the Reasonable Runaways strategy. Stacy, who thinks she's too young to have to worry about saving for her retirement, takes a wait-and-see attitude.

Ten years later, Katie has contributed $20,000 to her IRA and is doing so well that Stacy takes notice and starts diligently putting $2,000 a year into her own IRA, also investing it in the Reasonable Runaways strategy. Just as Stacy starts saving her money, Katie stops. She never puts another dime into her IRA, even though she continues to invest the money in Reasonable Runaways.

Fast-forward to the year 2037. The twins are 65 years old. Katie contributed only $20,000 to her IRA, putting away $2,000 a year between ages 25 and 35, whereas Stacy contributed $60,000 to her IRA as she aged from 35 to 65. Who has more money, Katie or Stacy?

Because of the power of compounding, Katie's IRA is worth $12.1 million when she turns 65. Stacy's is worth only $2.6 million—even though she contributed three times as much money! Katie's account is so much larger simply because she started saving her money 10 years earlier. No wonder Einstein said that nothing was as powerful as compounding.

According to the Social Security Administration, among Americans over 65 today, 45 percent are dependent on relatives, 30 percent live on charity, 23 percent are still working, and just 2 percent are totally self-supporting. If you want to be self-supporting, *start saving your money today.*

If you do nothing else, put $1, $5, or $10 into a jar every day. At the end of the week, deposit the money in a bank; at the end of the year, start investing it using the strategies described in this book. If that's all you do to save for your retirement, you'll be vastly better off than if you do nothing.

Let's meet four couples who are at different stages in their lives and see how rich their retirements will be if they save their money and invest it using our time-tested strategies.

How Four Couples Define *Rich*

Each of these couples has different ambitions and ideas about what it means to be rich. They all have the same goal, however, which is to retire rich—or at least rich enough to be free of financial worries.

For the sake of simplicity, the couples accumulate all their savings in their IRAs and make the maximum contribution of $2,000 per person per year. As we'll see later in the book, this is the bare minimum contribution if you want to retire rich. What's more, by increasing the amount of money you save and utilizing tax-advantaged vehicles like your company's 401(k) plan, you can vastly boost your net worth at retirement. While our overall recommendations are more complicated than these simple examples, by just looking at the four couples' IRA savings we get a clear picture of the power of compounding and the supreme importance of the investment decisions all four couples make.

Bill and Nancy Robinson

Both Bill and Nancy Robinson are 32 years old. Recently married, they have saved exactly nothing. Bill, an administrator at the Rock & Roll Museum in Cleveland, makes $32,000 per year. Nancy is a nurse and already makes $44,000 per year. They have no children yet but would like to have at least two. Bill and Nancy are pretty careful with their money and rarely carry any balances on their credit cards. Their monthly mortgage payment of $1,100 on their condominium is well within their means. Nancy has a student loan outstanding, but it will be paid off in less than a year.

For Bill and Nancy, rich means having the ability, when they are tired of working the long hours they so often do, to kick back, relax, and travel the world. They don't want to own a large house or fancy cars; nor do they want to leave much money to their kids when they die, although they want to be sure they have enough money so that they are never a burden to their children. They would like to be able to give their kids money while they're alive, to help them buy a car, start a business, or put a down payment on their first house.

Right now, Bill and Nancy have the combined income and minimal debt that allows them to start a savings plan immediately. The first thing each of them should do is open an IRA account and start making the maximum annual contribution of $2,000 every year from now until they retire. They should do this even if their contributions aren't fully tax deductible, because their money will still compound tax free.

The biggest choice Bill and Nancy face is how to invest their savings. Let's look at some hypothetical numbers that will illustrate the importance of their decision. If they are Nervous Nellies—always worried about the current state of the stock market or the political climates here and abroad—they might be inclined to keep their money in cash, earning only the interest rate that Treasury bills pay. If they diligently start saving their money and put $2,000 a year in their tax-advantaged IRAs, by the time they're 65 they will each have made contributions of $68,000 to their IRAs, and each of their IRAs will be worth $192,000. (I'm assuming that they make a $2,000 contribution when they are 65, as well.) When you take inflation into account (currently about 4 percent), you see why Treasury bills are a dismal investment over the long term. Over the last 45 years, their real return—after inflation—was just over 1 percent!

Now, even though the Robinsons do not want to leave money to their heirs, Bill and Nancy's combined savings of $384,000 isn't going to provide them with a carefree retirement. If they were lucky enough to earn 6 percent interest per year on their savings, their combined income would be only $23,000 a year. Rich? Hardly. Strapped is more like it. Even if Bill and Nancy were willing to spend principal, their savings could very likely run dry before they die, leaving themselves a burden to their children. And that's the last thing they want to happen.

Now, let's assume that Bill and Nancy are willing to take a little more risk. They decide to invest their savings in the bond market, where they can earn a little more interest than they can with cash. Unfortunately, the news here isn't much better. Again, they each contribute $68,000 to their IRAs. By investing in bonds, their accounts each grow to about $242,000. Now, $484,000 doesn't sound like such a bad nest egg, but at 6 percent interest Bill and Nancy are earning only $29,000 a year, less than Bill was making at age 32!

Let's now assume that instead of keeping their money in cash or investing in bonds Bill and Nancy decide to invest their IRA savings in the stock market. They do some homework and discover that 80 percent of professional money managers fail to beat the S&P 500 index, a simple index of 500 of the largest companies in the country. Rather than trying to outsmart the pros, Bill and Nancy decide to keep things simple and put all their savings in an S&P index fund. Assuming they receive a rate of return similar to the S&P 500's return over the past 45 years, the $68,000 they each invested in their IRAs would have grown to $892,000. Their combined savings would be almost $1.8 million, providing them with an annual income of about $108,000. The Robinsons are starting to feel rich.

Now let's assume that Bill and Nancy have read *How to Retire Rich* and invest their IRA savings in the simple, easy-to-understand growth strategy I call Reasonable Runaways. The $68,000 that each contributed to their IRAs grows to $4.4 million by the time they turn 65. Bill and Nancy have a combined net worth of almost $9 million, and this generates, at 6 percent interest, an annual income of $528,000. *Bill and Nancy Robinson are rich.*

What if Bill and Nancy want to retire before they turn 65? Indeed, if they implement the aggressive Reasonable Runaways strategy right now, and the strategy performs as well as it has over the past 45 years, their IRAs would each be worth $1 million by the time they are 57. At 6 percent interest this would generate a combined income of $120,000 a year, which they feel is enough for them to live on comfortably. The Robinsons could retire a full eight years earlier than they had anticipated—simply by sticking to this strategy. That is immensely rich.

But what if Bill and Nancy can't bear the volatility of the Reasonable Runaways strategy? Nancy can't sleep at night when the stock market is doing poorly, and this strategy can be very volatile, making her doubly nervous. In this instance, the Robinsons might prefer the more conservative and less volatile Leaders with Luster strategy (also covered in chapter 3). By taking less risk, Bill and Nancy will have a smoother ride, making it easier for them to stick with their investment program through the ups and downs of the stock market. The $68,000 they each saved in their IRAs would grow to $1.9 million, and their combined annual income would be just over $230,000. Bill and Nancy still feel plenty rich.

The message in the Robinsons' story is very clear. An investment in only cash or bonds is close to disastrous. You must invest in the stock market until you retire, and while an investment in the S&P 500 might provide you with an adequate income in your retirement, if you really want to retire rich, you must use superior investment strategies.

GEORGE AND THERESA RAMIREZ

Let's next consider the situation of George and Theresa Ramirez, both 38 years old. George is a computer programmer earning $60,000 a year, and Theresa is a part-time graphic artist earning

$30,000 a year. With a combined income of $90,000, they can each make an annual $2,000 contribution to their IRA accounts without much difficulty. To date, they have each saved $5,000 in their IRA accounts.

George and Theresa have a completely different idea of what it means to be rich. For them, being rich is having a legacy to pass on to their two young sons, Robert and Carlo. Both George and Theresa grew up in families that struggled to make ends meet. They put themselves through college and spent many years paying off their student loans and saving for a down payment on their home in San Jose, California. They have worked very hard to get where they are today and would like their sons and perhaps even their grandchildren to inherit some of the fruits of their labor.

Once again, we see that the Ramirez couple certainly won't get rich by investing in cash. If they each add $2,000 per year to their IRAs (again, like the Robinsons they also contribute $2,000 to their IRA accounts when they are 65), the $61,000 they each contribute will be worth a mere $152,000 when they turn 65, and their joint income will be a pathetic $18,200 per year. The same holds true for bonds. If they invest their savings in intermediate-term bonds, their IRAs would each be worth about $185,000. Again, not enough to live off—much less have anything left over to leave to their sons.

If George and Theresa consistently put their money into an S&P 500 index fund, they are certainly going to be much better off. Their IRA accounts would grow to $563,000 apiece, and if they earn 6 percent interest, their combined annual income would be $68,000.

Now let's look at the Reasonable Runaways strategy. If the Ramirezes diligently invest their money using this strategy, they would each have $2.2 million in their IRAs when they turn 65. Earning 6 percent, their combined income would be $262,000 per year, not to mention their $5 million net worth. George and

Theresa can retire rich, leave money to the boys, and have no financial worries.

But what if, like the Robinsons, George and Theresa just don't have the stomach for the volatility of the Reasonable Runaways strategy? An investment in Leaders with Luster could also perform well for them. Their IRAs would grow to $1.1 million each, providing them with a comfortable annual income of $132,000 and a legacy for their children.

TOM AND SARAH O'NEIL

Both Tom and Sarah O'Neil are 45 years old. Tom is an executive at Ford Motor Company, and Sarah is a homemaker. They have four children and live in a suburb of Detroit, Michigan. Tom and Sarah are very concerned about their retirement. They have been so busy working and raising their family that they've had little time for retirement planning. Though Tom has always made a good salary and currently earns $150,000 a year, they have managed to save only $15,000 in each of their IRA accounts. Although Tom did start making the maximum contribution to his 401(k) at age 40, he's left the money in cash, since he doesn't understand investing.

The O'Neils have become accustomed to an upper-middle-class lifestyle. They have a nice home, travel with their family to Saint Martin once a year, and go skiing whenever they can. Sarah is worried that they won't be able to maintain their lifestyle when Tom retires. Although he will receive a pension if he stays with Ford, without some additional income their finances will be tight. Sarah believes that when they retire they won't have enough money for trips to Saint Martin. Perhaps they won't even have enough income to afford to stay in the house where they raised their family.

Sarah knows that she has come a lot further in life than her parents ever did. Her mother was a waitress all her life; her father, a telephone repairman. While her parents are getting by on Social Security and her father's pension, they are always worried about money. Sarah is particularly worried about her father and his failing health. Her parents simply don't have enough money for a quality nursing home if her father should need it.

Sarah does not want to end up in the same boat as her parents, but she is terrified to commit to an investment program. Being an executive at Ford, Tom knows a lot about cars but little about investing. Both Tom and Sarah are baffled by the number of available investment alternatives and have kept their savings in cash because the stock market has always seemed too complex and frightening.

The O'Neils decide to do a little belt-tightening and commit to adding $4,000 a year ($2,000 each) to their IRA accounts over the next 20 years, also making their final contributions when they are 65. By doing this, they will have each put $57,000 in their IRAs by the time Tom retires. However, if they continue to keep their savings in cash, their IRAs will grow to only $123,000, and many of Sarah's worries will be justified. There will be no trips to Saint Martin. There will be little extra cash for the children and grandchildren. Heaven forbid Tom or Sarah ends up in a nursing home. Their combined annual income from their savings will be a paltry $15,000, which doesn't do much to supplement Tom's 401(k).

Again, the story is the same with bonds. Tom and Sarah's IRAs grow to $145,000 apiece, and the income they generate does little to enhance or support their lifestyle when they retire.

If Tom and Sarah are willing to invest in the stock market and keep their money in an S&P index fund, their IRA savings will grow to $353,000 by the time they turn 65. The O'Neils are finally convinced that keeping their money in cash or bonds is foolhardy. If Tom and Sarah have the confidence to invest in strategies rather than just the S&P 500 index, their return could be truly amazing. The $57,000 they save could grow to just over $1 million if invested in Reasonable Runaways. That is certainly enough for them to maintain a great lifestyle in their later years.

What if Tom and Sarah just can't face the volatility of Reasonable Runaways? An investment in Leaders with Luster would still outperform the S&P 500, and their IRAs would grow to $596,000 each.

STEVE AND BETSY JOHNSON

Our fourth couple is Steve and Betsy Johnson. Steve, 55, is a plumbing contractor who earns an average of $140,000 per year. Betsy, 49, is going back to work as a real estate broker. She expects to earn about $25,000 her first year. To date, they have saved $30,000, but Steve hopes to retire in only 10 years. They have three grown children and a nice home in Fort Lauderdale, Florida, but both Steve and Betsy wish they had more money in the bank. The Johnsons have been paying college tuition for one child or another for the past 10 years, preventing them from saving as much as they would have liked.

Steve and Betsy are each going to make the maximum $2,000-per-year contribution to their IRA accounts from now until they retire. Steve knows that he can sell his business if need be, but if he and Betsy fail to make an investment in the stock market right now, their financial future might be pretty bleak. Because their time frame is relatively short, they can't hope to make the amount of money that the Robinsons and the Ramirezes plan to, but they certainly can improve their financial situation considerably by investing wisely in the stock market.

If they put all their money in Treasury bills, their combined $74,000 savings grows to only $114,000 by the time Steve is 65. Once again, bonds aren't much better, in this instance growing to $125,000. Because their money has only 10 years to compound, an investment in the S&P 500 grows to only $199,000.

Steve and Betsy are in a more difficult position than our other couples in regard to risk. Because of their ages, they can't afford to take as much risk as our younger couples, but they also have a very pressing need to maximize their savings. Investing in the more aggressive Reasonable Runaways strategy would net Steve and Betsy $342,000 in 10 years. If they were more conservative and chose to invest it in the Leaders with Luster strategy, their money would grow to $261,000.

Are Steve and Betsy rich? Not just yet. But remember that we've looked only at their IRA savings. In chapter 6 we'll see how the Johnsons can retire rich by setting up pension accounts and wisely investing additional personal savings.

It's not too late

Whatever your age, *now* is the time to take control of your finances. It would be easy for the Johnsons to throw up their hands and say that it's too late, that there's nothing they can do to retire comfortably, much less rich. Steve might plan to forgo retirement; Betsy could plan to work full-time. But remember that the Johnsons were saving just $4,000 a year. Later we'll see that if the Johnsons increase their savings and invest it wisely, they too can retire rich.

No matter how old you are or how much planning you've done to date, if you decide *right now* to take action, your future will be much brighter. It is never too late to begin saving. It is never too late to begin an intelligent investment program based on long-term evidence and diligent research. But you have to do it right now. Not tomorrow. Not next week. *Now.*

It can be very hard to jump feet first into the stock market. Nobody wants to invest all their hard-earned savings in the market right before it goes down 15 percent. But the biggest mistake you'll ever make is to delay and delay and delay. Yes, the market could go down 15 percent next year, but what if it goes up 25 percent the year after that and the year after that? If the market's current gyrations scare you, focus on what *should* terrify you— hitting age 65 and not having any money. If you don't save your money and don't invest it in the stock market, you'll never retire rich. Accept that the stock market will have some bad years that you may find frightening—but not nearly as frightening as bagging groceries when you're 70 years old.

Since the founding of the New York Stock Exchange (NYSE) in the late 1700s, stock prices have gone up 71 percent of the time. As a long-term investment, the stock market can't be beat. But we don't live in the long term—we live in the present. As we'll see in the next chapter, the pain often associated with short-term volatility makes many people want to stick all their money in "safe" investments like T-bills or bonds. That safety is an illusion, however. The real long-term threat to your financial health is inflation, which can almost completely eat away your gains from an investment in cash or bonds. Inflation is a silent but potent threat because we don't feel inflation like we feel stock market gyrations.

In the blink of an eye, 10 years go by. Think of how fast the last 10 years went in your life. Do you remember the market correction of 1990 or the market meltdown of July 1996? At the time, people were truly terrified about what might happen to their investments. But a study of the stock market's long-term performance helps you understand that it doesn't matter what the stock market did yesterday or what it might do tomorrow. What matters is that over the long term, investing in the stock market using the strategies in this book is the best way to ensure a rich retirement.

CHAPTER TWO

THE STRATEGY REVOLUTION

Have you ever wanted to lose weight? Thousands of diet books are available, many of them filled with useful information on how to lose weight, but as a nation we're fatter than ever. Why? Because we don't *use* the information these books provide. How come so many of us can never lose weight even though simple, easy-to-understand diets can get us to our desired weight? The answer can be summed up in one word: *discipline.* Sadly, our habits and emotions can easily overpower our discipline and good intentions. In the showdown between a diet and a brownie, the brownie always wins.

In my office, the receptionist keeps a bowl of candies on her desk as a treat for office workers and visitors. When I'm dieting, I'll diligently avoid these goodies for the first few weeks. Soon after, however, I fall back to my old habit of grabbing a handful as I pass her desk. Gee, I wonder to myself, I've been so good on this diet and yet I'm not losing weight. It must be my genes. No, it's those 450 calories in three handfuls of jelly beans!

And then there are all those new diet books. I keep buying them to see if losing weight might get any easier. But it doesn't. I need the discipline to keep my hands out of the candy bowl. People are fatter than ever because they're following the wrong map for losing weight. In dieting, no amount of gimmicks or good intentions can substitute for the disciplined use of an effective strategy. The same is true for successful investing in the stock market.

YOU NEED A MAP
TO GET WHERE YOU WANT TO GO

Most investors do vastly worse than simple indexes like the Dow Jones Industrial Average and the S&P 500 because they have no coherent, underlying strategy for purchasing stocks. It's as if they were in Kansas City and wanted to get to New York but had no map to plan their trip. Imagine how foolish it would be to get in your car in Kansas City and say, "I'm going to trust my instincts and intuition to get me to New York." You might get there, or you might not—either way, it's not going to be a smooth trip. What if you head in the wrong direction, or get caught in a tough neighborhood, or find yourself stuck on a highway with no exit in sight? The fear and uncertainty of such a journey might prevent you from going at all.

Yet investors do this all the time. Instead of using a good strategy, they go in search of the next hot stock that will bring them untold riches. A search of the Dow Jones News Retrieval service, which covers nearly every news source imaginable, proves my point. Log on and type in "hot stock." When I recently did that, I found 1,391 stories containing references to hot stocks. Next I typed "stock market investing and discipline." How many stories did I find? Three! Hot stocks appeal to our emotions— disciplined strategies appeal to our intellect. Guess which one wins? In a nutshell, the largest problem investors have today is that they invest with their hearts rather than their heads.

THE ACCIDENTAL INVESTOR
Virtually everyone approaches a decision to buy or sell a stock in a haphazard manner, based not on a coherent underlying strategy but on the story about that individual stock. Is it going to in-

crease its earnings dramatically? Will a new management team shake things up? Is the overall industry going through a big restructuring? Far too often, investors focus on hunches or the story behind each stock that they buy. They end up with a portfolio filled with great stories—not great stocks! We're accidental investors, buying and selling stocks based on whatever story is appealing at the moment. What's more, we're often willing to listen to anyone who seems to have a good idea about an investment.

It's dinnertime. The phone rings. You answer and say, "Yes," you have five minutes to listen to a stockbroker tell you about an exciting opportunity. You wind up buying the stock because you find the story enticing. Yet you don't even wonder why or whether it's a great opportunity. Your brother-in-law, Bill, tells you about a hot stock that he thinks will soon double in price. You love his story and buy 100 shares the next day. It is our nature to want to invest stock by stock and to base our decisions on the stories behind the stocks we buy. Whether the story is accurate seems secondary. Unfortunately, most people spend more time studying *Consumer Reports* trying to decide what microwave to buy than researching whether a stock is a good investment.

We're also inclined to think about how our individual investments and stocks have performed, rather than about our entire portfolio. I was at a party, and a fellow who knew of my work told me about how well he was doing in the stock market. He had done twice as well as the S&P 500, which was up substantially that year. I joked that with his portfolio compounding at such a rate, he was sure to be listed on the Forbes 400 in no time. But when I said *portfolio,* the look on his face changed. He said that I had misunderstood him—he was talking about just some of the stocks he had bought. He then lamented about why his other investments had faired so poorly! It turned out that the majority of his money wasn't even invested in the stock market and that his overall portfolio had badly trailed the performance of the S&P 500.

IT'S NOT A GAME—IT'S A SCIENCE

Investing in the stock market is the *only* way to ensure that you will retire rich. We've seen that our strategies always outperform bonds and cash over the long term. So how do they compare with other investments, like gold or real estate? Once again, stocks blow the competition out of the water. Many people view their homes as the biggest—and best—investment they've made. Yet the *Chase Investment Performance Digest* reports that over the last 30 years, an investment in the typical one-family house in America compounded at 5.71 percent a year, way behind any of our time-tested stock strategies. Such an investment even lags T-bills! Commodities haven't done much better: over the last 35 years, an investment in gold returned 7.11 percent a year; silver, 5.04 percent a year; and crude oil, 6.73 percent a year. Clearly, the stock market is the place for your money if you want to retire rich.

It doesn't matter whether the market has a great year or a lousy one, because successful investing is a long-term endeavor. The sad truth is that people often treat the stock market like a giant game, darting in and out of investments based on gut feelings and emotions. Investors who methodically approach the market more like a science and use unambiguous, straightforward rules for investing will be much richer than those who treat it like a crapshoot. Indeed, history shows that the stock market has always rewarded patience and methodical behavior.

As mentioned earlier, the New York Stock Exchange has gone up 71 percent of the time. It has recovered from every downturn, going on to new highs. It has beaten cash and bonds in virtually every long-term period. But because of the way we approach the market, we rig it against us from the start. We habitually fall back on our worst impulses when trying to make good investment decisions. Fear, ignorance, greed, and hope conspire to rob us of our ability to make sensible, intelligent decisions about the market. We continually let our feelings overcome reason and try to take shortcuts that violate all logic. We live in the here and now, not the past or future—and this is our greatest roadblock when trying to make good investment choices. Because today's information and catchy headlines get filtered through our emotions, we give them the greatest importance. By doing this, we rob ourselves of perspective. If you can focus on the big picture, you'll see that the circumstances of today are quite meaningless to long-term investment performance.

Turn on the news and listen to which stocks are up and which are down, and you will feel the inexorable pull of your emotions if a stock you own is doing poorly. You may be tempted to sell it because of one day's drop in price. Or you might hear the chairman of the Federal Reserve say something negative about the market or about investors' "irrational exuberance" and want to sell all your stocks. Rest assured that you're not alone. Virtually everyone reacts this way, and it costs them a fortune.

SHORT-TERM THINKING DESTROYS PERFORMANCE

Two recent studies show how badly people's emotions and short-term thinking affect their investments. Dalbar Financial Services is a Boston-based consulting firm. In a recent 10-year study, it found that while the S&P 500 had a gain of 293 percent, investors in equity mutual funds earned only 70–90 percent! That's a three-to-one difference. The huge chasm between the two was attributed to investors trying to time the market, failing to keep their money in stocks for the entire 10 years. What if it were your own money? Instead of your $10,000 growing to $39,300, as it would have if you'd invested in the S&P 500, it grows to only $17,000–$19,000. Think of all the things you could do with that extra money—pay a year of college expenses for your son, take a grand tour of Europe, buy a new car.

Using data from Morningstar, a mutual fund rating service, Fundminder, Inc., a Los Angeles consulting firm, conducted a study with similarly disappointing findings. It evaluated the performance of 199 growth mutual funds over a six-year period and found that the average annual return was 12.01 percent. How did the owners of those same 199 funds do over the same six years? They did much, much worse, earning an average of just 2.02 percent a year!

For investors unwilling to back off from the tree of the here and now and walk up to the hill to see the forest of the future, successful investing and a rich retirement will forever remain a dream. What causes you to pull all your money out of the market is the same as what causes you to eat the brownie—lack of discipline. Short-term indulgences are very enticing but lethal to your long-term success.

STAYING IN THE MARKET IS 90 PERCENT OF THE BATTLE

As we saw in the Dalbar and Fundminder studies, one of the greatest secrets to successful investing is simply keeping your money in the stock market, whether times are bearish or bullish. It is a fact of life that stocks go down as well as up (remember, they go up 71 percent of the time). To the best of my knowledge, no one has yet learned how to accurately time the market. If someone had found a way, he or she would surely be on the Forbes 400 list of the richest people in the country by now! So until some lucky person finds a great market-timing strategy that proves itself over many years and market cycles, bet on the rising tides of the stock market—and keep your money there. If you manage to learn just this lesson and stay invested in the stock market despite short-term fluctuations, you'll end up doing better than 90 percent of all investors.

When some short-term bit of news makes you certain that it's time to sell, dwell on this. According to a study by Ibbotson Associates, a financial consulting firm, had you invested $1 in the stock market in 1926, it would have been worth $1,114 at the end of 1995. But if you remove the best 35 months from those 69 years, your dollar would be worth only $10.16! A University of Michigan study had similar results. Analyzing the 7,802 trading days between 1963 and 1993, researchers found that an investor trying to time the market but missing the best 90 days—just 1.1 percent of the total—lost out on 95 percent of the stock market's gains. A long-term investor investing $1 at the start of the study saw it grow to $24.30, whereas someone who missed just the 90 days with the biggest gains saw his $1 grow to just $2.10. There are no traders or market timers on the Forbes 400, but there are many, many investors.

EVEN THE PROS SUCCUMB TO HUMAN NATURE

OK, you're convinced that you must ignore short-term fluctuations and stay in the market. But the stock market is so complex, and humans are so prone to react emotionally—shouldn't we put our savings in the hands of a professional manager who supposedly knows much more than we do?

Unfortunately, professional investors are just as prone to the same mistakes the rest of us make. Over the long term, 80 percent of the mutual funds covered by Morningstar fail to beat the S&P 500. In a study I did for my book *What Works on Wall Street,* I found that of the 20 percent of conventionally managed funds that manage to beat the S&P 500, only one-third do so by more than 2 percent a year. This failure rate is astounding and should send most professional money managers back to the drawing board (or the dartboard!).

When engineers build a bridge that falls down, they don't build a bridge that way again. They learn from their mistakes, adding them to the body of knowledge that all engineers rely on when designing bridges. Unfortunately, the same is not true with investing. Amateurs and professionals alike consistently make the same errors because they let their emotions and fears override their intellect. Successful investing runs contrary to human nature.

It's natural to follow the crowd, let your emotions dictate decisions, buy stocks based on tips and hunches, and approach investing with an attitude that doesn't involve underlying cohesiveness and consistency. This has been proven by a number of scientific studies on human decision making. A number of studies cited in *House of Cards: Psychology and Psychotherapy Built on Myth* by Robyn M. Dawes compare the predictions of experts with predictions made by simple actuarial formulas; the simple models almost always outperformed the human experts! From doctors trying to diagnose cancer, to college admission committees trying to pick good students, to bookies trying to handicap the next horse race, the experts always lost to a consistently used model. Although they used perceptive and intelligent criteria when trying to diagnose cancer or pick graduate students, they couldn't take full advantage of the criteria's predictive ability. Why? Because their overwhelming human impulse allowed them to let other, unrelated information influence their decisions. The experts themselves were to blame for their own poor performance.

One study in *House of Cards* looked at the predicted grade point averages (GPAs) of a group of incoming college freshmen. Would these new students get good grades? Researchers contrasted the predictions made by admissions officers—who looked at letters of recommendation, results of personal interviews, SAT scores, and high school GPAs—with predictions based on simple models that used just high school GPAs and SAT scores. The researchers found that high school GPAs and SAT scores were the best predictors of the incoming freshmen's future GPAs. This simple model always outperformed the forecasts made by the admissions officers. In some instances, the interview process was found to subtract predictive value! The admissions officers undoubtedly knew how important high school GPAs and SAT scores were but didn't always use this simple, useful information to the fullest. The same is true in other fields.

I think that the reason 80 percent of traditional mutual funds fail to beat the S&P 500 in the long run is that many professional money managers have good ideas about how to choose successful stocks but don't use their ideas consistently. Again, their emotions get in the way. My first book, *Invest Like the Best,* shows you how to clone successful money managers by taking the stocks in their portfolios, putting them on a computer, and analyzing the different factors they possess. Using these factors as guidelines, you can then choose a group of stocks that look, act, and, most important, perform like those in the portfolio of the successful money manager. Since the book was written (1993), all the clone portfolios are outperforming the managers they were designed to copy! These portfolios have done better than the human managers for the same reason other experts are routinely beaten by simple models. The clone portfolios never deviate from their good investment ideas—they are unemotional and use a consistent and disciplined approach to investing.

One case is particularly interesting. In 1994, one of the very successful growth managers I cloned was having a tough year. As of June 30, 1994, his portfolio was down more than 15 percent. He wasn't necessarily a bad manager, but the growth stocks he bought were out of favor on Wall Street. Indeed, the manager's clone portfolio was also down about 14 percent. But here's where the story takes an interesting turn. No doubt the manager felt tremendous pressure to get his portfolio back on track. He was probably taking angry calls from shareholders and questioning his own reasons for buying and holding certain stocks. I think he was overwhelmed by the emotion of the moment, because he stopped buying the growth stocks that had worked so well for him and started buying a whole different class of stocks—in his case, large, heavy-industry companies; real estate investment trusts; and manufacturing companies. These stocks are the opposite of the growth stocks he had bought before. At the end of 1994, the manager's reworked portfolio was down another 9 percent, and he lost more than 22 percent by year's end.

Here's the rub. The clone portfolio, which was still invested in growth stocks, roared back 16 percent, managing to close that tough year with a loss of only 0.3 percent. Why? Because the clone portfolio used an effective strategy in a disciplined and consistent manner, unsullied by human panic.

I HAVE MET THE ENEMY, AND HE IS US

If you want to know the single greatest obstacle to stock market success, look in the mirror. Models and strategies beat humans because they reliably and consistently apply the same criteria time after time. They have no emotions to lead them down the wrong path. In almost every instance, it is the total reliability of application of a model that accounts for its superior performance. Strategies never vary. They are never moody, never fight with their spouse, and never get bored. They don't favor vivid, interesting stories over reams of statistical data. They never take anything personally. They don't have egos, feelings, fears, and hopes. And most important, they don't second-guess themselves.

WHAT'S THE BATTING AVERAGE?

It's not going to be easy to overcome your impulse to second-guess these successful investment strategies, but it can be done.

The best place to start is to understand your odds. Base rates are one of the most valuable bits of information you can use when looking at different savings vehicles and investment strategies, but because people prefer responding to gut reactions and colorful stories, they are often ignored.

Base rates are like batting averages. Most statistical predictions are based on these rates: 75 percent of students with GPAs above 3.5 go on to do well in school; smokers are three times as likely as nonsmokers to get cancer; over the long term, market-leading stocks with high dividend yields do better than the average stock 95 percent of the time. Basically, a base rate tells you how often something happens. The best way to predict the future is to bet with the base rate, provided it's gathered from a large sample over a long period of time.

The fundamental problem with base rates is that we love to ignore them. Even when we're fully aware of them, we'll throw base rates out in the presence of more interesting, descriptive information. Researchers have found this to be true in study after study of human behavior. For example, take a fictional town with a population of 100,000 people. If 70,000 of them are lawyers and 30,000 are engineers, the base rate for lawyers in that town is 70 percent. If you randomly select 10 names from a phone book and are asked to guess whether they are lawyers or engineers, you're forced to use the base rate information to make your guess because you have no other information to go on. You should guess that all 10 are lawyers because you'll be sure to get 70 percent right. Researchers have found that people do use the base rate information in this situation, guessing that all 10 are lawyers and getting 70 percent correct.

But look what happens when meaningless descriptive information is added to the equation. Say you're asked whether Bill is a lawyer or an engineer and all you're told is that he is 32 years old, plays tennis, and is well liked. In this type of situation, people largely ignore the base rate, though they should again guess that Bill is a lawyer. Researchers found that people tend to go with their gut feelings about whether Bill sounds more like a lawyer or an engineer.

Finally, researchers added stereotypical information, such as that Bill is quiet, likes mathematical puzzles, and avoids big parties. The underlying base rate still indicates that there's a 70 percent chance that Bill is a lawyer, but almost everyone guesses that he's an engineer. Even when you increase the base rate, making 90 percent of the townspeople lawyers, people will continue to say that Bill is an engineer because the description fits with people's preconceived ideas about engineers. We do the same thing with stocks, preferring a great story about a company to an analysis of the underlying reasons that it is a good investment.

Unfortunately, researchers and statisticians have been far more diligent with baseball statistics than they have been with investment strategies. Up until my book *What Works on Wall Street* appeared, there was almost no information about the long-term base rates of various stock selection strategies. The father of modern securities analysis, Ben Graham, lamented such lack of data in a speech that he gave in 1946! He said:

> It is amazing to reflect how little systematic knowledge Wall Street has to draw upon as regards the historical behavior of securities with defined characteristics. . . . Where is the continuous, ever growing body of knowledge and technique handed down by the analysts of the past to those of the present and future? When we contrast the annals of medicine with those of finance, the paucity of our recorded and digested experience becomes a reproach. We lack the codified experience that will tell us whether codified experience is valuable or valueless.

In the past, you had no way to know which investment strategies performed well over the long term. Even if you were committed to not being an accidental investor, you had no knowledge of the base rate—the batting average—of any particular investment strategy. Lucky for you, this is no longer the case.

The Strategy Revolution

Open almost any book about investing and you'll find some guru touting his or her brilliance. "I bought Microsoft before anyone else," or "Those Internet stocks will make you rich!" Another guru tells you why his stock picks are the best and why he was the only one to get out of the market before the crash in 1987. There is a stultifying sameness to these books. They all tout stocks, not strategies. The authors pump up their own egos without looking at the real results, even when they tell you to look for stocks that soared in value, conveniently ignoring their stock picks that failed. They offer no empirical support for their recommendations and give you no reason to believe that the same types of stocks will do well in the future. How can you know whether their advice is valuable?

What Works on Wall Street

I was the first independent researcher to be granted full access to Standard & Poor's Compustat database, the most comprehensive stock market database available today. It contains computerized information on almost 10,000 stocks going back to 1951. The data was given to me so that I could conduct tests on Wall Street's most popular strategies. My goal was to see what worked and what didn't, separate the winning strategies from the losers, and put into perspective why certain strategies are profitable and why others cause pain and lost profits. This was the first study ever done on the full Compustat database and the results were published in *What Works on Wall Street*.

This study is important because of the length of time covered. Respected researcher Richard Brealey estimates that to get valid results you need more than 25 years' worth of data about any particular investment strategy. Anything can work over a short period of time. Sometimes the zaniest ideas will work in the market, arousing interest in the press and then in the general public. I have a joke portfolio made up exclusively of stocks whose ticker symbols (the one to four letters that identify any given stock) are the vowels A, E, I, O, U, and Y. This portfolio beat the S&P 500 by over 11 percent in 1996, but that doesn't mean it's a good way to invest your money! It simply means that in 1996, chance led it to outperform the S&P 500.

Unfortunately, ultimately bad ideas often don't sound zany at all. That's why it's so dangerous to let good, short-term performance entice you. Look at the late 1960s. During that time, the hottest mutual funds were pouring money into stocks that had the greatest earnings gains in the previous year. The fund managers got nicknamed "gunslingers" because they were buying and selling stocks faster than a quick-draw could get his gun out of his holster. These managers were widely covered in the press, which showered them with superlative praise. They were geniuses, wunderkinder, brilliant boys who would forever change the way the investment game was played.

Had you been around then, you'd most likely have been easily seduced by the performance of those funds. Between December 31, 1963, and December 31, 1968, the performance of stocks with the greatest one-year earnings gains trounced the performance of the S&P 500, with $10,000 soaring in value to almost $35,000, generating a compound return of more than 28 percent a year. During those same five years, the S&P 500 had a comparatively modest gain of just over 10 percent, turning $10,000 into about $16,000. What's more, the gunslingers beat the S&P 500 in each of the five years.

Imagine that a fund that you own has beaten the S&P 500 for the past five years, and you've earned twice as much as your friend who put his money in a poky S&P 500 fund. Say that after personally experiencing these great returns and beating the S&P in every year for five years, I come along and tell you that, over the long term, your strategy is a bad way to invest? You'd think I was an idiot! After all, your personal experience proves I'm wrong. But that's the problem. Short periods of time are experienced personally, preventing us from seeing the bigger picture revealed by longer periods of time.

Over the long term, buying stocks with big earnings gains is a volatile, unstable investment strategy that does slightly worse than the S&P 500 while taking substantially more risk. Over the last 44 years, buying the 50 stocks with the highest one-year earnings gains has compounded at 11.68 percent, whereas the S&P 500 has compounded at 12.01 percent.

See how misleading those five years in the 1960s were? The sad thing is that many people believed that the gunslingers were geniuses and piled their money into those funds just as the strategy was starting to swoon. Over the next five years, the strategy got slaughtered, with $10,000 invested at the end of 1968 worth just $4,979 at the end of 1973! That's a loss of more than 50 percent, during a time when the same investment in the S&P 500 grew to $11,046! By then, the press had gleefully reported the gunslingers' demise, lavishing praise on the newest hot managers.

Only the Fullness of Time Can Show You What to Expect

Had this long-term research been available to investors in 1968, they would have known not to bet with the gunslingers. They would have known that a strategy based on big earnings gains was a poor long-term performer because of its high volatility. Its chances of beating the S&P 500 are 50–50—no better than flipping a coin. They would also have had realistic expectations about what they could expect to earn from the strategy. Someone expecting to earn 28 percent every year would be seriously misled. The more time studied, as was done for *What Works on Wall Street,* the more likely a strategy will continue to work in the future. We can once and for all separate the winners from the losers.

The S&P 500: A Simple Large-Capitalization Strategy

One of the first things I discovered when conducting research for *What Works on Wall Street* is that the mighty S&P 500, slayer of 80 percent of traditionally managed mutual funds, is an extremely simple index that can be duplicated using just one factor: market capitalization. If you simply buy all the stocks in the Compustat database that have a market capitalization greater than the average stock in the database—usually the upper 16 percent of those stocks—you virtually duplicate the returns of the S&P 500. Over the past 45 years, the S&P 500 compounded at 12.15 percent a year, whereas all the large stocks from the Compustat database grew at 11.92 percent a year, a miniscule difference of .23 percent! What's more, the risk was virtually identical. The S&P 500 had an annual standard deviation of return of 16.66 percent, while the deviation for the large-stocks group was 16.00 percent.

The mighty S&P 500 index is an exceedingly simple strategy, yet it continues to beat 80 percent of actively managed funds. It does so because it makes a consistent, disciplined investment in large-capitalization stocks. More important, I found other relatively simple strategies that do much better than the S&P 500! (More on these strategies in later chapters.)

Be a Bargain Hunter . . .
A key finding in *What Works on Wall Street* is that investors who insisted on getting some bang for their buck did well, while those willing to overpay for a great story did poorly. Investors buying stocks with low price-to-earnings, price-to-book, price-to-sales, and price-to-cash flow ratios did very well historically. These stocks are great values for long-term investors.

. . . Not a Spendthrift!
On the other hand, I found that the surest way to underperform the market is to buy the trendiest stocks of the moment—the ones that everyone talks about and whose valuations have gone to the moon. These are stocks with high price-to-earnings, price-to-book, price-to-sales, and price-to-cash flow ratios. Frenzy fuels their prices, and investors are willing to pay almost anything

to get in on a good thing. Whether they buy a stock like Polaroid in the 1960s or Netscape today, investors consistently get burned when they bet on these overvalued stocks.

When investors buy hot stocks with extremely high price-to-sales ratios, they often end up paying $1,000 or more for each $1 of a company's sales. In these investors' hearts, hope springs eternal. They're hoping the company will expand so quickly that their investment proves worthwhile. But if you strip the name and story from a stock, you'd never be willing to pay such an outlandish price. If I asked you whether you wanted to buy my store on the corner and all you had to do was pay me $1,000 for every $1 of my sales, you'd say I was crazy. But slap a sexy name and concept on it—say, Cybercash, which has a hot story about how it's going to make the Internet a safe place to transact business—and investors gladly pay 2,000 times sales! The power of a good story is unbelievable, and in the past, investors who paid these ridiculous sums suffered greatly. The laws of economics suggest that if you do the same, you'll suffer greatly as well.

All the strategies that invested in the trendiest stock of the moment did terribly. In my study of 45 years of market data, none came close to the S&P 500's return. In particular, the stock's price-to-sales ratio (how much you have to pay for every $1 of a company's sales) emerged as the single best ratio to pay attention to. Low price-to-sales ratios are one of the key factors in the Reasonable Runaways strategy described in the next chapter.

Let's look at how two investors would have fared over the last 45 years by buying stocks with low price-to-sales ratios versus stocks with high price-to-sales ratios. An investor who put all his or her money into the 50 stocks with the lowest price-to-sales ratios would have seen a $10,000 investment in these bargain stocks grow to $8.3 million—a compound return of 16.09 percent per year. Conversely, an investor who consistently bought the 50 stocks with the highest price-to-sales ratios would have seen a $10,000 investment in those overhyped-story stocks grow to just under $92,000! That's a compound return of 5.04 percent, worse than the return on Treasury bills over the same period. That's $8.2 million lower than the amount earned by an investor who bought the low price-to-sales ratio bargain stocks.

Just look at the base rates of each of these strategies. Investors buying the low price-to-sales stocks never had a 10-year period when they lost money, but investors in the high price-to-sales stocks had some 25-year stretches when they lost money! The high price-to-sales ratio group had one 10-year period, ending in 1990, when they lost 7.38 percent per year—and that was when the overall market was doing quite well and the S&P 500 had a compound annual gain of 13.93 percent! No sane person should ever stick with a high price-to-sales ratio strategy. Yet this is exactly what investors do when they buy overvalued stocks with great stories.

It's *NOT* DIFFERENT THIS TIME

Investors who buy pricey, overhyped stocks are deluding themselves—and their investing habits will eventually cause them real pain. Hot-story stocks have individual years when they skyrocket, and investors inevitably get caught up in the hoopla. In 1995, high price-to-sales ratio stocks jumped 46 percent, trouncing the S&P 500. Think of how difficult it would be to sit at a party and listen to a friend who invested in these stocks tell you about how much money he was making—and, by the way, they're in such sexy new industries! You'd feel behind the times with your stodgy, bargain-basement, low price-to-sales strategy. "Maybe your strategy used to work, but it's different this time. It's a brand new world," you'd hear.

People have been saying "It's different this time" for hundreds of years. But not much has changed since Isaac Newton lost a fortune in the South Sea Trading Company fiasco of 1720. This trading company had all the characteristics of a contemporary hot-story stock, with investors creating a mania over the company's prospects for success. Investors' dreams that the company would gain trade monopolies in the South Seas sent the company's price into the stratosphere. And, as we've seen in the more recent past, the story ended the way it had to—badly. Many investors were wiped out. Newton lamented that he could "calculate the motions of heavenly bodies but not the madness of men."

Using a disciplined, consistent approach to investing is the only way to retire rich. Stock prices are still determined by people, and as long as the madness of men and women determine stock prices, people who use simple disciplined strategies are going to do well. Names change. Industries change. Styles come in and go out of fashion. But the underlying characteristics that identify good investments remain the same. It's *not* different this time.

The laws of economics remain the same. Whether it's the South Sea Trading Company in 1720 or today's Internet companies, overpriced stocks are overpriced stocks. Only a study of history helps you understand this. All the strategies that failed to beat the S&P 500 over the last 45 years bought overpriced stocks with high price-to-book, price-to-earnings, price-to-cash flow, or price-to-sales ratios. And all the strategies that beat the S&P 500 bought stocks with low price-to-book, price-to-earnings, price-to-cash flow, or price-to-sales ratios. What's more, several other strategies that use more than one of these single ratios do even better.

The most important thing to remember is that successful investment strategies are quite simple. Many people fear that investing is complicated and hard to understand. As a matter of fact, it's part of human nature to believe that the more complex an explanation, the more intelligent it is. A clever study, described next, neatly makes the point.

THE STORY OF SMITH AND JONES

Professor Alex Bavelas, founder of the Group Network laboratory at the Massachusetts Institute of Technology, designed an experiment in which two subjects, Smith and Jones, face individual projection screens. Smith and Jones can't see each other or communicate in any way. They're told that the purpose of the experiment is to learn to recognize the difference between healthy and sick cells. They must learn to distinguish them using trial and error. In front of each are two buttons marked Healthy and Sick, along with two signal lights marked Right and Wrong. Every time a slide is projected, Smith and Jones must guess whether the cell is healthy or sick by pressing the button so marked. After they guess, their signal light will flash Right or Wrong.

Here's the hitch. Smith gets true feedback. If he's correct, his light flashes Right; if he's wrong, it flashes Wrong. Since he's getting true feedback, Smith is soon getting around 80 percent correct, since it's a matter of simple discrimination.

Jones's situation is entirely different. He doesn't get true feedback based on his guesses. Rather, the feedback he gets is based on Smith's guesses! It doesn't matter whether he's right or wrong about a particular slide—he's told he's right if Smith guessed right, and he's told he's wrong if Smith guessed wrong. Of course, Jones doesn't know this. He's been told that there is a true order that he can discover from the feedback. He ends up searching for order where there is none.

The moderator then asks Smith and Jones to discuss the rules they use for judging healthy and sick cells. Smith, who got true feedback, offers rules that are simple, concrete, and to the point. Jones, on the other hand, comes up with rules that are, out of necessity, subtle, complex, and highly adorned. After all, he had to base his opinions on Smith's guesses and hunches, not true feedback.

The amazing thing is that Smith doesn't think Jones's explanations are absurd, crazy, or unnecessarily complicated. He's impressed by the "brilliance" of Jones's method and feels inferior and vulnerable because of the pedestrian simplicity of his own rules. The more complicated and ornate Jones's explanations, the more likely they are to convince Smith.

Before the next test with new slides, the two are asked to guess who will get the most right the second time around. All Joneses and most Smiths say that Jones will. This time, Jones shows no improvement at all. Smith, on the other hand, does significantly worse than he did the first time, since he's now making guesses based on some of the complicated rules he learned from Jones.

The Best Strategies Are Simple

Just as with Smith and Jones, people yearn to make the simple complex. My findings in *What Works on Wall Street* illuminate simple rules about successful investing. Of course it makes sense that you'll do well if you don't overpay for a stock. Of course it's silly to pay $50 for every $1 of a company's sales. Of course it makes sense that big companies paying healthy dividend yields are better investments than big companies with high price-to-earnings or price-to-sales ratios. But this is information stripped of all the color and stories—you have only the base rate to go on, and it's easy to use the commonsense measurements that have withstood the test of time. But start talking about the individual stocks and their industries, and people are happy to throw base rates out the window.

I've given many presentations about the results of my study. During every talk, I watch as people nod their heads in agreement and get visibly excited about using the information to improve their investment performance. Inevitably, someone in the audience will ask me to name some of the stocks or industries that are currently chosen by the best-performing strategies.

When I tell them, their facial expressions change dramatically. They'll say things like, "I hate that stock," or, "That industry is in the doldrums," or, "That company will never turn around, its CEO is a megalomaniac!" It's like throwing a magic switch. The minute I speak the name of the stock or industry, most people in the group forget everything I just told them, reverting to their old habits of basing decisions on prejudices, gut feelings, and, sometimes, extremely misleading personal experience.

When building a stock portfolio, we all need to be like Joe Friday from the TV series *Dragnet*. Whenever anyone wanted to give Joe a personal read on a situation or digressed into a story about an event, Joe would stop them and say: "Just the facts, please, just the facts." When you insist on just the facts, you often end up buying stocks when everyone else is selling. For example, one strategy would have forced you to buy Union Carbide just after it had blown up a town in India and Exxon while the oil was still glistening on Prince George Sound. Those were not easy times to stick with the facts, ma'am!

Empires rise and fall, Democrats replace Republicans, computer companies displace steel companies in the American marketplace. The beat goes on. The late newspaperman Walter Winchell said that the same thing happens today as yesterday, only to different people. William of Ockham, a 14th-century Franciscan monk, developed the Principle of Parsimony, now called Ockham's Razor. For centuries it has been a guiding principal of modern science. Its axioms—such as "What can be done with fewer assumptions is done in vain with more" and "Entities are not to be multiplied without necessity"—boil down to this: *keep it simple, sweetheart.* Ockham's Razor shows that, most often, the simplest theory is the best.

BE HUMBLE IN FACE OF THE MARKET

There are really two ways to approach investing—the proud way and the humble way. The proud way is for those who believe that they're smarter than everyone else and can use their insights and abilities to make superior investment choices. The humble way is for those who believe that they don't know everything; this leads them to study what has worked over the long term and then use it. The path to achieving investment success is in studying long-term results and finding a strategy or group of strategies that make sense. It is the humble way, but it works. Remember to choose a comfortable level of risk, or you won't be able to stick with your chosen strategy.

You now have the long-term data that show you what works on Wall Street. To succeed, you must let this data guide you. Successful investors look at history. They understand and react to the present with knowledge of the past. Something as simple as looking at a strategy's best and worst years is a good example. In the past, investors had nothing to go on but tips and hunches. You now have a map to get you where you want to go, giving you a tremendous advantage over the uninformed. You know what the potential parameters of a strategy are, which can help you stick out the bad times and not get too excited by the good. If the maximum expected loss in a strategy is 35 percent, and the strategy is down 15 percent, instead of panicking, an informed investor can feel happy that things aren't as bad as they could be. This knowledge tempers expectations and emotions, giving informed investors a perspective that acts as an emotional pressure valve. Thinking historically, they let what they know transcend what they feel. This is the key to successful investing.

JUST DO IT!

It's all well and good to know about your strategies, but knowing and doing are distant cousins. As Goethe said, "To think is easy. To act is difficult. To act as one thinks is the most difficult of all." The reason that amateur and professional investors can't do better than the S&P 500 index is that they may have good ideas about successful investing but they don't always act on them. I hope your understanding of the strategies I'll cover in the next chapter will give you not only the power of knowledge but the will to action. Put the two together and you can retire rich.

CHAPTER THREE

THE STRATEGIES

Now that we know why most investors—amateur and professional alike—don't beat a strategy as simple as the S&P 500, let's take a look at some amazing strategies that have regularly outperformed the S&P 500 over the past 45 years. These strategies are so easy to understand that you can fit them on the back of a business card. But don't let their simplicity fool you. They have withstood the test of time and, if history is any indication, will continue to perform beautifully in the future.

These strategies will guide your stock selection. The important thing is that you will always know why you are buying or selling a particular stock. One of the reasons investors underperform the S&P 500 is because they invest on a stock-by-stock basis, without a coherent, underlying strategy. Apart from the story behind the stock, most investors really can't articulate why they bought a certain stock or how it fits their portfolio. You'll also know the various strategies' historical base rates. This means you'll never have to guess whether your portfolio's performance is normal, because you'll have 45 years of data to compare it with.

I highly recommend that you use these strategies in an IRA account. Not only is the first $2,000 a year you save in an IRA tax deductible but also everything you earn compounds tax free.

THE STRATEGIES | 45

Later, in chapters 4, 5, and 6, we'll see how you can utilize mutual funds, 401(k) plans, and other savings to enhance your wealth even more. For now, these strategies are your roadmap for successful investing.

CHANGE THE WAY YOU THINK

I'm going to try to change the way you think about stocks. Thousands of newsletters, magazines, newspapers, TV shows, and Web sites are devoted to the stock market. Some of them offer useful information, but for the most part all they do is add to that anxious feeling that you'll never be able to keep up with all the news. Don't let yourself fall into this trap.

Forget about a stock's industry. Disregard the most recent news stories praising or criticizing corporate management. Pay no attention to insider trading at the firm. Avoid what the latest stock market guru is saying about the prospects for a stock or an industry. Don't get wrapped up in what the company's president says in the annual report. Above all, don't let the stories about any stock influence your investment decisions.

Look instead at the attributes, or factors, that stocks possess. What is XYZ Corporation's PE ratio? What is its market capitalization? Does the stock have attributes that are similar to those of stocks that have done vastly better than the S&P 500? First I'll define these terms for you. And when you understand the factors, you will easily understand the actual investment strategies. Then we'll take a look at the winning strategies—how they have performed over time, how risky they are, and whether they are right for you.

Whenever you crave more serious detail, go to the Performance Appendix at the back of this book. There you'll find a comprehensive list of how each strategy performed in every year since 1951 and how they compare with other investments.

FACTOR DEFINITIONS

Some of the terms we'll be defining, like *market capitalization* and *price-to-sales ratios,* sound a lot more daunting than they really are. Wall Street pros, to make themselves sound like they're earning their high commissions, like to make you think it's complicated, but it's not. Let's get going!

MARKET CAPITALIZATION

Market capitalization is simply the **total dollar value of a company.** Total dollar value is the current price of each share times the common shares outstanding for that company. If a company has 100 shares outstanding and is trading at $10 per share, the company's market capitalization is $1,000. As you might expect, many well-known companies have huge market capitalizations. Coca-Cola is a giant, with 200,504,000 shares outstanding, each currently selling for $61. That translates to a market capitalization of over $151 billion. The company really could buy the world a Coke!

Coca-Cola dwarfs a company like Winnebago, the maker of recreational vehicles and motor homes. Even though Winnebago has a healthy 17 percent share of its market, it has a market capitalization of $181 million—modest in comparison to Coca-Cola's. Again, calculating Winnebago's market capitalization is simple. There are 25.3 million shares of Winnebago stock, at the time of this writing trading at $7.12 per share—25.3 × $7.12 = $181 million. (I'll show you where to get the information about market capitalization in chapter 8.)

Market capitalization is important because the stock prices of big companies bounce around a lot less than the stock prices of smaller companies, making them much less volatile. Generally, larger companies are better established, have been around a lot longer, and therefore have the wherewithal to sustain themselves in an economic downturn. Smaller companies are usually younger and have a more difficult time during a recession. However, when the economy is booming, the stock prices of smaller companies tend to do better than those of larger companies. This makes sense. It's much more unlikely for Coca-Cola's price to double than Winnebago's. When we get into the strategies, remember that market capitalization is the size of a company in absolute dollar value.

PRICE-TO-EARNINGS (PE) RATIO

In the last chapter we saw how stocks with high price-to-earnings ratios performed poorly compared with stocks with lower PE ratios. But exactly what is a price-to-earnings ratio? It is the **price of a stock divided by its annual earnings.** For example, if a stock is selling for $10 per share and has $2 of earnings per share, its price-to-earnings ratio is 5 ($10 ÷ $2). You are paying five times the earnings of the company for that stock. In reality, PE ratios of 5 are very low and very rare. The PE ratio of the S&P 500 in early 1997 was about 21 times earnings. When a stock has a very high PE ratio, it means that its price is high in relation to earnings. Conversely, the price of a stock with a low PE ratio is low in relation to earnings. Most of the time, you won't even have to calculate the PE ratio, since it's already reported in most major newspapers.

Price-to-earnings ratios have varied over time, generally being low during recessions and high when the economy is strong. They are also a handy gauge of investor expectations. When a stock has a high PE ratio, it is usually a signal that investors have very high expectations for that stock. They are willing to pay the moon for the stock because they expect future earnings to be even higher. Sadly, while hope may spring eternal, high expectations are generally dashed. Historically, high PE-ratio stocks have been very poor investments. Over the last 45 years, an investor annually buying the 50 stocks with the highest PE ratios would have seriously trailed the S&P 500 while taking much more risk, earning just 9.23 percent a year, compared with 12.15 for the S&P 500.

Our winning strategies focus on companies with low price-to-earnings ratios. Modest expectations are more often rewarded, and if a stock doesn't quite live up to these expectations, it's rarely punished as much as a stock with very high expectations that fails to deliver. The higher they climb, the harder they fall!

PRICE-TO-SALES RATIO

The next factor, the price-to-sales ratio, I've dubbed "King of the Value Ratios." You get the price-to-sales ratio by **dividing the price of a stock by the sales per share.** Another method is to divide a company's total market capitalization by its annual sales. For example, if a company has a market capitalization of $500 million and annual sales of $1 billion, it has a price-to-sales ratio of 0.5 ($500 million ÷ $1 billion).

The price-to-sales ratio differs from the price-to-earnings ratio in that it measures revenues rather than earnings. It looks at the top of the balance sheet rather than the bottom. But why do we want to focus on price-to-sales as opposed to price-to-earnings ratios? After all, I've never heard someone say, "Let's get down to the top line."

A joke can be illuminating here. A company wanted to hire a new chief financial officer. The board of directors asked each applicant just one question: "What is two plus two?" Each person except the woman who got the job answered four. Her answer was: "What number did you have in mind?" The joke illustrates how easy earnings are to manipulate—it's not uncommon for companies to do just that to look more appealing to investors. Sales figures are difficult to tamper with and therefore give a more truthful picture of the health of a company. That's why you're better off focusing on price-to-sales ratios rather than price-to-earnings ratios.

As with PE ratios, stocks with low price-to-sales ratios are better investments than stocks with high price-to-sales ratios. In early 1997, the average price-to-sales ratio of a stock in the S&P 500 was 1.7; in other words, the average stock was selling for $1.70 for each $1 of sales. But sometimes these dry ratios are difficult to get your arms around. Remember the corner store from chapter 2? I asked you to pay $1,000 for every $1 in sales that the store generated. You'd never be able to make any money if you paid such a high price, but that's exactly what investors do when they buy stocks with a hot story and superhigh price-to-sales ratios. What's more, even if these high price-to-sales ratio companies do prove to be wildly successful, investors often don't make any money, since even the brightest outcomes are already priced into the stock.

The story of Alcohol Sensors International is a fantastic example of how people are seduced into paying ridiculous price-to-sales ratios for a hot-story stock. Alcohol Sensors was a brand-new company in early 1995. It had just come out with a line of automobile ignition devices that would prevent a car from starting if a drunk driver was at the wheel. For a car with one of these devices to start, the driver must breathe into a sensor that measures alcohol on the breath. If an unacceptable level of alcohol is detected, the device disables the car's ignition. No doubt, many investors felt that this was a great invention, because by the end of 1995 the price-to-sales ratio of the stock was an astounding 1,486! Investors were paying $1,486 for every $1 of Alcohol Sensors International's sales! How could any company possibly live up to such high expectations? Alcohol Sensors surely couldn't—its price took an incredible beating in 1996, plunging 71.3 percent in one year. Clearly, investors weren't looking at the company's price-to-sales ratio when they bought the stock. They were more likely listening to news stories touting the stock, heeding the warnings of the Mothers Against Drunk Driving campaigns, believing the device was a great invention—but paying absolutely no attention to the fact that the stock was ridiculously overpriced. Alcohol Sensors may have had a good story, but it was a bad investment.

High price-to-sales ratio stocks are among the worst investments you could have made over the last 45 years, earning less than T-bills. Avoid them like the plague.

RELATIVE STRENGTH

Another important factor is relative strength. It may sound daunting but really is a very simple concept. The easiest way to understand it is to think about how well the stock price did over the previous year. Did it win? Did it lose? By how much? Let's say XYZ stock cost $50 a year ago but is worth $100 today. That's an increase of 100 percent. If the market had gone up just 10 percent during the same year we could say that XYZ stock has very strong relative strength, since it did 10 times as well as the overall stock market. An even simpler description of relative strength is **price appreciation.** The stocks whose prices appreciated the most last year have the strongest relative strength.

Strong relative strength is an important component of many of the successful investment strategies in this book, though it seems counterintuitive. You may be saying to yourself, Why would I want to buy a stock after its price has gone up so much? Isn't the whole point of this exercise to buy low and sell high? Author Damon Runyon once said that the battle is not always to the strong and the race not always to the swift—but that's the way to bet. Buying stocks with strong relative strength is just like betting on a fast horse. For a number of reasons, when a stock has very strong relative strength, it's usually a signal that investors have positive expectations for the company.

But again you say, "I don't want to buy a stock *after* it has gone up 100 percent! It can't sustain that kind of growth. I'll lose money." Intuitively, I agree with you, but the facts don't support us. In a fascinating 1989 study of stocks that went up 300 percent in any single calendar year, Professor Marc Reinganum of the University of Iowa found that 85 percent of them were at two-year highs before they tripled!

As I found in my research for *What Works on Wall Street,* relative strength is the only single growth variable that beat the market over the past 45 years. It's also a component of the 10 best-performing strategies over the last 45 years. It's not wise to use it alone to pick stocks, however. The strategy is far too volatile, with wild fluctuations that would make even a thrill-seeking investor queasy. As we learned last chapter, the inability to stick with a strategy is what causes most people to underperform the market over the long term. Successful strategies can't be so volatile that no one can stick with them. Relative strength is a particularly good tool to use in conjunction with low price-to-sales ratios. That is the essence of our Reasonable Runaways strategy, which chooses cheap stocks on the mend.

DIVIDEND YIELD

Several strategies we'll look at focus on dividend yield. A dividend is what a company pays out to its shareholders. The dividend yield is the **dividend per share divided by the price per share, times 100** (to make it a percentage). If a company pays a cash dividend of $1 per share and its shares sell for $10, the dividend yield is $1 \div 10 \times 100$, or 10 percent. Thus, you make 10 percent on your money. In addition to the dividend, of course, the prices of your shares may also increase.

Buying big, well-known companies with higher dividend yields is an excellent way to make money over the long term, especially for investors who don't like to take big risks. The Leaders with Luster and Dogs of the Dow strategies we'll cover shortly use high dividend yields as their final criteria. These strategies had the best risk-adjusted returns of all the strategies I studied over the past 45 years, because their high dividend yields reduced their overall risk so much.

Buying stocks with no dividend yields or low dividend yields is not necessarily bad. The aggressive strategies that we'll cover have little or no yields. That's because we want growth from those companies, not beefy dividends.

CASH FLOW

The final factor you need to understand is cash flow, which is the **income of a company after all expenses are paid, plus depreciation, except for provisions for common and preferred dividends.** Whew! That's a definition only an accountant could love! All you need to remember is that the cash flows of companies with large market capitalizations tend to be much greater than the cash flows of companies with smaller market capitalizations.

WINNING STRATEGIES: THE GROUND RULES

Now that you understand the factors, let's finally look at the investment strategies that can help you retire rich. Remember that you must stick with these strategies through thick and thin, in good times and in bad. All these strategies have years when they don't do as well as the S&P 500, and you will face years when you will lose some money. But my research has shown that these strategies can't be beat over the long term.

In chapter 6 I'll cover the mechanics of setting up accounts and putting together your portfolio, but for now I strongly advise that you use an IRA to hold the stocks in these strategies. Even if your $2,000 contribution isn't fully tax deductible, the investments compound on a tax-free basis, which will greatly enhance your returns over the long run. Also, using these strategies in your IRA will force you to think of them as long-term investments. Because you're penalized for withdrawing money from your IRA before you are 59½ years old, you'll be more likely to leave your money untouched and less likely to panic about short-term gyrations in your portfolio.

Setting up an IRA is simple. Just ask for an IRA application from whatever broker or mutual fund company you've decided to use; then send in your check. From then on, all the money in the IRA account compounds tax free, until you start withdrawing it after age 59½.

THE IMPORTANCE OF 25- TO 50-STOCK PORTFOLIOS

First of all, at least for our most aggressive strategies, you must buy between 25 and 50 stocks for your portfolio and rebalance your portfolio once a year, selling the stocks that no longer meet the strategies' criteria and buying those that do. (All the returns I quote in this book are from 50-stock portfolios unless otherwise noted.) Now, I can hear you howling, "O'Shaughnessy, you're crazy! How will I ever be able to buy, much less follow, 25 to 50 stocks? I'll never be able to read all those annual reports or know whether to keep or sell any particular stock in my portfolio!" Yet that's exactly why I want you to buy so many. Owning between 25 and 50 stocks is one of the key reasons these strategies work so well. It diversifies your investments and protects you from your own worst impulses. When you buy 25 to 50 stocks, you pay much less attention to individual stocks and their stories and more attention to the strategy that helped you choose them in the first place.

. I've said it before and I'll say it again: human nature makes it very difficult for us to ignore the story behind a stock. We're interested in *this* stock, or *this* industry, not in how a class of stocks performs over a long period of time. Remember the story in the last chapter, where people based their guesses about whether a person was a lawyer or an engineer entirely on their preconceived notions about what lawyers and engineers are like? We do the same thing with stocks. A stock-by-stock approach wreaks havoc with our ability to buy stocks successfully, since it virtually guarantees that we'll base our decisions on emotions and short-term thinking. People who buy stocks on a stock-by-stock basis almost never beat the S&P 500. Buying 25 to 50 stocks helps you short-circuit the impulse to follow each and every stock or to be seduced by their stories. The law of large numbers becomes a kind protector, helping you remove your emotions from your investment decisions.

A recent study underscores why you shouldn't put all your eggs in one small basket. Gerald Newbould and Percy Poon are professors of finance at the University of Nevada who studied the effect that the number of stocks held in a portfolio has on overall volatility and total return. They found that holding between 8 and 20 stocks—a common recommendation—wasn't enough to adequately diversify a portfolio. They found that to be within 20 percent of the commonly quoted risk and reward figures, an investor has to expand the number of stocks he or she owns to at least 25. And if your portfolio contains smaller-capitalization stocks, you should hold even more.

Yet the strategy revolution wouldn't be possible without the current revolution in the brokerage industry. Buying 25 to 50 stocks would have been extremely difficult and expensive for an individual a few years ago. But with the advent of deep discounts in the brokerage industry and on-line trading via the Internet, today it is a much more manageable task. You can now buy a few shares of stock at a time for a reasonable transaction fee and not get gouged on the price while you're doing it. (In chapter 9 I'll discuss in depth the mechanics of trading your portfolio.)

#1: REASONABLE RUNAWAYS

Let's start with our most aggressive strategy, Reasonable Runaways. This stock-picking strategy is one of the best I've found in my research of 45 years of stock market data. It delivers eye-popping returns. For example, had you invested $10,000 at the end of 1951 and faithfully stuck with the program year-in and year-out, your investment would have been worth $23 million by the end of 1996! The same $10,000 invested in the S&P 500 would have grown to only $1.7 million. And don't forget that the S&P 500 beats 80 percent of traditional mutual funds and professional money managers over the long term! The Reasonable Runaways strategy compounded at 18.81 percent per year since 1951, whereas the S&P 500's return was only 12.15 percent over the same time period.

Not only does Reasonable Runaways do extraordinarily well over long periods of time, it also works better than the S&P 500 over almost all 5- and 10-year periods, beating the S&P 500 in 80 percent of all 5-year periods over the past 45 years. Look at any 5 years over the last four decades—say, 1961 through 1966, 1973 through 1978, or 1980 through 1985. During 80 percent of these periods, Reasonable Runaways beat the S&P 500. So what does this mean? Well, if history is a good guide and you're reading this in 1998, by using the Reasonable Runaways strategy you have an 80 percent chance of beating the record of the S&P 500 by the end of 2002. Those are good odds!

The news gets even better when you look at Reasonable Runaways over 10-year periods. To retire well, you must invest long term, and it is over the long term that Reasonable Runaways really shines. In only one 10-year period did this strategy fail to beat the S&P 500—the 10 years ending December 31, 1990. During those years the S&P had an average annual compound return of 13.93 percent, whereas Reasonable Runaways' return compounded at 13.53 percent. That's a miniscule difference— I'd call it a draw.

Again, what does this mean? It means that if you invest your money in the Reasonable Runaways strategy and don't deviate from it for 10 years, you can be 97 percent certain, based on past performance, to do better than the S&P 500. By using this strategy you can compound your money at a tremendous rate. But remember, it is a long-term strategy.

Watch Out for Volatility

The negative side of this strategy is its volatility. It is considerably more volatile than the S&P 500, bouncing around a lot more than the S&P in any given year, just like the smaller-capitalization companies we discussed earlier. To use this strategy successfully, you must commit to it for 5 to 10 years and accept its volatility.

There were 15 separate years since 1951 when Reasonable Runaways did worse than the S&P 500, sometimes by significant amounts. In 1987, for example, Reasonable Runaways lost 12.9 percent, compared with the S&P 500's gain of 5.23 percent. And during the bear market of 1990, while the S&P 500 lost 3.5 percent, Reasonable Runaways lost 12 percent.

Never underestimate the power of volatility, because in real time, these losses can be very hard to stomach. If a strategy is too volatile, you're not going to be able to stick with it and then you won't make the money you had hoped to. If the ride is too frightening for you, and you just can't stand a 12 percent loss when the market is up, you should use a more conservative strategy that's easier for you to stay with through thick and thin. However, if you know the record of Reasonable Runaways over the last 45 years and make a long-term commitment to it, you will be handsomely rewarded.

To help people stay in the market when the sailing gets rough, I like to compare these investment strategies with keeping your money in cash or Treasury bills. Let's say you decide to keep your retirement savings in cash because you're terrified the market is going to collapse. We've already seen how deadly this can be for your retirement plans. Over the last 45 years, an investment in cash returned virtually nothing after inflation. More important, there was never a 10-year period when the returns on Treasury bills beat the Reasonable Runaways strategy! The worst 10-year return that this strategy had was 7.52 percent per year for the 10 years ending December 31, 1974. Over that same time period, the S&P 500 compounded at just 1.24 percent. So no matter when you started over the past 45 years, if you stuck with Reasonable Runaways for 10 years, you'd always be better off than if you kept your savings in cash. This is an extraordinary statistic. Remember it, and it will be much easier to stick with Reasonable Runaways through thick and thin.

Let's continue this exercise, because I think it is profoundly important. Let's say it's the end of 1974 and you have $10,000 to invest. The market has lost almost 50 percent in just two years. It has been the most devastating period for the stock market since the great crash of 1929 and the Great Depression in the 1930s. No one wants to invest in the stock market. The prophets of doom are predicting that inflation will wipe out all your savings, telling you that gold is the only place to put your money. OPEC controls the world's energy supply. The United States has just gone through one of the biggest constitutional crises in its history, resulting in the resignation of the president and the assumption of the office by a man who was not elected but selected—by his disgraced predecessor.

Clearly, it was a difficult time to commit any money to the stock market. Lacking any long-term understanding of the investment strategies outlined in this book, it would take incredible courage to invest in the market during such a grim economy. Nevertheless, had you invested $10,000 in Reasonable Runaways in 1974, by the end of 1984 your investment would have grown to $114,000 and you'd have earned an annual compound return of over 27 percent! The same $10,000 invested in Treasury bills grew to $23,000, a return of 8.71 percent a year. Remember that the worst 10-year period that the Reasonable Runaways strategy experienced was the 10 years ending December 31, 1974. Even then, a $10,000 investment grew at 7.53 percent a year to $20,000, comfortably ahead of the 5.47 percent return earned by Treasury bills over the same 10 years.

If you are worried about where the market is headed right now, focus on any time in the past when people were afraid to put their money in the stock market. You'll see that the stock market is always the best place to put your money over the long term. Look at the early 1980s, when T-bills were yielding over 14 percent. Anyone not jumping at those rates had to be a fool, right? Wrong. Anyone keeping his or her money in 90-day Treasury bills since the end of 1981 would have earned only 6.45 percent a year. Investors using Reasonable Runaways would have every reason to gloat—their returns would have been 19.53 percent a year.

Commit for the Long Term

A 10-year commitment to Reasonable Runaways is essential, particularly if you are going to invest most or all of your IRA savings in it. This is a volatile strategy that's not appropriate for people who are unwilling or unable to commit to it for 10 years. We will see later in this chapter that mixing Reasonable Runaways with other, less volatile, strategies is appropriate for people with a shorter time horizon or less risk tolerance. Make sure you look at the Performance Appendix at the back of this book to gauge your ability to withstand those years when the stocks go up or down dramatically.

How Does Reasonable Runaways Work?

Let's look at exactly how Reasonable Runaways works. First, all the stocks that we will consider—our universe—must have market capitalizations greater than $150 million. This eliminates all the very small stocks, often called micro-caps, which can be very tricky to actually buy at a fair price. Next, we're going to buy only stocks with price-to-sales ratios of less than 1. We want to buy a dollar's worth of sales for less than a dollar. Finally, we're going to buy the 25 to 50 stocks with the best price appreciation last year. That's it. It's literally as easy as one, two, three, four.

1. Market capitalization must exceed $150 million.
2. Price-to-sales ratios must be lower than 1.
3. Buy the 25 to 50 stocks from numbers 1 and 2 above that have the best one-year price appreciation.
4. Rerun the selection process once a year.

Not only is it that simple; there's also no wondering whether that new management team will turn the company around. No listening to your brother-in-law tout his latest hot stock. No countless hours sifting through financial magazines trying to make sense of conflicting advice. No guessing and hoping. This is a time-tested strategy with results based on 45 years of market history. Let history be your guide—ignore the noise of today's market opinion and speculation.

Let me remind you how important it is to buy between 25 and 50 stocks if you are using the Reasonable Runaways strategy. This is an aggressive strategy with significant volatility, and to buy just a few stocks is suicide. The diversification that comes from a larger portfolio is essential to your success.

Why Does It Work So Well?

So why does Reasonable Runaways work so well? Think about it. How could it *not* work? Essentially, you're buying a diversified group of bargain-priced stocks on their way back up. You're buying one dollar's worth of sales for less than one dollar. Even if that were the only factor you used, you'd eventually make money! Investors have very low expectations for these stocks, yet you are buying them when investors are reassessing their prospects, indicated by the tremendous price appreciation over the previous year. Investors are saying, "Should we really be paying only 50 cents for every $1 of this company's sales?" It could be a tremendous computer maker like Dell or a popular West Coast fast-food chain like Karls Jr.—*the name of the stocks you'll buy each year doesn't matter.* What matters is what you get for your money—in this case, cheap stocks that investors are reassessing. It is a one–two punch that has worked very well over the long term.

Reasonable Runaways is what I call a blended strategy, uniting elements of both value and growth investing. Using a low price-to-sales ratio involves a component of value strategies because it selects bargain-priced stocks. Relative strength measures the price momentum of stocks, traditionally a factor used by growth investors. Uniting the two gives us the best of both worlds. You don't have to wait forever for your bargain stocks to be discovered because their price appreciation in the previous year indicates that they are already being noticed, yet because their price-to-sales ratios are below 1, they are still reasonably priced.

Discipline Is the Key to Success

The key, of course, is discipline. You must have discipline when using these strategies to invest in stocks. Every year, you must rebalance your portfolio to once again hold the 10, 25, or 50 stocks that meet your chosen strategy's criteria. Don't play favorites and keep any stocks that no longer qualify. Rebalance your portfolio each year; sell all the stocks that no longer meet your criteria and buy the new stocks that replace them. Once again, weight the stocks equally, so that you stay absolutely true to your strategy. Remember, *most traditional actively managed funds do not do as well as the S&P 500!* You, too, will have years when you do not do as well as the S&P if you are using Reasonable Runaways. But if you stick with it year-in and year-out, you will succeed.

Let's have some fun and look at the upside of Reasonable Runaways. Look at just a few years. In 1982, Reasonable Runaways returned almost 40 percent, almost double the S&P 500's very healthy 21.4 percent gain. In 1965 the S&P 500 was up 12.45 percent, whereas Reasonable Runaways returned a dazzling 55 percent! And in 1971 Reasonable Runaways earned 32 percent compared with 14 percent for the S&P 500.

More often than not, this strategy beats the S&P 500 by a wide margin. But I hope I've made my point about the potential dangers of the volatility of Reasonable Runaways. You're going to have to live through some bad years to reap the rewards of the strategy. Never underestimate the power those losing years can have over you, because when the strategy is down, you're going to want to jump ship.

Look at 1987. The market has crashed, and Reasonable Runaways did even worse than the S&P 500. At that time, your desire to abandon this strategy would have been overwhelming, and the news media would have fueled your fears even more. In years like that, you need to review the Performance Appendix at the back of this book. Photocopy the historical returns of Reasonable Runaways and tape the page to your refrigerator. Study the numbers every morning before you grab your orange juice. Constantly remind yourself that you are investing for the long term. That is the only way you will succeed. Remind yourself, when the market is down, that this is a strategy that has never, ever underperformed Treasury bills over a 10-year period. If you stick with the Reasonable Runaways strategy, you can retire rich. But the volatility of the strategy doesn't make it easy.

Because they are young and have time on their side, Bill and Nancy Robinson are ideal candidates for Reasonable Runaways. Even if the strategy has a decade when it earns returns similar to those of the worst decade in the last 45 years, they'd still have more than 20 years to let Reasonable Runaways shine. If you're young like the Robinsons, this is clearly the strategy for you.

The Lazy Man's Reasonable Runaways

OK, you're sold on the idea that you must use a great stock market strategy if you want to retire rich. But I'm lazy, you say, and don't have the time or inclination to go to the library to look up the price-to-sales ratios that are integral to the Reasonable Runaways strategy. Can I use the PE ratios I find in the newspaper instead? You most certainly can. While PE ratios aren't as true an indicator of a company's value, they are far better known to the general public than price-to-sales ratios and easy to find in most major newspapers.

The PE version of the Reasonable Runaways strategy is almost as profitable as the low price-to-sales ratio version, turning a $10,000 investment at the end of 1951 into $22.7 million by the end of 1996, a compound return of 18.74 percent a year. The two are very similar in other ways as well. Like the original Reasonable Runaways, the PE version was never outperformed by cash in any 10-year period, and the worst compound annual return over any 10 years was 6.15 percent. Its base rate is not quite as good as the original version, beating the S&P 500 67 percent of the time in any single year, 85 percent in any 5-year period, and 92 percent of the time in any 10-year period. The fundamental reason to use this version of the strategy is convenience.

#2: Leaders with Luster

But what if, try as you might, you just can't stand the risk and volatility associated with the Reasonable Runaways strategy? Tom and Sarah O'Neil are perfect examples. Sarah, in particular, gets queasy just thinking about the stock market. Even after reviewing the long-term returns of Reasonable Runaways, the O'Neils are certain they can't stomach its volatility. What if you, like the O'Neils, want to use a strategy that lets you sleep more soundly at night? Or what if you are nearing retirement and need a more conservative strategy?

A Less Volatile Strategy

Leaders with Luster is a tremendous strategy that buys well-known, market-leading companies with high dividend yields. Unlike Reasonable Runaways, which holds smaller and lesser-known stocks, the stocks in Leaders with Luster are household names like Mobil, Exxon, General Motors, Ford, Chrysler, GTE, and DuPont. The Leaders with Luster strategy is a large-capitalization strategy, with much lower risk than Reasonable Runaways as a result. The worst Leaders with Luster ever did in any single year over the past 45 years was a loss of 15 percent, compared with a loss of almost 26.5 percent for the S&P 500.

If you invested $10,000 in Leaders with Luster in 1951, that money would have been worth $6.4 million at the end of 1996, compared with the $1.7 million you'd have earned from the same investment in the S&P 500. I know this return is not as enticing as the return of Reasonable Runaways, but it is amazing when you consider that you are taking virtually the same risk as the S&P 500—and making a lot more money. Imagine, instead of the $1.7 million you'd earn from an investment in the S&P 500, you'd make $6.4 million without taking any additional risk! But that's not all. This strategy beats the S&P 500 95 percent of the time over all 5-year periods and 97 percent of the time over all 10-year periods.

The strength of this strategy is in how well it performs over 5-year periods. Leaders with Luster never lost money over any 5-year period in the past 45 years. Because of this, it's a fabulous strategy for people whose overwhelming impulse is to keep their savings in cash. If history is a reliable guide, and you stick with this strategy for at least 5 years, you are almost 100 percent certain not to underperform the S&P 500. This is a conservative strategy that never lost a dime over any 5-year period, beat cash 95 percent of the time, and beat long-term corporate bonds 100 percent of the time over all 10-year periods and 95 percent of the time over all 5-year periods. Leaders with Luster is a strategy that just about anyone can stick with, which, as I've pointed out time and time again, is the key to successful investing.

A Great Strategy for the Bear in You

What's more, if you're really nervous that the next bear market is around the corner, this is the strategy for you. One of the worst 5-year periods in stock market history was from 1969 to 1974. The S&P 500 lost 2.35 percent per year during that time, so $10,000 invested there at the end of 1969 would have been worth only $8,877 at the end of 1974. But look at Leaders with Luster. The same $10,000 invested in this strategy would have been worth $12,125, a return of 3.93 percent a year. It may not be much to brag about, but it's a lot better than a loss.

For those of you with shorter time horizons, these numbers are very important to understand. If you need to use your savings in five years or less, Leaders with Luster makes more sense than Reasonable Runaways, and it is the strategy that I recommend.

How Does Leaders with Luster Work?

So how does Leaders with Luster work? We'll start by creating a universe of stocks that I call market leaders. Market leaders are big, well-known companies that most people are happy to invest in. Here is how to determine whether a stock is a market leader: First, the market capitalization of a market-leading company has to be greater than that of the average stock, usually about $1 billion. Second, the cash flow has to be greater than average. Third, the number of common shares outstanding also must be greater than average. Next, annual sales should be 50 percent higher than those of the average stock. Finally, I exclude electric utility stocks. While they usually pay very high dividend yields, their share prices don't appreciate as much as those of nonutility stocks. (We'll look at a wonderful utility strategy later in this chapter.)

To arrive at the Leaders with Luster strategy, we simply take our market-leading companies and once a year buy the 25 to 50 stocks with the highest dividend yields. Again, it's a simple strategy, so why does it work so well? Many market researchers have found that the stock prices of most large companies tend to do as well as the stock prices of other large companies. So, if Exxon is compounding at a rate of 10 percent, it's likely that GE or any other large company will have similar returns. Leaders with Luster works so well because of the high dividend yields that the stocks pay, giving those safe, market-leading companies a nice boost in performance. It's a strategy you could gladly recommend to your grandmother or Aunt Esther, since its focus is on safe and solid companies.

Getting the Best of Both Worlds

But wait a minute, you say. Both strategies sound great—I love Reasonable Runaways' great performance but prefer the lower risk and lower volatility of Leaders with Luster. What happens if I put Reasonable Runaways and Leaders with Luster together? Now you've hit on something! In my study of the last 45 years, I found that blending these two strategies was absolutely the best thing you could do if you want great rewards with lower risk. If you had split your money between Leaders with Luster and Reasonable Runaways, an investment of $10,000 on December 31, 1951, would have grown to $13.6 million by the end of 1996.

This blended portfolio is consistently profitable, beating the S&P 500 in 34 of the last 45 years. That's a success rate of 76 percent in any given year! The worst one-year loss was 24.3 percent—less than any one-year loss suffered by either the S&P 500 or the Reasonable Runaways strategy. The worst 5-year period for this strategy was virtually a wash. It lost slightly more than 1 percent for the 5 years ending December 31, 1973. What's more, this strategy beat bonds and T-bills 100 percent of the time over all 10-year periods.

Combining Reasonable Runaways and Leaders with Luster is

a great strategy for people who crave comfort and stability. That's why George and Theresa Ramirez have decided to use it. They want to leave money to their children and grandchildren and think Reasonable Runaways would help them do that, but they just don't think they can stick with such a volatile strategy. By combining Leaders with Luster and Reasonable Runaways, they can be 75 percent certain to do better than the S&P 500 in any given year.

Remember that you still have to accept that 25 percent of the time you won't beat the S&P 500, even with this safe and stable blended strategy. To use any of these strategies successfully, you must accept that there will be years when you lose money and years when your portfolio won't perform as well as the S&P 500.

None of these strategies are for people who are interested in only next quarter's or even next year's performance. Those who think that they can always do better than the market or never lose money in stocks are delusional. People who think like that usually end up with virtually nothing to show for all the time and effort they spend trying to jump in and out of the market or trying to find the next red-hot money manager. If you do that, you'll never beat the market over long periods of time.

Blending Leaders with Luster and Reasonable Runaways gives you the best of both worlds. You own big, well-known companies with high dividend yields, as well as smaller, reasonably priced companies whose prices are really starting to appreciate. It's an all-around strategy—you get value, you get growth. You get big, you get small. You're so diversified that when one strategy is down, the other is often up.

If you decide to use this blended strategy, you don't have to buy 100 stocks. Buying 25 stocks from each strategy—for a total of 50 in your portfolio—is actually slightly more profitable than buying 100 stocks, although the risk is slightly higher. And again, if you use a discount broker, buying these 50 stocks is manageable and affordable.

THREE 10-STOCK STRATEGIES

All right, so now you're a believer, but you just can't commit to buying 25–50 stocks. Try as you might, and despite evidence to the contrary, you still think buying so many stocks is too much of a hassle. Is there any successful strategy that lets you buy fewer stocks?

You can build a portfolio of 10 stocks, but it's a little like a dieter being willing to carry a few extra pounds so he can enjoy those tasty brownies. You're not going to be as thin, but you're not going to have to work as hard either. Provided you don't expect to make as much money as you would with Reasonable Runaways and prepare yourself for a little extra volatility, you can choose from three excellent 10-stock strategies. The only time it's acceptable to buy fewer than 25, however, is when you're using conservative strategies focusing on big, well-known companies.

Steve and Betsy Johnson are keen on these variations. They would like to keep their investment program as simple as possible, and they just don't have the time to learn about the new deep-discount stockbrokers and trading via the Internet. They want to keep their account at the discount broker they've used for years, where they can do business over the phone. Here are three 10-stock strategies—Dogs of the Dow, the Utility strategy, and Core Value—that would work well for the Johnsons.

#3: DOGS OF THE DOW

Dogs of the Dow is a 10-stock strategy that has become very popular in the last several years. I wrote an article for *Barron's* in 1992 featuring its returns over the previous 63 years. *Barron's* now writes quarterly articles on the Dogs, keeping interest in it high. The strategy is ridiculously simple. Start with the 30 internationally famous blue chip stocks in the Dow Jones Industrial Average (the current stocks are listed in the Performance Appendix at the back of this book). Rank them by dividend yield, from high to low. Then, every year, buy the 10 stocks with the highest dividend yields, replacing any that have fallen off the list. That's it! Over the last 15 years this simple strategy has beaten 95 percent of all traditionally managed mutual funds! When you look at longer periods of time, it's done even better.

Since 1929, the Dogs of the Dow strategy has beaten the S&P 500 in every decade—from the depression in the 1930s to the restructuring in the 1990s. In only two 10-year periods did it fail to beat the S&P 500. Its 5-year base rate isn't as good as Leaders with Luster's, but remember that you're buying only 10 stocks. For an easy-to-use 10-stock strategy, Dogs of the Dow is truly phenomenal.

That's Some Track Record!

The beauty of Dogs of the Dow is that you can look at its performance all the way back to 1929. I always recommend looking at a worst-case scenario before choosing an investment strategy, because it shows you what to expect.

Say it's 1929. On the eve of the biggest crash in market history, you've decided to put your money in Dogs of the Dow. You stick with it, and by 1938 you have not lost money, although the crash ushered in the worst depression this country has ever experienced and many other investors are financially ruined. The $10,000 you invested on December 31, 1928, was worth $10,888 in 1938. And that's just if you made a lump sum investment of $10,000 before the market crashed. Had you put $2,000 a year in Dogs of the Dow between 1928 and 1939, your $22,000 investment would have grown to $38,765, a gain of 76 percent in one of the worst 10-year periods in American economic history! During that time, you would have lost money had you invested it in the S&P 500.

The Awesome Power of Compounding

The Dogs of the Dow strategy demonstrates the awesome power of compounding. What if you'd been lucky enough to have a grandparent open an account for you in January 1929 and invest it in Dogs of the Dow? Even though the ensuing decades brought depressions, world wars, runaway inflation, price controls, and every conceivable type of economic boom and bust, you would be enormously rich. A $10,000 investment in the S&P 500 at the start of 1929 would have been worth just over $6 million by the end of 1996. The same $10,000 invested in Dogs of the Dow would have been worth almost $34 million—a difference of almost $28 million. The amazing thing is that when you compare the compound returns, they don't look that much different. The Dogs of the Dow compounded at 12.7 percent a year, while the S&P grew at 9.89 percent a year. You'd have $28 million more just because your annual compound rate of return was 2.81 percent higher. To retire rich, it's essential to reach for some of the higher returns our strategies offer.

The Dogs of the Dow and Leaders with Luster both buy large, well-known companies with high dividend yields. The primary difference between the strategies—other than the number of stocks they hold—is that Leaders with Luster fishes from a larger pond of stocks, owning stocks outside the Dow Jones Industrial Average as well as overseas companies that are traded on U.S. exchanges. Grand Metropolitan PLC is a high-yielding company that owns all-American businesses like Burger King, Green Giant, and Pillsbury, but because it is a foreign company it would never show up in the Dogs of the Dow strategy. It could, however, be included in Leaders with Luster.

Another difference between the two strategies is that Leaders with Luster's overall dividend yield is higher than that of the Dogs of the Dow. Again, this is because Leaders with Luster reaches beyond the 30 stocks in the Dow Jones Industrial Average. Just because Ford Motor Company and Kellogg's aren't Dow stocks doesn't mean they are bad investments. As a matter of fact, many times they offer higher yields than many Dow stocks.

Both Leaders with Luster and Dogs of the Dow have similar 10-year base rates, but Leaders with Luster has better 5-year base rates. The trade-off is ease. With Dogs of the Dow, you buy fewer stocks and they are easier to find, making the portfolio less complicated.

#4: Utility Strategy

Leaders with Luster and Dogs of the Dow are wonderful conservative strategies with high dividend yields. If you're retired—or close to retirement—you may want an even higher dividend income than either one of those strategies can provide. One way to do this, while still having the benefit of owning stocks, is to invest in utilities. The next 10-stock portfolio I recommend focuses on utility stocks, whose yields are traditionally very high.

This simple 10-stock Utility strategy is a great way to earn high yields while still having the opportunity for capital gains. Note that this strategy doesn't limit you to just utility stocks, but 95 percent of the time utility stocks are what the strategy chooses.

Safety First

Never make the mistake of buying a stock just because it has a high dividend yield. You must make sure that the company will actually be able to keep up its dividend payment. Many financially insecure companies pay high dividends, but they can rarely keep up rich payouts when times get tough. You need to buy only the safest companies with high dividend yields. To find them, go to the library and look at the *Value Line Investment Survey,* a quantitative rating service that provides information on around 1,700 stocks. *Value Line* assigns safety ranks to the stocks it covers. This rank is awarded on a scale of 1 to 5. Stocks that *Value Line*'s formulas deem safest are ranked 1, and those deemed riskiest are ranked 5. *Value Line* bases the safety rank on the stability of the stock's price, as well as a host of other factors, including company size, market penetration, product market volatility, financial leverage, earnings quality, and the overall condition of the balance sheet.

This Utility strategy is the best utility stock strategy I have found in my research of 45 years of data. Like Dogs of the Dow it's very simple. Start with the *Value Line* stocks with a safety rank of 1. From this list (usually about 120 stocks), once a year, buy the 10 stocks with the highest dividend yields. That's it! Because you're using yield as your final criterion, you almost always end up with a portfolio of high-quality utility stocks. And because of their safety ranks, the stocks in the portfolio are far less risky than the average stock.

Income and Capital Gains, Too

What singles this Utility strategy out is that it has a dividend yield that rivals bonds. Over the last 12 years, the average yield of the portfolio has been above 6 percent! (Because only 12 years' worth of safety rank information is available, I have results for this strategy since only 1985.) And the Utility strategy has done fairly well in total return. For the 12 years ending December 31, 1996, the strategy earned an annual compound return of 14.74 percent, compared with an annual gain of 16.80 percent for the S&P 500. Note that trying to outdo the S&P 500 is not the point of this strategy. Rather, it's designed to act as a substitute for bonds, offering high income. Yet, unlike bonds, it offers investors something more—the opportunity to earn capital gains as well.

Say it's 1986, and Bill and Nancy Robinson decide to retire early. They've saved $2 million and are comparing an investment in bonds with an investment split evenly between bonds and the stock market. Their primary concern is to generate enough income for a rich retirement while protecting themselves from the ravages of inflation. In 1986, the yield on a 10-year Treasury bond is about 8 percent. If they put the entire $2 million into bonds, their annual income will be $160,000. Bonds, however, won't protect them from inflation. While $160,000 was a great income in 1986, it may not be so great after 10 or 15 years later. But when Bill and Nancy look at the various strategies I've covered, only this Utility strategy offers a yield high enough to generate a good income. At the end of 1986, this 10-stock strategy had a yield of 6.9 percent, just 1.1 percent lower than the Treasury bonds!

They decide to split their money evenly between the Utility strategy and Treasury bonds. They plan to spend all the income that they earn. They're going to travel, spend money on their children, have fun, and relax. If the Robinsons put all their money in Treasury bonds, they would never have more than $2 million, since they plan to spend all their income. But since they have decided to put $1 million of their savings into the Utility strategy, in addition to the dividend income they'll receive, they'll earn a compound annual return of 5.78 percent per year, and their $1 million will grow to $1.7 million. As a result, by the end of 1996 they have $2.7 million, almost 50 percent more money than if they had put it all in Treasury bonds. What's more, their income is growing as the years go by, protecting them from inflation.

If you're an income-hungry investor who doesn't want to risk losing your savings to inflation, this Utility strategy is a wonderful tool. Remember, though, that if you don't need income from your savings right now, you're going to be much better off using one of the other strategies I've covered, since they compound at a much higher rate and will make you far richer in the long run.

#5: CORE VALUE

While you're still in the library with the *Value Line Investment Survey,* let's look at one more conservative strategy that has done tremendously well over the last 12 years. Again, we only have data on this strategy from the last 12 years, but the criteria we're using have withstood a longer test of time.

The Robinsons used the Utility strategy because they needed a portfolio that generated enough income for them to lead rich and rewarding lives in retirement. They didn't want to risk losing any capital by buying any old stock with a high dividend yield, so they stuck with stocks that *Value Line* rated highest for safety. What if they could get a slightly lower yield in return for even more safety?

The Core Value strategy is another 10-stock portfolio ideal for conservative investors. Because it consists of only 10 stocks, it's very important that all of them be safe, sound investments. To create Core Value, we'll again use the *Value Line Investment Survey*, but this time we will look at financial strength ratings rather than safety ranks. Many rating services rank the financial stability of stocks and bonds; *Value Line*'s system is different because it rates each stock's financial strength relative to all others in the database. The ratings range from A++ to C in nine steps. Companies with the best financial strength are rated A++ because they have the ability to weather hard times better than almost all the other companies in the database. The ratings continue from A++ to A+ to A, then B++ to B+ to B, all the way down to C, the lowest of the nine ratings. *Value Line* gives its lowest rating to companies with very serious financial problems.

Since Core Value buys just 10 stocks, we'll insist on an A++ rank. By limiting our choices to those with the best financial strength, we eliminate all but about 40 stocks in the *Value Line* universe. And you'll recognize them all—such as Boeing, Bristol Myer Squibb, Coca-Cola, General Electric, and Lilly. Next, since 45 years of data show how well big companies with high dividend yields perform, we'll eliminate all the A++ stocks with dividend yields below the average A++ stock. Thus, if we see that the average A++ company has a yield of 3.1 percent, we'll require all Core Value stocks to have yields greater than that.

Finally, from the approximately 20 stocks that remain, we'll annually buy the 10 stocks that are expected to increase their dividend the most in the next three to five years. You find this figure by looking at the projected dividend growth rate figure within the *Value Line* report. The 10 remaining stocks constitute a wonderful core holding in any equity portfolio.

Great Performance Over the Last 12 Years

If you think this financially strong, high-yielding portfolio sacrifices returns, think again—over the last 12 years, the Core Value portfolio had a compound return of 21.17 percent, considerably higher than the S&P 500's return of 16.80 percent over the same time period. Keep in mind that if you could test Core Value's returns back to 1951, they would probably be closer to the returns of Dogs of the Dow or Leaders with Luster, as stocks have performed particularly well over the last 12 years. Nevertheless, this strategy is a standout performer, offering exceptional returns from the most financially secure stocks.

PUTTING IT ALL TOGETHER

We've covered a lot of ground, but I'm sure that by now you understand that you don't have to settle for the returns of an index like the S&P 500. History shows that market capitalization is not the best factor to use when building a successful portfolio; rather, it's quite average. Just because the folks at Dow Jones and Standard & Poor's focus on market capitalization doesn't mean we have to. Imagine if, back in the 1950s, Dow Jones decided to base its Industrial Average on low price-to-sales ratio stocks rather than large blue chip companies. The Dow Jones Industrial Average would be four times higher than it is today! Imagine how the performance of most conventional managers would look compared with that!

HISTORY IS THE BEST TEACHER

These five time-tested strategies, singly or in combination, have strongly and consistently outperformed the S&P 500 over the past 45 years. Remember, when I say "strongly outperformed," that can mean as little as 2–3 percent per year. It's the compounding effect of those returns that can make a vast difference to your wealth. By saving your money and investing it in a strategy that earns just a few percent more a year than the S&P 500, you can retire rich.

I strongly believe that these strategies will continue to shine. They make a great deal of sense. On the aggressive side of the market, it pays to be a cheapskate and focus on reasonably valued stocks that are rebounding from a setback. On the conservative side, all roads lead to high dividend yields. It makes sense to buy financially strong companies with higher dividend yields.

The key to your success is discipline. All these strategies had years when they didn't beat the S&P 500. Let's say you decided to invest in Dogs of the Dow in 1972. You read an article in *Barron's* showing you that a $10,000 investment in Dogs grew to over $500,000 between December 31, 1928, and December 31, 1971, whereas the same investment in the S&P 500 grew to just $324,000. But then you take a look at the last five years. Ouch! Not only did Dogs of the Dow trail the S&P 500, it underperformed it in each of the last three years. In 1971 alone, the Dogs of the Dow did only half as well as the S&P 500. Even after seeing all the long-term data, you'd be inclined to say, "Well, the strategy used to work, but it doesn't anymore."

Of course, we now know that Dogs of the Dow was a dragon-slayer during the ensuing five years, doing almost three times as well as the S&P 500—$10,000 invested in Dogs at the end of 1971 (right before the worst bear market since the 1930s) grew to $27,700 by the end of 1976, while the same $10,000 invested in the S&P 500 grew to just $12,700. The Dogs actually showed a gain during the worst bear market since the 1930s!

Above all, remember that these strategies won't make you rich if you don't stick with them. Like the real estate mantra "Location, location, location," ours is "Discipline, discipline, discipline."

CHAPTER FOUR

MUTUAL FUNDS:
What to Look For—and Look Out For

Mutual funds are the most popular investment vehicles available to investors today. Their growth has been truly sensational. Between 1994 and 1996 alone, investments in U.S. equity funds nearly doubled, growing from $870 billion to $1.5 trillion dollars! And there are plenty to choose from—in 1997 there were more mutual funds in existence than there were stocks trading on the New York Stock Exchange!

Mutual funds are as vast in scope as they are in number. Currently, you can get a mutual fund for virtually any purpose, from the conservative to the outlandish. Want a fund that doesn't invest in tobacco stocks? No problem. How about a fund that invests all its money in computer stocks? There's a ton of those. Believe that the stars foretell the future? Go ahead and plunk your money into a fund that picks stocks using astrology!

In chapters 5 and 6 we'll see how you can best integrate mutual funds into your overall campaign to retire rich. For now, let's see what you should look for and look out for when considering mutual funds.

WHY MUTUAL FUNDS CAN BE A GOOD INVESTMENT

It is not a perfect world, and mutual funds are not a perfect investment, but they can be a very good bet for a careful investor. They have several things going for them.

EASY DOES IT

The first and foremost advantage of mutual funds is ease. The PITA (pain in the ass) factor is much lower when you buy a mutual fund than when you put a portfolio together yourself. Do I think you *can* put a great portfolio together yourself? Absolutely—all you need to do is use the strategies I described in the last chapter. Do I believe you *will* do it yourself? I hope so, especially now that you have 45 years of data showing you just how well these strategies work. But experience has taught me that even true believers often lack the time, inclination, and interest to fully implement these strategies. Even though our portfolios need to be revisited only once a year, it can be difficult to follow all the paperwork, problems, and proxy statements that come from owning 25 to 50 stocks. What's more, if you're starting out with $2,000 or $3,000, it can be pretty tricky and relatively expensive to buy 25 to 50 stocks. If you're starting out with just a couple thousand dollars, you should probably put your money into a mutual fund until you've accumulated enough money to buy 25 to 50 stocks with greater ease.

Steve and Betsy Johnson face the same problems when looking at the Reasonable Runaways and Leaders with Luster strategies. They feel they just don't have the time to build a 25- or 50-stock portfolio on their own. They prefer investing in mutual funds because it's relatively easy.

DIVERSIFICATION: A SAFETY NET FOR THE PRUDENT INVESTOR

The second good reason to own mutual funds is that they enforce a diversified investment. By law, mutual funds are forbidden to own more than 5 percent of any one stock, which means they must own at least 20 stocks. I cannot overstate the importance of diversification. Many of you might find that the strategies in this book make a lot of sense but you say, "I only have the time and money to buy five stocks from the list." *Don't do it.* I can't tell you how many times we hear this at O'Shaughnessy Capital Management and how many times it ends badly. Indeed, as I mentioned in the last chapter, I think 10 stocks is the absolute minimum for a portfolio, and then only if you are buying conservative, well-known stocks with high dividend yields. Buying a minimum of 10 stocks keeps you focused on strategies rather than stories and helps you diversify away some of the risk that comes with investing in the market.

Let me give you a great example of why diversification is so important. Get a pencil and break it. That wasn't very hard, was it? Now find 50 pencils, put them all together with a rubber band, and try to break them at once. I'll bet you can't do it. Even if you smash the bundle on the side of your desk you'll probably break only a couple and the rest will survive unscathed. Diversification acts like that bundle of 50 pencils, protecting you from the pain of the price declines of a few "broken" stocks.

A few years ago, technology and semiconductor stocks were red hot. And rightly so, since they shared many characteristics of the stocks in Reasonable Runaways at the time. But investors panicked, thinking that enthusiasm got out of hand as the prices of those stocks soared to new highs. Even though many of the stocks were still attractive because of their underlying factors, the inevitable corrections came, of course, and the technology and semiconductor stocks got hit hard. Many lost more than 50 percent of their value in less than six months.

Right before their swoon, however, those stocks were at the top of many buy lists. If you had tried to cherry pick just 5 or 10 hot stocks from those lists, you might have ended up with nothing but semiconductor and technology stocks, and your portfolio would have suffered a horrendous blow.

If you have a portfolio of 50 stocks, when a few stocks go down in value you're not going to suffer too much. Any single stock—or group of stocks from one industry—can blow up, even if it meets all the criteria of one of our strategies. But the likelihood of many or all of the 50 stocks in a carefully constructed portfolio doing poorly is very slim indeed. Thus, a diversified portfolio is a wonderful safety net for any prudent investor.

WHY MUTUAL FUNDS CAN BE A BAD INVESTMENT

THE S&P 500 BEATS MOST MUTUAL FUNDS

Sadly, many mutual funds are not good investments. Why? Because *80 percent of them fail to beat the S&P 500* over the long term, as well as the short term. According to the *Washington Post,* in addition to losing to the S&P 500, the average mutual fund in 1996 was also beaten by the S&P 1,500 Super Composite Index, the S&P 600 Small Cap Index, the New York Stock Exchange Composite Index, The Dow Jones Industrial Average, and the NASDAQ Composite Index. Whew!

As we now know, the S&P 500 is nothing more than a large-capitalization strategy. Buying all the stocks in the Compustat database, whose market capitalizations are greater than the database mean, can easily duplicate its returns. So, you say, if the S&P 500 strategy is so simple, why can't more than 20 percent of mutual fund managers beat it? Good question.

FUND MANAGERS FACE THE SAME DEMONS WE ALL FACE

Nearly every traditional mutual fund manager working today is subject to the same whims and passions and the same emotional decision-making process that makes regular investors underperform the S&P 500. Stocks are bought and sold on hunches, feelings, hope, and greed, not with underlying strategies that are consistently implemented.

As a matter of fact, many professional managers end up doing worse than more patient individuals who simply stick with simple strategies. Professional fund managers live and breathe the market, minute by minute. If you think day-to-day market fluctuations can make you panic, think about what minute-to-minute movements must do to the emotions of professional managers! Moreover, it's a rare money manager who doesn't believe he or she is uniquely gifted in picking good stocks. They believe they have the ability to sift through each great story for the few that will lead to riches.

Unfortunately, the facts are against them. Far from adding value by making subjective decisions about individual stocks, they are subtracting value, often by huge percentages. They, too, are victims of their humanity—and, in many cases, their over-sized egos.

Style Drift

The traditional mutual fund management system contributes to the poor performance of many mutual funds for several reasons. The first basic problem is something called style drift, which is just a fancy way of saying that fund managers don't always stick to their knitting. They don't do what they say they are going to do, usually because they let their short-term focus cloud their thinking. They say they are using one type of investment method and end up using quite another. It's not unusual to invest in what is billed as a growth fund only to open up a quarterly or annual report to find 40 percent of the fund invested in the bond market! Now that's style drift! The style of the fund drifts away from its stated purpose, often leaving you with your money managed quite differently than you originally intended.

Imagine how costly this can be to someone who has carefully planned his or her overall portfolio. For example, assume that before reading *How to Retire Rich,* George and Theresa Ramirez carefully did their homework and decided to allocate 40 percent of their portfolio to a growth mutual fund, 40 percent to a conservative value fund, and 20 percent to cash. If the funds they select perform as well as the average growth and value funds currently on the market, they can expect their portfolio to earn about 12.7 percent a year. But what happens if they open their statements and find that the growth fund manager they chose has switched 40 percent of his assets to bonds because he was nervous about the market? This single change would reduce their expected return to 11.81 percent—*without their consent*. The situation has gotten so bad that the Morningstar mutual fund rating service no longer categorizes funds based on what the fund itself says it does. Rather, Morningstar does its own factor analysis of the mutual funds it follows, so that it can categorize the funds more accurately for investors. Thus, if a fund calls itself a small-cap growth fund, but Morningstar finds that the fund is really invested in larger-cap value stocks, that's how it will list it. Unfortunately, in far too many cases, you really have no way to know whether the growth or value fund you are buying really is a growth or value fund, unless you do the homework yourself.

Incubator Funds: What You See Is Not What You're Going to Get

Another thing that can seriously mislead investors is an all too common practice known as fund incubation. A mutual fund company will start up a new fund with a couple hundred thousand dollars of its own money, operating the fund without making it available to the public. Its goal is to generate huge gains that it can advertise when it opens the fund to the public. These returns are often artificially high and misleading, since they are frequently generated by investments that the fund company can't continue to make when it has larger sums of money to invest. Essentially, the strategy used to generate the fabulous returns will not be the same as the one used after the fund starts investing money for the public.

Here's an example. A fund company opens the Whizbang Growth Fund with $1 million of its own money, investing it in tiny growth stocks. The small fry soar, and the fund opens its doors to the public while boasting about its fabulous track record. Surprise, surprise—$500 million pours in. But Whizbang's manager can no longer buy the tiny stocks that fueled the fund's performance because there's now too much money to invest. The fund winds up with a portfolio of larger-cap stocks, and the manager can't possibly duplicate the returns that enticed investors into Whizbang in the first place!

What's more, many big mutual fund companies take advantage of their buying power to muscle in on hot initial public offerings (IPOs). They then put these IPO stocks into their incubator funds, artificially beefing up their performance numbers even more.

It's not unusual for a fund company to set up as many as five separate incubator funds, offering the public only the one or two that performed well. Those that didn't cut muster are unceremoniously dumped. Investors are left with funds that can't possibly live up to their past records or to your expectations. Fund incubation is a horribly misleading practice, yet it remains a pervasive problem because it helps mutual fund companies attract huge sums of money. Sadly, many of these fund companies are far more concerned about attracting assets than generating great returns for their investors.

Indeed, one of the reasons Tom and Sarah O'Neil are so nervous about the stock market is that they were burned in the past when they invested their money in an incubator fund that had just gone public. Those advertised red-hot returns turned ice-cold quickly, making Tom and Sarah believe that the stock market was rigged against them.

Window Dressing

Another problem with conventional mutual fund management is something referred to in the trade as window dressing. In reality it is blatant deception.

In far too many mutual funds, trading volume picks up at the end of a quarter or the end of a year. Why? Because the fund managers are selling all the losing stocks that they don't want to admit owning and they're buying the winners that they wished they had owned. Hey, it makes the quarterly and annual reports look so much better! After tearing open their semiannual reports, investors are thrilled to see that their fund owned all the hot stocks of the moment and that the real clunkers are mercifully absent. What they don't realize is that the hot stocks were bought and the clunkers were sold just days before the quarter ended!

The practice is pure deception and sleight of hand, and it makes no sense for the investor. It's done to make shareholders believe that their fund manager was in the right place at the right time. Unfortunately, it happens all the time. It can also be quite costly to investors, since many of the stocks that are sold for purely cosmetic reasons are often still good values for the long term, and many that were suddenly bought have already had their day in the sun.

MUTUAL FUND FEES: READ THE FINE PRINT

Next is the issue of mutual fund fees. It is completely fair that a mutual fund company charges you a management fee, typically between .75 and 1.5 percent. What is not fair, in my opinion, is the inclusion of a 12b-1 fee, which is a marketing expense that the fund charges you so it can sell itself to other people. In other words, you are paying for the fund's advertising. Of the approximately 4,000 equity funds covered by Morningstar, 2,500 charge their shareholders a 12b-1 fee. If you are a long-term shareholder, there is no good reason to pay a fee to market the fund to other people. It's a lot like having to sit through a series of advertisements after paying $7.50 to see a movie!

Some mutual funds also charge a load, or an up-front commission. However, load mutual funds are a dying breed, for good reason. Say you invest $1,000 in a mutual fund with a 4 percent load. Instantly, you lose 4 percent, and your investment is worth only $960. (My goal here is to help you make money, not lose it!) The only reason you should consider a mutual fund with a load fee is if you work with a full-service broker who will keep you in a good fund through hell or high water. The Dalbar study I talked about in chapter 2 found that many investors who bought load funds actually made more money than did investors in no-load funds. Again, it's a matter of discipline. The fee that load investors paid helped them keep their money in the market longer, and they ended up doing better as a result, even after paying the load. Brokers who can keep nervous investors in good portfolios when the market hits a rough patch are rare commodities, however. Most are the first to jump ship at the first sign of rough seas. It is worth buying a mutual fund with a load fee only if you want to use a broker and find one who can show you that he or she has kept clients in well-managed funds over long periods of time.

If you want to use a full-service broker to help you build and keep a portfolio of good mutual funds, try to find one who charges an overall wrap fee, similar to what fee-only financial planners charge. Then you can ask the broker to recommend no-load funds. Remember that a good full-service broker can be a great help when times get rough in the market and is thus well worth the fee.

Beware the Taxman

Mutual funds can present unwanted tax consequences for the unwary investor. When you buy shares in a mutual fund, you could be buying a huge capital gain and not even know it. For example, you could invest in a fund that has a large position in a stock that has appreciated dramatically over the previous five years—say, Microsoft or Intel. The day after you buy the fund, the manager decides to sell those shares. The fund incurs a big capital gain, and even though you didn't pocket the money, you're responsible for the taxes! Always watch out for funds with big undistributed gains. Services like those from Morningstar and *Value Line* (both available at your local library) can help you identify those funds, since they list that figure in their commentaries on individual mutual funds.

Rock Stars, Sports Heroes, and . . .
Mutual Fund Managers?

Another concern for investors is that the mutual fund world is beginning to look a lot like the free-agency system in professional sports. Mutual fund managers are starting to move from fund to fund like athletes move from team to team—and, not surprisingly, they're often being lured by bigger and bigger salaries. This turnover in management wreaks havoc with your ability to track the record of a fund, since rarely does a new manager come to a fund and leave everything exactly as it was! You have no way to predict the performance of funds when managers leave, because their strategies leave with them. For example, of Fidelity's 248 managers, 95 have been at the helm for only a year or less! That's why it's much better to stick with funds that follow a fully disclosed strategy. You'll know what to expect, even if the turnover in management is high.

The way mutual fund managers are compensated can also cause problems, since their annual bonuses are frequently tied to their fund's performance. A manager with this kind of bonus incentive who is lagging the market has nothing to lose and everything to gain from taking big risks that may not benefit the long-term interests of shareholders. After all, bonuses are based on this year's returns and don't take into account how much risk the manager took with your money or whether he or she stuck to the style that you wanted in the first place.

Say a manager is paid a $100,000 salary and has a $1 million bonus contingent on his or her performance relative to the S&P 500. Put yourself in the shoes of a conventional value manager who is trailing the S&P index by 2 or 3 percent come July or August. You'd probably be inclined to do the same thing many money managers do. You'd buy a couple growth stocks, hoping to bolster your performance. That million-dollar bonus looms large, and it is nearly impossible not to focus on short-term performance when it is tied to such an enticing reward. The sad fact is, however, that when fund managers make decisions this way, they almost always hurt their long-term performance. Never forget that it's your money they're gambling with, and this unnecessary focus on the short term can really hurt your carefully made plans to retire rich.

Case Study: The Fidelity Magellan Fund

A look at the past decade for Fidelity Magellan—perhaps the best-known mutual fund in the country—uncovers an excellent example of the pitfalls inherent in traditionally managed mutual funds. It is not my intent to vilify the Fidelity Magellan Fund or any of its managers, and I believe Fidelity's management is doing its utmost to get the fund back on track. Nevertheless, the case beautifully illustrates many of the issues I have been discussing in this chapter.

It is interesting that Fidelity Magellan was started as an incubator fund in the 1960s but did not fully open to the public until 1981. It was the king of all mutual funds for most of the 1980s—thanks to the excellent investment strategy used by its manager, Peter Lynch. Between 1981 and May 1990, when Lynch retired, Magellan swamped the performance of the S&P 500, earning an average annual compound return of 23.83 percent. Lynch turned a $10,000 investment into $75,000 during his tenure! In the same period, an investor in the S&P 500 would have earned a compound annual return of only 15.66 percent, with $10,000 growing to $39,000. Under Lynch's leadership, the investment strategy of the Magellan Fund was highly defined—he bought classic, large-capitalization growth stocks.

But look what happened when Lynch's successor, Morris Smith, stepped in. In an effort to tighten up the Magellan Fund and move it to an even stronger growth profile, Smith sold some 400 stocks. A year later, he left and was replaced by Jeff Vinik, who previously ran Fidelity's Growth and Income Fund. It wasn't long before Vinik made his mark, and soon Magellan started to look much more like a big-cap value fund than the growth fund investors still believed it was.

In addition to changing the types of stocks the fund bought, Vinik made a huge bet that bonds would do well, shifting some 40 percent of the fund into bonds. Talk about style drift! Even if Vinik had been right about bonds—which he wasn't—he shouldn't have put any money in bonds for a fund that was still being billed as the best growth fund in America. All of a sudden, Magellan looked much more like a balanced value fund, which offers investors a far more sedate mix of conservative stocks, bonds, and cash.

Vinik left the Magellan Fund to start a hedge fund and was replaced by Bob Stanski, yet another manager from the Fidelity stable. Four managers in four years—the turnover has left the Fidelity Magellan Fund reeling. All continuity was lost. Since Peter Lynch left, Magellan has barely outperformed the S&P 500. A $10,000 investment in the fund made on May 1, 1990, was worth only $28,000 at the end of 1996, barely ahead of the S&P 500, which turned $10,000 into $27,000 over the same period.

I still think Fidelity is a great company, and I hope its problems prove transitory. But this case study illuminates many of the weaknesses inherent in traditionally managed mutual funds. The past performance of any fund with such style drift and high management turnover will probably have little to do with its future performance.

None of these problems affect funds that use empirically tested strategies in a disciplined fashion. That's why using great strategies leaves so many traditional mutual fund managers in the dust.

What to Look For in a Mutual Fund

Discipline, Discipline, Discipline

The first thing to look for in a mutual fund is a disciplined investment style. Simple index funds, based on market capitalization, are the first that come to mind. The Vanguard Index 500 is the best-known fund that replicates the S&P 500 index, but there are a number of others. The DFA Funds, offered by Dimensional Fund Advisors, offer a whole range of indexes keyed to market capitalization, from very-small-cap indexes to very large ones. Other index funds include the Schwab 1000, which invests in the 1,000 largest stocks in the market, and the Vanguard Small Cap Fund, which attempts to replicate the performance of the Russell 2000, an index of small-capitalization stocks. When you see the word *index* in a fund's description, you're almost certain to get a rigorously implemented strategy, unsullied by the whims of a money manager.

Enhancing Those Indexes

Enhanced indexing is a method by which a fund company tries to enhance the performance of an underlying index, by either emphasizing an underlying factor it believes is a key to success or using options and other derivatives to enhance the index's performance. Some of your choices are the Bear Stearns S&P Stars portfolio, which rigorously invests in only those stocks awarded five stars by S&P analysts, and the Fidelity Disciplined Equity Fund, which uses an artificial intelligence program to identify stocks that may be undervalued because of short-term price gyrations (note that this fund seriously underperformed the market recently—according to a Morningstar analyst, this was because the manager was allowed to override the model!).

Strategy Indexes: Uniting Active and Passive Management

My company, O'Shaughnessy Capital Management, offers the O'Shaughnessy Funds, a family of mutual funds based on the time-tested strategies discussed in chapter 3. We call our funds Strategy Indexes, because they unite the best qualities of active and passive money management. They're like actively managed funds because they pick stocks using strategies tested over more than four decades. But they're similar to index funds because they can never and will never override the underlying strategies. No doubt, if I were allowed to override my own strategies I'd be like every other conventional manager and screw things up! The O'Shaughnessy Funds are highly disciplined and rigorously implemented, and they always use my time-tested strategies to guide their stock selection.

I created the O'Shaughnessy Funds because the evidence supporting these strategies was so overwhelming. I believe that investors deserve easy access to superior investment strategies, and for those of you who don't have the time or inclination to put together your own portfolios, the O'Shaughnessy Funds may be an easy solution. Current funds include the Cornerstone Growth Fund (very similar to Reasonable Runaways), the Cornerstone Value Fund (Leaders with Luster), the Dogs of the Market Fund (a fund that expands the Dogs of the Dow strategy to a larger number of stocks), and the Aggressive Growth Fund. What's more, all employees at O'Shaughnessy Funds put their money where their mouths are, investing the entire equity portion of their portfolios in these time-tested strategies.

Lexington Corporate Leaders: Sticking to Their Knitting
The Lexington Corporate Leaders Fund, started back in the 1930s, is an interesting fund that takes stick-with-it-ness to the extreme. Its founding managers bought stock in the 30 companies that they believed were the corporate leaders of their era, including stocks like Mobil, Sears, and General Electric. The fund has simply held these stocks, never adjusting nor rebalancing the portfolio to make room for new corporate leaders.

It's amazing how well the fund has done both recently and historically. In the 10 years that ended in 1996, the fund compounded at 14.89 percent a year, just slightly behind the S&P 500 but well ahead of the average equity income fund in the Morningstar Mutual Fund Survey. Longer term, it does a bit better than the S&P 500. Between 1975 and 1996 the fund compounded at 15.27 percent, ahead of the S&P 500's 14.91 percent compound annual return. Remember that *the fund has never changed stocks in its portfolio!*

The performance of the Lexington Corporate Leaders Fund shows that discipline alone can help you beat the market. But discipline applied in a cohesive and ongoing way can really knock the lights out. Imagine how much better the fund might have done had it annually reapplied its original criteria for selecting corporate leaders, replacing Columbia Gas with Intel or Burlington Northern with Microsoft. The fund's performance could have been truly outstanding.

Nevertheless, the success of the Lexington Corporate Leaders Fund makes this much clear—stick with an idea or a strategy and you'll do much better than a hyperactive trader or someone always moving in and out of the market.

Quantitative Funds: The Black Box Approach

Quantitative funds also may be worth considering, but they present a dilemma. Pure quantitative funds are superior to conventionally managed funds because they *consistently* use a strategy the manager has found successful. The problem is that they are often shrouded in secrecy and have come to be known as black boxes. (On the other hand, I call the strategies in this book lucite boxes, because they're fully explained.) Perhaps black box quantitative managers are afraid you won't be willing to pay for their services if you know how simple their successful strategies really are. It's a little like not wanting to see the magician David Copperfield if you know how all his tricks are done. Of course, some quantitative funds are so complex mathematically that the management thinks the model is too difficult to explain to investors. Trust me, they say. If they do indeed stick with it, at least you'll be getting a fund that's consistent and disciplined.

I believe you should know exactly how your money is being managed—that's why I'm writing this book. A level playing field is always best; you need and deserve to know exactly how your money is being managed. Only then will you have the confidence to stick with a long-term investment program. Whether you invest in the mutual funds my company offers or build a portfolio on your own using these strategies, you should know exactly what to expect. Knowledge is power.

Children are afraid of the dark, not because it is dark but because it is unknown. To show a child that there's nothing to be afraid of, all you have to do is flip on the light. I believe the only time you should consider a black box quantitative fund is when you see that procedures are in place that force management to stick to its model despite short-term fluctuations. If you hear that the fund is changing its strategy in some manner, seriously question the manager's ability to stick with his or her strategy.

WHAT IT ALL BOILS DOWN TO

If you want the ease of owning a mutual fund, I recommend any of the disciplined funds mentioned in this section. They enforce discipline, remove emotion from the investment process, and have been tested over long periods of time. They are much better investments than traditional hit-for-the-fences mutual funds. And although they may not seem as exciting, they're a lot more reliable.

HOW TO FIND THE BEST CONVENTIONAL MUTUAL FUNDS

Let's say that you have a friend who hasn't seen all this research and insists on investing in conventionally managed mutual funds. Can you tell your friend anything that will give him or her a better chance to do well? Yes. Get them to always look for the *consistent use of a disciplined strategy.*

The best thing to look for is a mutual fund that has had the same manager for a long time who has been doing the same things the same way, over and over. In my first book, *Invest Like the Best,* I found that the one thing great money managers share is a disciplined and consistent investment strategy. Managers like John Neff and Peter Lynch fit the bill, sticking with their approach through thick and thin.

To find whether a mutual fund has a disciplined and consistent investment style, first read its prospectus and marketing literature. Look for the investment objective section. It should clearly describe how the fund invests its money. Look for easy-to-understand language, unambiguous and clearly written. Is the objective of the fund concrete? Do the managers offer proof or reasons for investing the way they do? Next, look at the stocks in the fund's portfolio. Has the fund invested in the kinds of stocks it claims to in its literature? If you buy a growth fund, does the manager really buy growth stocks, or has he or she decided to invest a huge chunk of the portfolio in cash or bonds? These questions can be difficult to answer, but in general the best thing to look for is a fund that clearly states its criteria for buying stocks.

Next, call the fund company and find out whether the portfolio manager responsible for the fund's performance is still at the helm. Does he report to an investment committee that can override his choices, or does he call all the shots? Then ask more questions. Was the majority of the mutual fund's returns generated when it had much less money under management? Will the manager be able to continue using his strategy if the fund gets a huge inflow of cash? Will the fund close to new investors so it can continue using the same strategy, or will it change the strategy as assets grow?

The answers to these questions will help you assess the underlying continuity of a mutual fund's management team, which is essential information if you want to choose a successful fund. In the traditionally managed mutual fund world, such information can guide you to a consistent manager.

INTERNATIONAL FUNDS

With international investing, you really have to use mutual funds. The day may come when there is as much data on foreign companies as there is on U.S. firms, but until then you should rely on mutual funds for any overseas investing. DFA, Vanguard, and Schwab all offer international indexes that try to duplicate the returns of various international markets. Also, look for funds like DFA's High Market-to-Book Foreign Fund, essentially a strategy index focusing on foreign companies with low price-to-book ratios. Low price-to-book ratio stocks do very well in America, and research I've done shows that they are highly likely to perform strongly overseas as well.

No matter what kind of international mutual fund you're looking for, always look for the same discipline and consistency you look for in domestic funds.

STRATEGIES ARE THE FUTURE

I think that as my study of Wall Street becomes more widely known, and as others pursue their own historical tests, strategy indexes will become as popular as traditional mutual funds and plain vanilla index funds are today. They make the most sense, provide historical proof of their efficacy, and remove emotion from the decision-making process to boot. They also give investors the ability to conveniently use a superior strategy with minimum hassle.

For now, if you want to invest in mutual funds, always make discipline and consistency your two most important criteria when selecting a fund. It doesn't matter whether you're looking for an aggressive fund or a conservative fund—the hallmark of top-performing funds is the consistent use of a superior investment strategy.

CHAPTER FIVE

HOW TO GET THE MOST OUT OF YOUR 401(K)

If you want to retire seriously rich, in addition to following one or more of the strategies in this book you will also need to take maximum advantage of your retirement plan at work. Remember that your primary vehicle for a rich retirement will be the use of these time-tested strategies in your IRA. But by maximizing your savings in your 401(k) at work you can turbocharge your savings and be assured of a happy retirement.

The best way to get the most out of your 401(k) plan is simple—put the most money into it that you can. Sadly, few Americans are doing this—recent statistics show that only one in four American workers are putting money into their 401(k) plans. What's more, according to a recent poll in *Fortune* magazine, 75 percent of Americans fear they aren't saving enough money for their retirement. Yet it is something everyone can do something about right away.

It's a travesty that so few people take advantage of their 401(k)s. The only way you are going to retire rich is to *invest right now*. Along with your IRA, 401(k) plans are a wonderful tool to help you retire rich, especially if you've put off saving for your retirement.

THE NEW PENSION PLAN

More than 95 percent of U.S. companies with over 5,000 employees currently offer a 401(k) plan, and smaller companies are adding them in droves. The catchy name, 401(k), comes from the section of the IRS code that spells these plans out. Using many words when a few will do, our government calls them cash or deferred compensation retirement plans. A 401(k) really is a defined contribution plan.

In chapter 1 I talked about defined benefit plans, the traditional pension plans that guaranteed you a fixed amount— usually not adjusted for inflation—throughout your retirement. 401(k) plans work differently. They define the contribution that you can make to the plan but say nothing about how much you can expect to get when you retire. That number is up to you and will be determined by the investment choices you make. With 401(k) plans, you make a defined contribution from your salary. The government regulates the amount that you can contribute, but as of 1997 you can contribute up to 15 percent of your salary, with the maximum contribution being $9,500 a year.

WHAT MAKES 401(K) PLANS GREAT

CONTRIBUTIONS ARE PRETAX DOLLARS

The main reason why 401(k) plans are great investment vehicles is because your contributions to them are pretax dollars. If you make $50,000 a year and contribute 10 percent to your 401(k) plan, that $5,000 contribution is treated as deferred compensation and is not subject to taxes other than Social Security. (Remember what dire straits the Social Security system is in—it needs your money!) As a result, when tax time comes, you'll be taxed only on an income of $45,000—your salary less your 401(k) contribution. *Every dollar you put into your 401(k) is de-*

ducted from your income taxes for that year. If you're in the 28 percent tax bracket, as someone making $50,000 a year would likely be, it's like making 28 percent on every dollar you put into your 401(k). That's a better return than even our best strategy!

Income Is Tax Deferred

The next great thing about 401(k) plans is that all the money you put in them compounds on a tax-deferred basis. Taxes and inflation are the enemy of investment success. Look at how seriously taxes affect returns. Assume you're using Reasonable Runaways in two accounts, one tax deferred and the other fully taxed. If you made a one-time $10,000 investment in each account and achieved a return similar to the Reasonable Runaways historical return, after 10 years you'd have $54,691 in your tax-deferred account but only $35,921 in your taxable account. That's a difference of almost $20,000, effectively dropping your after-tax returns in the Reasonable Runaways strategy from 18 percent to 14 percent. Granted, you'll have to pay taxes on your 401(k) savings when you start taking it out of your account, presumably when you retire. In some instances, if your planning is poor or you've done too well with your investments, the tax hit could be considerable. But that's not such a bad problem. Clearly, the power of compounding your money without the taxman taking his pound of flesh is overwhelming. I highly recommend IRA contributions for the same reason—even though they're not always fully tax deductible, they too compound on a tax-deferred basis, which enhances your returns considerably.

Matching Contributions from Your Employer

There's yet another tremendous reason to take advantage of your 401(k) plan. In most cases, your employer will match a portion of your contribution—typically, 50 cents for every dollar you contribute. To use our earlier example, your $5,000 contribution would be matched by a $2,500 contribution from your employer. That's like getting an instant 50 percent return on your investment! If you work for a company that matches a portion of your 401(k) contribution, you'd be foolish to pass it up.

You Can Take Them with You

Finally, 401(k) plans are today's retirement plan of choice because they're portable and follow you from job to job. All your contributions are yours alone, and, after you become vested—typically, after a certain number of years with your company—all the money your employer contributed is yours as well. All together, 401(k) plans are a great tool to use in your campaign to retire rich.

The Basics

Now let's learn about your 401(k) and look at the best ways to invest the money you put in it. The government allows your employer to restrict who gets to participate in its 401(k) plan, but the restrictions are usually not a big deal. The most important eligibility standards are simple: your employer can prohibit you from joining until you've been with the company for a year or until you are 21. Your employer might not offer a 401(k) plan to all employees. If you work for a big company, for example, only certain employees or certain divisions might be eligible. While that's far more unusual today than it was in the past, it can still be a problem. It's important to learn as much as you can about what your company offers.

Finding Out About Your Company's 401(k) Plan

The first thing you need to do is get the specifics on your company's plan. Don't be surprised if your personnel manager or human resources manager gives you a blank stare when you ask about it, as it's not unusual for 401(k)s to be delegated to a plan administrator. Depending on the size of your company, the plan administrator is either someone within the human resources department or an outside firm that specializes in plan administration. The administrator's job is to educate you about your company's 401(k) plan and the options available to you. He or she should sit down with you and find out when you're going to retire, how aggressive you're willing to be, and whether you understand different types of risk. The administrator should then help you build a mix of investments that's right for you.

Brace yourself for the number of names and reports involved. You'll hear about plan sponsors, trustees, summary plan descriptions, individual benefit statements, and more. It may sound complicated, but it isn't. Let's get the players in order to see who's who.

Who's Who in the Bureaucracy

The *plan sponsor* is your employer, or the company offering the plan. The sponsor has the final say on how the plan is structured, what investments are offered to you, how you can invest your money, and whether it is going to match a portion of the money you contribute. The *trustee* of the 401(k) plan is either an individual or a committee that has overall responsibility for the plan and reports to the plan sponsor. As mentioned earlier, the *plan administrator* is the person or outside company that provides you all the information you'll need to get your 401(k) started. The *investment managers* are usually outside firms that offer mutual funds or money management services. They buy and sell securities, bonds, or Treasury bills on your behalf. Finally, the *record keeper* is usually an outside firm that keeps track of all the paperwork, contributions, investments, and other information having to do with the plan and its participants.

The Paperwork

When you inquire about your firm's 401(k), you'll usually receive a *summary plan description* that tells you what your company's plan provides and how it operates. It will outline your investment choices, from investing in outside mutual funds to purchasing company stock. It explains such things as when you can start participating, how to contact the plan administrator, and how to make contributions. Hardly thrilling reading that will keep you awake at night, but the summary plan description will give you the nuts and bolts about your company's 401(k) plan. The *summary annual report* summarizes the financial reports that the plan files with the U.S. Department of Labor.

The *individual benefit statement* is more interesting. It is a document that describes how much money you've accrued and what percentages of your benefits are vested. It's essentially a summary detailing how much money you have in your retirement account.

The *material modifications document* is a summary of any changes in your company's plan. If it changes the plan by adding or dropping a mutual fund or making a new asset class available to you, you will find out about it in this report.

Don't let any of these technicalities daunt you or prevent you from beginning *today* to put as much of your salary as you can into your 401(k). The time you'll spend getting all this set up will be about as gratifying as a visit to the Department of Motor Vehicles, but the payoff will be great.

How Much Should You Contribute?

As I mentioned earlier, the maximum 401(k) contribution you can make as of early 1997 was 15 percent of your salary, up to $9,500 a year. The IRS usually adjusts this every three years by a few hundred dollars to account for inflation. The $9,500 is a limit on *your* contribution, not on any matching contribution from your employer. If your employer decides to match you at 50 cents on the dollar, you would add another $4,750 annually.

Now let's see what an unbelievable addition a 401(k) can be in helping you retire rich. Assume that a strategy index fund isn't available but that you can invest in an S&P 500 index fund. Let's say, like Tom and Sarah O'Neil, you've got 20 years to go until you retire. But, unlike them, you've saved absolutely nothing. Don't panic. You can still plan for a rich retirement if you make the maximum contributions to your 401(k). Let's say Tom hadn't saved anything and started making annual contributions of $14,250 to his 401(k)—his maximum allowable contribution plus his company's contribution. Assume that there are no increases for inflation. If he does as well as the S&P 500 has over the past 45 years, at age 65 his 401(k) is going to be worth $1.3 million. That's starting at age 44 and not using any of the power of our time-tested strategies!

Let's look at another example. What if you make $60,000 a year and you don't qualify for your company's matching contributions? You don't think you can swing the maximum 15 percent contribution, but you know you can save 10 percent of your salary, $6,000. Even in this case, you'll be pretty well off by the time you retire at 65. You'll make a total contribution of $126,000 over those 21 years, but because you are saving pretax money and it's compounding tax free, if you get the same return as the S&P 500 your account will be worth $560,000 when you retire—that's in your 401(k) alone. The power of these numbers is unbelievably compelling.

Where to Invest Your 401(k)

OK, let's say you're contributing the most that you can to your 401(k), and you're taking full advantage of every matching benefit that your employer offers. Now what do you do? Generally, your investment options are fairly limited. Until a few years ago, insurance companies controlled a large portion of 401(k) investments. As a result, most 401(k) funds were invested in Guaranteed Investment Contracts (GICs), sometimes called *stable funds* in 401(k) lingo. GICs are contracts between you (acting as lender) and the issuer (normally, an insurance company or bank, acting as borrower). Under the terms of the contract, you receive your original investment plus a specified rate of return over the term of the contract. Now, as I've mentioned already, these contracts will never make you rich. For the most part, they're certificates of depreciation. Most people invest their retirement money far too conservatively, fearing the loss of principal. But we've already seen that the biggest risk is not loss of principal but loss of purchasing power. Money invested in GICs, T-bills, and bonds provides very modest returns and should be used only to reduce your overall portfolio's volatility or to provide you with a reliable income after you've retired.

Equities—Still the Best Place for Your Savings

Most 401(k) plans now allow you to choose among money market funds, bond funds, GICs, company stock, and several equity mutual funds. If your goal is to get rich, you'll want to put most of your savings in equity funds. Remember that your 401(k) savings are a long-term investment. If you're not going to retire for 20 years, you should not care whether your portfolio declines a bit next year! You should care about having the most money possible waiting for you at retirement, and the only way to do that is to invest in the stock market.

But look before you leap. Investigate the equity funds available in your 401(k) like you investigated mutual funds. Decide which are based on stories and which are based on discipline. You know that to maximize your chances of getting rich, you'll have to invest in the most disciplined funds available. If you have a strategy index available, by all means use it. As mentioned in chapter 4, the O'Shaughnessy Funds are strategy indexes, although they are currently available on only a few 401(k) plans. But as more people learn of the power of these strategies, I expect that disciplined funds will become more widely available on 401(k) plans throughout the country.

If a disciplined strategy fund isn't available through your 401(k), look for simple index funds. Is an S&P 500 or a Russell

2000 index fund available through your 401(k)? If so, use it. If there are no strategy index funds, no regular index funds, and no funds that easily spell out their methods, pick a fund that invests in high-yielding blue chip stocks or one that describes itself as an equity income fund. Such funds have the greatest chance of sticking to their underlying strategy because they usually have a straightforward investment style. Yes, they'll probably manage to screw up, change style somewhat, and move to cash when they ought not, but because of their charter, they'll probably do it a lot less than a gun-slinging growth fund manager who chooses stocks more capriciously.

If, however, you do have a growth mutual fund that outlines a strategy that sounds sensible and has a reasonable degree of consistency in returns and tenure of the manager, it might be a good choice. Always try to find a fund that clearly states its stock selection method.

What About My Company's Stock?

Many 401(k) plans let you invest in your company's stock. For all the reasons already covered, I recommend not making a large investment in a single stock. Typically, people feel it's the loyal thing to do, and they will put too much of their 401(k) savings in their company's stock. This is a huge mistake. Indeed, in many 401(k) accounts, the company's stock accounts for 50 percent of the equity allocation! You never want to take the exponential risk that is associated with investing in a single stock. Think of how an IBM employee who diligently invested all her money in IBM stock must have felt as she watched its price drop 50 percent in the early 1990s!

There are only two reasons you might want to invest a small percentage of your 401(k) in your company's stock—either the company is selling it to you at a reduced price or the stock meets the criteria of one of our successful time-tested strategies. Take a look at the underlying factors of your company's stock. Is it a market-leading company with a high dividend yield? If so, it fits our Leaders with Luster criteria and should be included for that reason. Remember to allocate only a small percentage of your money to a single stock, even if it is your firm. You should allocate the same dollar amount to the stock as you would if it were one of the 25 to 50 stocks in the Reasonable Runaways or Leaders with Luster strategies.

BONDS AND CASH

Unless you're about to retire, you shouldn't have more than 50 percent of your 401(k) invested in cash or bonds. Investing in bonds or T-bills will help *keep* you rich, but I think you know by now that they're not going to *make* you rich. When used in moderation, bonds and cash can help reduce the overall risk and volatility of your portfolio. Look for funds that invest in intermediate-term Treasury bonds, high-quality corporate bonds, or short-term T-bills. Over the past 45 years, intermediate-term bonds have been a better investment than long-term bonds, returning 6.42 percent compared with 5.87 percent. What's more, long-term bonds had some five-year periods when they lost money, whereas intermediate-term bonds never had even a three-year period when they didn't make money.

HOW MUCH CAN YOU EXPECT TO MAKE?

Let's revisit three of the couples we met in chapter 1 and look at some examples of how their 401(k) accounts might grow. Remember Bill and Nancy Robinson? They're both 32 and have 401(k) plans available to them at work. (Again, we'll assume that everything is in constant dollars and no upward adjustments are made for inflation.) Bill makes $32,000 a year and contributes the maximum 15 percent to his 401(k), $4,800. Nancy makes $44,000, and she makes her maximum contribution of $6,600. Let's say Bill and Nancy put all their money in an S&P index fund and earn 12.15 percent a year—the same as the S&P 500's compound return over the past 45 years. At age 65, Bill will have amassed $2.1 million and Nancy will have $2.9 million, for a combined total of $5 million! And that's assuming they never get raises or better-paying jobs.

Bill and Nancy have 33 years until they retire. What if they're not so lucky, and instead of earning 12.15 percent a year they earn returns from the S&P 500 that are the same as the worst 33-year period from our study? The worst 33-year return for the S&P 500 was 9.8 percent, between December 31, 1955, and December 31, 1988. In this case, Bill's 401(k) would be worth $1.2 million and Nancy's would be worth $1.7 million, for a total of $2.9 million. This is a less appealing scenario, but it's still a nice chunk of change!

Don't Treat Your 401(k) Like a Bank

What if Bill and Nancy Robinson make the common mistake of keeping all their 401(k) savings in a money market fund, earning returns similar to those of U.S. Treasury bills? Earning the average 5.35 percent that T-bills provided over the last 45 years, Bill's 401(k) would be worth $462,000 and Nancy's would be worth $635,000, a total of almost $1.1 million. That's five times less than if they had invested in the S&P 500 and earned a return of 12.15 percent.

The same holds true for bonds. If the Robinsons put all their money in an intermediate-term bond fund that invested in government bonds maturing in five years, and they earned the same 6.42 percent these bonds have historically returned, Bill's 401(k) would be worth $580,000 and Nancy's would grow to $800,000, for a total of $1.38 million.

The case is quite clear that, for the foreseeable future, the Robinsons should take advantage of their youth and invest as much of their 401(k) savings as they can in the stock market. There's never been a 20-year period when an investment in stocks failed to make money, as Jeremy J. Siegel points out in his excellent book *Stocks for the Long Run*. And this is since the early 1800s! Twenty years from now, the Robinsons might want to add bonds to their portfolios, particularly if they've earned higher than average returns. But for now, stocks are the best investment for them.

When Bonds Make Sense

As you approach retirement, you'll want to increase your investment in bonds and cash. Why? Because you may not want to risk earning returns similar to the lowest of those in the past. For example, assume Steve and Betsy Johnson have decided they will use Reasonable Runaways in their IRAs but are uncomfortable committing all the money in Steve's Simplified Employee Pension (SEP) plan—a 401(k) plan for those who are self-employed—to the stock market. Steve is 55, and both he and Betsy are worried about how high stock prices are. To ease their worries, they've decided to put 70 percent of Steve's retirement savings in an S&P 500 index fund, 20 percent in intermediate-term government bonds, and 10 percent in Treasury bills. Every year, they'll make sure their portfolio has this 70–20–10 mix.

Since 1951, this mix has compounded at 10.6 percent a year and has had a maximum one-year loss of 16.6 percent, compared with a one-year loss of 26.5 percent for the S&P 500. It's also less volatile than the S&P 500 over three-year periods, and it never experienced a loss in any five-year period. That's something that Steve and Betsy are more comfortable with.

Steve is, however, investigating how he can use some of our strategies in his plan, since the returns are so much more appealing to him. He currently has his SEP at his local bank and is planning to move it to a brokerage firm that offers strategy index funds so he can use these time-tested strategies directly.

Keep in mind that Steve and Betsy Johnson are paying a price for their less volatile portfolio, since their annual compound return will be 1.53 percent lower. But if this more conservative overall approach is easier for them to stick with and, most important, keeps them invested in the stock market through ups and downs, it's better for them in the long run. Remember that investors who can't stomach a lot of risk usually end up selling out of the market at *exactly the wrong time*. In the Johnsons' case, they might even be better off allocating 50 percent of their portfolios to stocks, 40 percent to bonds, and 10 percent to cash. This really reduces their portfolio's volatility and gives them a rate of return that's not much lower than that of the 70–20–10 mix mentioned earlier.

Because Steve has his own business, he can make larger contributions to his SEP than many can to their 401(k)s. As of 1997, he can contribute up to $24,000 a year to his SEP. Since they haven't saved much to date, Steve and Betsy have decided to contribute the full $24,000 to Steve's SEP. Betsy's anticipated $25,000 annual income from her new job selling real estate will certainly help ease the savings burden.

That's a lot of money, and the Johnsons must invest it so that fluctuations in the market don't make them panic and sell out. Since they have only 10 years to go, the power of compounding has less time to work its magic. But with a conservative portfolio containing 50 percent stocks, 40 percent intermediate-term bonds, and 10 percent T-bills, Steve and Betsy's $240,000 worth of SEP contributions grows to $545,000. And their risk is half that of the S&P 500!

STOCKS FOR THE LONG HAUL

I know I sound like a broken record, but when time is on your side stocks always do better than other investments. Let's look at the various returns George and Theresa Ramirez would earn depending on how they allocate their savings. As you'll recall from chapter 1, George and Theresa are 38 years old and have a combined income of $90,000 a year. They both plan to contribute the full 15 percent a year to their 401(k) plans. (Once again, we'll look at these examples in constant dollars.)

At George and Theresa's current salaries, their combined 401(k) contribution is $13,500 a year. Their employers match their contributions at 50 cents for every dollar, so together they're putting away $20,250 a year! That's a serious commitment, and the Ramirezes hope to be richly rewarded for their diligence.

If George and Theresa put all their savings in a GIC or an intermediate-term bond fund that earns 6.42 percent a year, the $547,000 they set aside would grow to $1.7 million, about three times the amount they put into their 401(k)s over the years. But if they put half their savings in an S&P 500 index fund and the other half in intermediate-term bonds, George and Theresa can increase their total retirement accounts to $3 million. Without taking much more risk, they now have combined accounts that are worth six times the amount they set aside.

Finally, if they invest all their 401(k) savings in the stock market and earn 12.12 percent a year (again, that's the historical return of the S&P 500 over the last 45 years), the Ramirezes will start racking up millions. By committing everything to stocks, they will have combined accounts worth just under $5 million when they are 65, approximately 10 times the amount they set aside.

The point is clear. Even if you're worried about the stock market, it's essential to invest in stocks if you want to retire rich. If you put just 50 percent of your money in stocks, your returns will be three times greater than if you keep your savings in cash or bonds! And that's with an extremely low level of risk and a lot less turbulence than a portfolio fully committed to stocks.

TIME TO GET GOING

If a 401(k) plan is available to you and you haven't yet put any money into it, *start doing so right now.* Call your company's human resources department or the plan administrator's 800 number for information about your 401(k). Know that for legal and monetary reasons, it's in your company's interest to get as many people as possible participating in its plan. Most companies try to make it easy to get started.

Get your 401(k) set up and start taking advantage of the tax savings it offers you. Again, each dollar you contribute is tax deferred, so depending on your tax bracket, it's like making an instant 28 percent on your money by doing nothing more than putting it in a 401(k) account. Get involved as well. If your plan has rotten investment choices, ask your company or plan administrator to add better ones.

Remember that the sooner you start and the more you save, the richer you'll be. From the put-your-money-where-your-mouth-is department, all employees at my company, O'Shaughnessy Capital Management, make the maximum 15 percent contribution to their 408(k) [similar to a 401(k)], investing their savings in the strategies featured in this book.

Finally, decide on a portfolio you can stick with through thick and thin. We've seen that timing the market is a fool's game. Time *in* the market is the only way to take advantage of its superior returns.

CHAPTER SIX

PORTFOLIOS FOR THE REST OF YOUR LIFE

Now that you understand the power of the investment strategies we've covered and know about the different savings vehicles you can use, let's revisit our four couples and see how, with diligent savings and superior investment strategies, they can all retire rich. We'll look at each couple's portfolios in light of how aggressive or conservative they are, and we'll see how their overall savings plans—IRAs, 401(k)s, and other savings—can work together to increase their returns and reduce risk.

You can use these couples' stories as models for your own plans to retire rich. You'll recall that the Robinsons, the Ramirezes, the O'Neils, and the Johnsons are different ages, have different goals, have saved different amounts of money, and have different risk tolerances. By relating your own situation to their stories, you'll be able to see how the money you save and the investment decisions you make *now* will affect your future.

(Please note that in almost every case, I don't include the impact of taxes. Tax laws are constantly changing, and everyone faces different tax rates. As a result, I cannot give you an accurate picture of what each couple's tax bite will be when they start removing money from their tax-advantaged accounts.)

Bill and Nancy Robinson: The Big Payoff of Starting Early

The Robinsons have an incredible advantage in their quest to retire rich—their age. You'll recall that Bill and Nancy are both 32. Like them, if you are in your 20s or 30s and start saving diligently and investing wisely now, there is almost no way not to end up rich. The magic of compounding will be on your side, and as long as you *stay in the market,* a rich retirement is easily within reach.

The Robinsons live in Cleveland, where Bill works at the Rock & Roll Museum and Nancy is a nurse. They haven't started saving yet but are convinced that they can't rely on Social Security and are therefore entirely responsible for their nest egg when they retire in 33 years. Bill and Nancy understand that they must take maximum advantage of their relative youth and make saving money a top priority. They are both happy with their professions and think they'll stay with them throughout their working lives.

Right now, Bill's salary is $32,000, but he expects it to increase as he moves up the management ladder. If Bill starts putting $2,000 into his IRA and contributing 15 percent of his salary to his 403(b) plan every year, he'll be saving $6,800 annually. [The museum is a nonprofit organization, and its version of a 401(k) is called a 403(b).] What's more, his $4,800 403(b) contribution will be tax deductible, thereby reducing his taxable income and lowering the taxes he pays.

Bill balked at first when he realized he'd be putting away 21 percent of his income every year, but Nancy reminded him that they were in this together and had her income to rely on as well. Nancy earns $44,000 a year and expects to continue her nursing career at the hospital where she currently works. Her goal is to become the head nurse in the maternity ward.

Tax Advantage Makes Saving Easier
Having done their homework, Bill and Nancy decide that, together, they can stick to their ambitious savings program. Even

when Nancy makes the maximum contribution to her 401(k), the Robinsons combined pretax income is $64,600. What really shocked Bill and Nancy was how little difference there was in their total take-home pay after they started putting 15 percent of their income into their 401(k) and 403(b) plans. For example, before Nancy started her automatic savings, her semimonthly gross pay was $1,833. After federal, state, Social Security, and Medicare taxes were taken out, she was left with $1,292.45. But when she started contributing $275—15 percent of her salary—to her 401(k) her paycheck came to $1,099.98 after taxes, just $192.47 less than before. But wait a minute—if she's saving $275, why is her paycheck only $192 less? Because by putting money into her 401(k), Nancy reduces her taxable income and pays fewer taxes.

This tax benefit was the extra boost that fully convinced Bill and Nancy to make the maximum contributions to their 401(k), 403(b), and IRA plans that they can, despite how difficult it seemed at times. They figured out a detailed budget, including everything from the basics—condo payments, car, food, and income taxes—to the unusual, including their combined $4,000 contribution to their IRAs. They figured that if they could stick with their budget they'd have about $5,000 at the end of each year to spend on a great vacation—a nice reward after such diligent budgeting and saving.

By making the full 15 percent contributions to their 401(k) and 403(b) plans, as well as contributing $2,000 each to their IRAs, the Robinsons will be saving around 20 percent of their income. Every time they're tempted to spend that 20 percent on a whim or a passion of the moment, they pull out their calculations of what their nest egg will be worth if they stick to their savings program. Let's take a look.

THEIR FUTURE LOOKS BRIGHT

Assume that things work out for Bill and Nancy as they hoped. Bill stays with the museum, getting his first 10 percent raise in

2001, when he's 36. He's promoted to senior operating officer at age 40, and his salary is increased to $65,000 a year. Bill finally achieves his dream in 2015, and at age 51 he is named director of the Rock & Roll Museum. Nancy ends up reaching her goal at the hospital sooner than she hoped, becoming head of the maternity nursing staff in 2003. She'd taken maternity leave herself two years earlier, when their first child, William Jr., was born. Nancy was receiving a 4 percent raise every year, but she grew restless at the hospital and wanted to have more time to spend with their son. She took a job with a home healthcare company catering to the growing elderly population, which allowed her to work fewer and more flexible hours. And although her hours went down, her pay went up. She was able to transfer her 401(k) to her new company and take time off to give birth to their second son, Jonathan, in 2004. Even though a big income was never something Nancy aspired to, she found that by just getting salary increases of 4 percent a year she could make the maximum allowable contribution to her 401(k) by the time she was 42.

Bill and Nancy realize that the percentage of their total income they are saving is declining each year, since they are earning much more than they did at 32. Each year's savings contributions are less and less painful, amounting to less than 10 percent of their income by the time they're in their 50s.

How to Invest for a Rich Retirement

How the Robinsons invest their money will determine whether they'll be duly rewarded for their careful budgeting and diligent saving. If Bill and Nancy had not read *How to Retire Rich*, they might have been like many others with little investing knowledge and remained nervous about the stock market. If that were the case, and they both stuck with their savings plan but kept the money in the bank—earning interest similar to the return on Treasury bills over the previous 45 years—they would each have a total of $193,000 in their IRAs. That's just about three times the $68,000 they each contributed over the years. But gosh, without taking any risk at all, their combined IRAs alone would be worth almost $400,000—not including the money in their 401(k) and 403(b) plans. Anyone should be able to live on that, right?

Don't forget that this is $400,000 32 years from now. If inflation rates were similar to those of the last 45 years, each of their accounts would need to be worth $147,000 just to keep up with inflation. When you realize this, you see that in real terms Bill and Nancy are barely keeping their heads above water by keeping their savings in cash. Assuming we experience inflation similar to what we've faced over the past 50 years—about 4.5 percent—in 32 years this book will cost $123.25! A café latte at Starbucks will set you back $12, a movie will be $34, and the average car will cost almost $90,000! Bill and Nancy could blast through their IRAs simply by buying two fancy cars! Clearly, keeping their savings in cash is a horrible strategy for the Robinsons.

Assuming they left their 401(k) and 403(b) savings in cash as well, Nancy's total nest egg would be worth $1 million and Bill's would be worth about $950,000. [Bill has less because when he was in his 30s, he made $10,000 less than Nancy and therefore couldn't contribute quite as much to his 403(b).] Their combined nest egg of almost $2 million doesn't exactly leave them in the poor house, but again, because of inflation, they don't have nearly as much money as they could if they had invested in the stock market. Remember how much of it was contributed, and not earned. In Bill's case, he contributed $68,000 to his IRA and $292,000 to his 403(b), for a total of $360,000. Nancy contributed $68,000 to her IRA and $307,000 to her 401(k), for a total of $375,000. That's a combined contribution of $735,000. Growth added just 169 percent to their accounts over 32 years. That's not a good return for such diligent savings over the years.

As you may recall from chapter 1, bonds [or, in 401(k) parlance, Guaranteed Investment Contracts], don't offer a much brighter picture. Putting all their savings into bonds would leave Bill with $1.18 million and Nancy with $1.2 million. Clearly, bonds and cash are investments that offer a cushion against market gyrations, but they are never engines of growth. They can be used in conjunction with stocks but will never get you truly rich on their own.

Aggressive Investing Pays Huge Returns

What if Bill and Nancy read this book and decide that the only way to do well is to commit everything to the stock market? Assuming they have no strategy indexes available in their 401(k) and 403(b) plans and simply invest them in an S&P 500 index fund, but they devote all their IRA savings to the Reasonable Runaways strategy, Bill and Nancy will be seriously rich. Their IRAs alone will be worth $4.4 million each! Nancy's 401(k) will have grown to $3.6 million and Bill's to $3.2 million, for a grand total of $15.6 million! Even with 4–5 percent inflation, that's serious money, and that's assuming they invest their entire 401(k) and 403(b)s in the S&P 500. They may actually have an option to invest in a strategy index like Reasonable Runaways or Leaders with Luster. If that were an option for Bill and Nancy, they would really be rolling in it. If Nancy received returns similar to those of the last 45 years, her 401(k) alone would be worth $7.9 million using the conservative Leaders with Luster strategy and $17.4 million using Reasonable Runaways! But don't forget that Reasonable Runaways often requires an iron stomach, which relatively few people possess. What's more, most people will want to reduce their exposure to risk as they get older. So let's look at a couple different ways the Robinsons can reduce their risk levels as they get closer to retirement and see how it affects their overall net worth.

A More Conservative Path

Let's first look at Bill's retirement accounts, since he always ends up with slightly less money than Nancy. What would happen if

Bill took more risk in his 30s and 40s but pulled in his reins and became more conservative as he neared retirement? Using this approach, Bill would invest his IRA in Reasonable Runaways and his 403(b) in an S&P index fund until he turns 50. After 50, he would invest 50 percent of his IRA in Reasonable Runaways and 50 percent in Leaders with Luster. He would also move 30 percent of his 403(b) out of the stock market, investing 20 percent in intermediate-term bonds and 10 percent in T-bills. Finally, after age 60 he would move his entire IRA into Leaders with Luster and invest 50 percent of his 403(b) in the S&P 500, 40 percent in intermediate-term bonds, and 10 percent in T-bills. This gives him an extremely conservative portfolio in the last five years of his working life, yet he still ends up with a pile of money. If he followed this plan, by the time Bill turned 65 his IRA would be worth $3.3 million and his 403(b) would have grown to $2.4 million, for a grand total of $5.7 million! While that's about $2 million less than if Bill always invested in Reasonable Runaways, it's a program that lowers his risk in his later working years, a prudent thing since he was smart enough to start saving when he was quite young. Indeed, Bill's age is such an advantage that if he chose to be aggressive only in his 30s—moving 30 percent of his 403(b) to cash and bonds when he turns 40 and 50 percent when he turns 50—he could still retire with $4.5 million!

What if the Robinsons decide that they aren't comfortable with the higher risk levels of Reasonable Runaways? They figure that by being more conservative with their 401(k) and 403(b) savings, they can afford to take more risk in their IRAs.

Bill and Nancy decide to invest 70 percent of their 401(k) and 403(b)s in equities, 20 percent in bonds, and 10 percent in cash now but move to 50 percent equities, 40 percent bonds, and 10 percent cash when they turn 40. This conservative scheme lets them be totally aggressive in their IRAs, where they decide to follow the Reasonable Runaways strategy until they retire. If the Robinsons follow this plan, they'll still be extremely rich when they turn 65. Provided Bill and Nancy earn returns similar to those of the past 45 years, their IRAs would be worth $4.4 million. And even with their more conservative portfolios, Bill's 403(b) would be worth $1.8 million and Nancy's would be worth $2 million, for a total of $12.6 million—all while taking very little risk in their 401(k) and 403(b) plans.

The Power of Youth

I cannot overstate the power of starting to save for retirement *as early as possible*. The earlier you start to save, the more conservative you can become as you get older without really hurting your overall return. Assume that Bill and Nancy are smart enough to use the Reasonable Runaways strategy in their IRAs but don't start until age 40. That eight-year delay seriously affects the value of their IRAs by the time they turn 65. Remember that if Bill and Nancy open their IRAs at age 32 and contribute $2,000 to them annually, the IRAs grow to $4.4 million using Reasonable Runaways. By starting at age 40, however, Bill and Nancy each contribute $52,000 to their IRAs, but it only grows to $1.1 million! That's a difference of $3.3 million—representing $400,000 a year for the eight years they didn't contribute to their IRAs. Would you turn down a job for $400,000 a year that required you to do nothing but save $2,000? Not many people would, but that's exactly what Bill and Nancy do by delaying their savings programs.

Bill and Nancy's case demonstrates the power of having time on your side. If you are in your 20s or 30s and haven't begun saving, you are literally throwing away a fortune. By starting early and being fairly aggressive throughout your 40s, you almost can't help being rich by the time you turn 65. What's more, if you start saving early, you can become quite conservative with your money while in your 50s without damaging your ability to retire in style. For example, if the Robinsons invest their IRAs in Reasonable Runaways until they are 55, then switch to the more conservative Leaders with Luster, each of their IRAs would still grow to $3.3 million.

If you're the type who falls asleep on roller coasters (and can easily stick with a successful strategy like Reasonable Runaways through its ups and downs), your youth can ensure that you'll have a small fortune when you turn 65.

GEORGE AND THERESA RAMIREZ: YOU CAN'T BE TOO PREPARED

George and Theresa Ramirez are six years older than the Robinsons, and at 38 they already face different challenges. They are committed to building a legacy to pass on to their sons, Robert and Carlo. George and Theresa grew up in families that struggled to make ends meet and don't want their sons to face the same fate. They also feel very strongly that a great education will be the best gift they can give their boys, and so a college fund must be part of their savings plan.

You might recall that George is a computer programmer and Theresa is a graphic artist. Their combined income is $90,000, and they've each saved $5,000 in their IRAs. They've got 27 years until they retire, so they can afford to be aggressive with their retirement savings. Like the Robinsons, the Ramirezes ran a budget to see how they could fund their 401(k)s, their IRAs, and the boys' college funds.

SAVING FOR THE COLLEGE YEARS

Ironically, the boys' college accounts proved to be the greatest challenge. The problem with college funds is that they are fully taxed by the government. George and Theresa immediately understood that taxes would make quite an impact and that the sooner they started saving for their sons' college, the better off they'd be.

George and Theresa start by setting up custodial savings accounts for Robert and Carlo's college funds. These are usually referred to as Uniform Transfer to Minors Act (UTMA) accounts, whereby an adult holds the savings in custody for the child until age 18. They decide to use an UTMA account for two reasons. First, they don't want their boys to be able to blow their money on video games. Second, minors are not allowed to buy stock or mutual funds, and the Ramirezes know by now how important it is for them to invest their sons' college funds in superior stock market strategies.

The Ramirezes were disappointed to learn about the "kiddie tax." In its infinite wisdom, our government penalizes you for having the foresight to help your children save for their futures! It works like this. The first $1,300 of Robert and Carlo's investment incomes is not taxed. After that, however, they'll be taxed at their parents' marginal tax rate, which in the Ramirezes' case is 31 percent. This happens only until the boys turn 14, when their investment income above $1,300 will be taxed at 15 percent. (Whew, time to take an aspirin!)

The Ramirezes opened their boys' college accounts with money that they had been saving for just that purpose. They set up one UTMA account for four-year-old Robert with a gift of $6,500 and another for two-year-old Carlo with a gift of $4,000. (They give more money to Robert because he is older, and they want their boys to end up with roughly the same amount of money when they are ready for college.) They plan to add $500 a year to each account and to invest the money using Reasonable Runaways.

If they achieve returns similar to that of Reasonable Runaways over the past 45 years, when Robert turns 18 his college fund will be worth $83,900. Over the years, George and Theresa contributed a total of $13,500 to Robert's college account. What's unfortunate is that Robert will have paid a total of $14,000 in taxes over the years—$500 more than all the money his parents contributed. Carlo, who started with $4,000, would have $86,000 at age 18. His parents would have contributed $12,000 to the account, and he would have paid a total of $14,000 in taxes to Uncle Sam.

Just to make sure they're doing the right thing by investing the boys' college funds in stocks, George and Theresa want to look at a worst-case scenario. They find that the worst 15-year period Reasonable Runaways experienced was that ending December 31, 1974, one of the most difficult periods for the stock market since the Great Depression. During that time, Reasonable Runaways earned 10.68 percent a year. At that rate, when Robert is 18 his account would be worth $42,000, and Carlo's account would be worth $40,000, considerably less than if they earned returns similar to those of the last 45 years. What George and Theresa find compelling is that Reasonable Runaways still vastly outperformed an investment in cash or bonds over the same period. For the 15 years ending December 31, 1974, T-bills returned 4.62 percent a year and intermediate-term bonds returned 5.05 percent. Had Robert's fund been invested in either cash or bonds, the most he could hope to have in his account would be $24,000, about half as much as he'd have using Reasonable Runaways.

This is just what George and Theresa needed to see. They know they're making an *informed choice,* not basing their decision on guesses or emotions. Moreover, they feel they can handle declines in the market or in their sons' portfolios, since they understand the worst-case scenario. Unlike many investors who pour money into mutual funds after a great year or quarter, the Ramirezes are committing to a *strategy,* knowing that it has ups and downs but that it still beats the pants off its competition. Since they understand that market declines are part of life, they'll be much more likely to stick with their superior investment strategy over the long haul.

Ensuring Their Future

Now that they have set up their boys' college funds, the Ramirezes want to make important decisions about their own retirement accounts. They are both pretty happy with their careers, with George earning $60,000 designing computer software and

Theresa bringing in $30,000 as a part-time graphic artist. George wants to work with computers for the rest of his career. He knows that he's living through an era that will transform the world, and he can't think of a better way to participate in that than by designing new software for the digital age. George is promoted to team leader of his software group in 2005, and in 2013 he is named director of programming. With only minimal cost of living increases in his salary, George can make the maximum contribution to his 401(k) in just two years, as his current 15 percent contribution is $9,000. If he also adds $2,000 to his IRA every year, he'll initially be contributing 18 percent of his gross salary to his retirement savings. But, just as with the Robinsons, George is getting a huge tax benefit by making the maximum contribution to his 401(k). What's more, he is extremely motivated to leave his boys a legacy, and this makes it much easier for him to put aside such a good-sized percentage of his income.

Theresa enjoys her work as a graphic artist for a large advertising agency in San Francisco, especially since she is often able to work out of her home. She thinks it's very important to have time with the boys when they are young, but she would love to start her own Web site design company when the boys are in school full-time. Because her part-time salary is only $30,000, she can contribute only $4,500 to her 401(k), but Theresa knows that when she starts working full-time she should be able to significantly increase her salary and her 401(k) contribution.

Theresa's dream comes true, and at age 44 she and three others found By Design, a Web site design firm. While she had been making contributions to her 401(k) of $4,000–$6,000 over the last six years, by the time she is 47 her salary reaches the level where she can make the maximum $9,500 annual contribution.

When They're 65

By now, we know that George and Theresa won't get rich investing in bonds or T-bills. By keeping their IRAs and 401(k)s in cash or bonds, George's savings would grow to $768,000 and Theresa's would grow to $653,000. That nest egg of $1.4 million is not going to make them feel rich 27 years from now, since it barely keeps up with inflation.

If, on the other hand, they keep their retirement savings in the stock market, using Reasonable Runaways in their IRAs and the S&P 500 in their 401(k) accounts, George's savings would grow to $4.3 million and Theresa's would grow to $3.7 million, for a grand total of $8 million! Again, you see the power of saving when you're young by looking at the returns from the Ramirezes' IRAs. If they started putting $2,000 a year in their IRAs at age 38 but didn't already have $5,000 saved, the final value of their IRAs would be $1.6 million compared with the $2.2 million they earn starting with $5,000 in each account. Think of it! $5,000 today might make your retirement account tomorrow worth $623,000 more when you retire.

Now that we've looked at the extremes, let's see how the Ramirezes will do somewhere in the middle. George decides to be aggressive, using Reasonable Runaways in his IRA and the S&P 500 in his 401(k). Theresa uses a more conservative strategy, investing her IRA in Leaders with Luster and her 401(k) in 50 percent stocks, 40 percent bonds, and 10 percent cash. Using those strategies, George would have a retirement fund worth $4.3 million. Theresa's IRA would be worth $1.1 million, and her very conservatively invested 401(k) would be worth $967,000, leaving her with about $2.1 million at age 65. The benefit of this more conservative stance is that it gives the Ramirezes an overall portfolio that's broadly diversified and lower in risk—giving them more peace of mind while still building their nest egg to $6.3 million.

THE POWER OF STRATEGY INDEXES IN A 401(K)

What if Theresa has access to a strategy index in her 401(k)? As one of the founders of By Design she can pick the funds available in her firm's 401(k) plan. If she selected something like

O'Shaughnessy Funds Cornerstone Growth (similar to Reasonable Runaways), Cornerstone Value (like Leaders with Luster), or another mutual fund group that invested in these strategies, she could really beef up the returns in her 401(k).

If Theresa invests in a mutual fund that duplicates the Reasonable Runaways strategy and achieves similar historical returns, after fees of 1.25 percent her return would be 17.5 percent. Her 401(k) would then grow to $3.9 million, compared with the $1.1 million earned in the S&P 500. By using a strategy index, Theresa can afford to be much more conservative overall and still beat the market. If she put half her 401(k) into a strategy index like Reasonable Runaways, 40 percent in intermediate-term bonds, and 10 percent in T-bills, her return would still be higher than if she had put all her money in an S&P index. Her average return would be 12.65 percent, and her 401(k) would be worth $1.6 million when she turns 65. What's great about this strategy is that it has lower risk levels than the S&P 500, and it never had a five-year period when it lost money! Now that's a plan Theresa can stick with!

How to Lower Risk and Still Retire Rich

By combining a strategy like Reasonable Runaways with an investment in bonds and cash, you can eliminate much of the risk of the stock market and still retire rich. While you won't have as much money as someone who commits all her savings to a strategy like Reasonable Runaways, you'll be sleeping better at night and will be much more likely to stick with the strategy through the ups and downs of the stock market.

Because Theresa is taking a large risk starting a business, she may want to invest her 401(k) even more conservatively. If she used Leaders with Luster in her 401(k), she'd end up with $2.1 million—while using a strategy that never lost money over any 5-year period. If she wanted to take virtually *no risk* in her 401(k), she could use the 50–40–10 allocation she used before but substitute Leaders with Luster for Reasonable Runaways as the equity investment. In this case, her 401(k) would be worth $1.1 million when she turns 65. Most important, this strategy is less risky than investing in long-term government bonds!

A MIDDLE-OF-THE-ROAD STRATEGY THAT'S HARDLY MIDDLE OF THE ROAD

In our final scenario, Theresa uses the nearly risk-free strategy just described, investing her 401(k) in Leaders with Luster, bonds, and cash. She also invests her IRA in the conservative 10-stock Dogs of the Dow strategy. George is a bit more aggressive, investing his IRA in Reasonable Runaways but putting 70 percent of his 401(k) in the S&P 500 and 30 percent in bonds and cash. At age 65, George will have $2.2 million in his IRA and $1.6 million in his 401(k). Theresa will have $1.1 million in her IRA and $1.1 million in her 401(k). They will have had a smooth ride and have $6 million in the bank, all while taking relatively little risk.

A wise thing for the Ramirezes to do when they retire is to invest half their IRAs in bonds and half in the stocks from our Utility strategy. In addition, they should allocate 70 percent of their 401(k)s to bonds and 30 percent to stocks. This would give them ample income to live on and capital appreciation to boot, adding to the legacy for their children. Remember that George and Theresa never had to spend too much of their annual income on the boys' future education, because they had made annual contributions to their college funds. Planning made the difference. Using simple strategies, they were able to meet all their goals and retire rich.

TOM AND SARAH O'NEIL: ALLOWING PERSISTENCE TO OVERCOME RISK AND FEAR

You probably remember that Tom and Sarah O'Neil are both 45 years old and live near Detroit, Michigan, with their four children. Tom earns $150,000 a year as an executive at Ford Motor Company, and he and Sarah have each saved $15,000 so far in their IRAs, which they have kept in cash. Sarah is partly to blame for this small sum. The stock market terrifies her, and she's always sure that the moment she invests, stocks will tumble and she'll lose a lot of money. She, like many of us often do, took one particular story to heart. Her brother-in-law invested $20,000 in a small start-up company and watched his investment soar to almost $1 million as the company's stock took off. But then the investment soured, and the company's prospects declined, along with the price of its stock. Her brother-in-law had bought the stock on margin, taking a loan from his broker to buy additional shares. When the stock's price declined, her brother-in-law had to post additional collateral to cover the loan. In less than a year he had not only lost his $1 million, he owed his broker more than $100,000.

Sarah saw all stock investments through this lens. Just as one good stock story can make some people feel invincible in their stock-picking instincts, one bad stock story can turn others off the market completely. Sarah was extremely worried about how she and Tom would support themselves when Tom retires. She sees her own parents struggling to get by on Social Security and knows that it will be just as bad—if not worse—for them. But her fear of the market has led them to keep both Tom's 401(k) and their IRAs in cash. While Sarah is an extremely intelligent person and realizes that she is being irrational, her fear of the stock market is very common.

Both Sarah and Tom read *How to Retire Rich,* but each has a quite different reaction. Tom gets fired up and is ready to invest his IRA money in Reasonable Runaways and his 401(k) in an S&P 500 index fund, since there are no strategy indexes available on his plan. His background in engineering made him instantly comfortable with the systematic, long-term method presented in the book. Sarah also finds the numbers compelling but can't help but focus on the worst-case scenarios. Look at how Reasonable

Runaways did in 1973 and 1974, the two worst years for the stock market since the Great Depression. If they faced a similar crash, their IRAs—now worth $15,000—would fall to $9,000. Worse, what if the next crash is followed by another depression, like in the 1930s? Sarah is sure their savings could be wiped out.

SARAH'S FEARS ARE ALL TOO COMMON

Tom was extremely frustrated with Sarah at first. He couldn't understand why she was so unwilling to invest in the stock market, especially after seeing all the evidence in *How to Retire Rich.* He thought she was being totally unreasonable. But then he saw a survey in the *New York Times* that showed that investing worries were incredibly common, especially among women. Indeed, half the women surveyed said stock market fluctuations made them very nervous. What really bothered him—especially after reading *How to Retire Rich*—was that while most men and women fear they will not have enough money when they are older, the majority will also only consider "safe," or guaranteed, investments. As we've seen again and again, these investments will never make you rich. Yet 73 percent of the women surveyed said that they would invest only in such safe instruments, and 65 percent said they wanted to earn nonvariable rates of return.

Tom suddenly understood that Sarah's feelings about the stock market were very common. So he asked Sarah what she thought separated the rich from the not rich. After disregarding those who had inherited their money, Sarah thought about people who had done well, from the computer geniuses in Silicon Valley all the way to her sister's husband, who had made a great deal of money supplying the big automakers with hard-to-find parts. She came up with the following traits. Smart. Creative. Risk takers. Persistent. Willing to accept failure and try again. Able to see opportunity where others see danger.

That list made Tom and Sarah understand *why most people aren't rich*. After all, 56 percent of men and 73 percent of women want only guaranteed investments—not vehicles for smart, persistent risk-takers willing to accept failure. Such investments are for risk-averse people who are either already rich or never will be. When Sarah saw investing in this light, her fears finally began to subside. She'd always been persistent—you don't raise four happy, well-mannered children without abundant persistence! But she was also smart, and she started to understand the value of taking a little risk with their retirement savings.

A Plan for Sarah

The first place Sarah looked when trying to decide how to invest was the Performance Appendix at the back of this book. What happens if both she and Tom continue to contribute $2,000 a year to their IRAs and Tom makes the maximum contribution to his 401(k)? If they keep their money in cash or GICs, the best they could hope for is a nest egg of about $800,000. Twenty years from now, things will undoubtedly cost a good deal more than they do today. If the O'Neils can earn 6 percent on that $800,000 when Tom retires, their annual income would be about $48,000 before taxes. Given their income and lifestyle now, that looks pretty meager.

So what if the O'Neils take the aggressive route, using Reasonable Runaways in both IRAs and investing Tom's entire 401(k) in an S&P 500 index fund? The picture becomes much rosier, and they'd likely have more than $2 million in their IRAs and $1.4 million in Tom's 401(k). Their combined net worth would exceed $5 million!

But this alternative made Sarah's fears return. She saw Tom's 401(k) as the bulk of their savings and thought that it was foolish to invest it all in the stock market, no matter what the numbers showed. By now, though, she knew that some of it had to be invested in stocks if she and Tom wanted to retire rich.

Sarah started by reviewing the current stocks in the Reasonable Runaways strategy. She didn't like that she didn't recognize many of the companies, but what unnerved her most were their daily price fluctuations. Tom pointed out that they had to ignore the short term and focus on the fact that Reasonable Runaways had delivered eye-popping returns over the long term. But Sarah knew that she could never stick with such a strategy because its volatility would be her undoing.

Next she looked at the stocks in Leaders with Luster. These she liked a lot more. She recognized them—household names like Exxon, Ford, and 3M. But Sarah still couldn't shake her fears that the market would have another 1929-style crash in prices, and Leaders with Luster's track record went back only to 1951. That left her with the Dogs of the Dow strategy, where she has a record back to 1929. So how would Sarah have done had she started investing her IRA in the Dogs of the Dow on December 31, 1928, right before the greatest stock market crash and depression in U.S. history? Sarah thought that this analysis would surely give her a good reason to avoid stocks and stick with the certainty of GICs or cash.

But it did just the opposite. Had Sarah started her IRA right before the crash, religiously contributing $2,000 a year for 21 years, by the time she was 65 her account would be worth $61,000 if invested in cash, $106,000 if invested in bonds, and over $200,000 if invested in the Dogs of the Dow strategy. This stock strategy—risky in Sarah's eyes—had more than doubled the returns of the so-called risk-free bond or cash strategy during the worst economic downturn in American history! She was absolutely floored. With this long-term perspective, Sarah finally understood that *the riskiest thing she could do was not invest her money in the stock market.* Indeed, even if the market was at an intermediate-term high, she knew she should still invest in stocks because she didn't need the money for another 20 years. She was sold on the 10-stock Dogs of the Dow strategy and at last could invest her IRA savings there with confidence. She also became much more comfortable with Tom using Reasonable Runaways in his IRA, as long as he was willing to diversify his 401(k), investing 30 percent of it in bonds and cash—just in case they needed a port in a storm.

The O'Neils' Future Transformed

Because Sarah was persistent enough to get to the heart of her fears and come to a decision about investing in the market, the O'Neils' future will be considerably brighter. Instead of letting irrational fears drive Tom and Sarah's investment decisions, their research has led them to the best investment strategy for them. It's more aggressive than an investment in bonds or cash, but Sarah is comfortable with it because it is quite conservative.

So what will their nest egg be worth using this more conservative strategy? Remember that Tom will use Reasonable Runaways in his IRA, put 70 percent of his 401(k) into an S&P 500 index fund, and put the rest in bonds and T-bills. Sarah will use the Dogs of the Dow strategy in her IRA. Once again, if they get returns similar to those of the last 45 years, when they retire Tom will have $1 million in his IRA and $1.1 million in his 401(k). Sarah will have $600,000 in her IRA, and their total savings will amount to about $2.7 million—compared with the $700,000 if they left all their savings in cash and bonds. They're now confident and at ease, knowing they'll have enough money to take vacations, give gifts to their grandchildren, and have the time to enjoy life. By facing their fears and taking action, Tom and Sarah can retire rich.

Steve and Betsy Johnson: Making Up for Lost Time

Last year, Steve and Betsy got a wake-up call from their accountant. Start saving the maximum allowable *right now,* she said, or you'll never be able to retire in style. They were shocked. How could retirement loom so near? They'd gone to Woodstock, for God's sake, and now they were facing retirement? What's more, they were actually proud of the $30,000 they had saved thus far in Steve's IRA and thought they were doing just as well as others in their generation. They also were counting on an inheritance from Betsy's mother when she died. Between the equity in her mother's home and other savings, Betsy expected to inherit about $100,000. But when Steve and Betsy took a hard look at the numbers, they saw how right their accountant was.

PUTTING A PLAN IN PLACE

The first thing Steve did was to start a Simplified Employee Pension (SEP) plan for himself. His plumbing contracting business was very successful, but he had never gotten around to setting up a pension plan. Because he could use a SEP instead of a 401(k), his maximum annual contribution was $24,000, which, after a great year for his business, he was able to make the year he opened the account.

The first thing Betsy did was open an IRA of her own with a $2,000 contribution. Having just gone back to work as a real estate broker, her goal was to increase her commissions on real estate sales by 10 percent a year until she could make the maximum contribution of $9,500 to her 401(k). With a lot of hard work and a strong Florida real estate market, she reaches this goal by age 59 and accumulates $126,000 in her 401(k).

But even with their newfound savings fervor, the Johnsons realize that they won't retire rich if they put all their money in riskless investments. If they keep all their savings in T-bills, when Steve retires at age 65 his IRA will be worth about $90,000 and his SEP (assuming he was always able to make the maximum contribution of $24,000 a year) will be worth $456,000, for a total of about $550,000. Betsy plans to work until she is 65, but her IRA invested in cash will still be worth only $87,000 and her 401(k) will be worth $106,000. All told, they would have $739,000. While that's a lot better than if they'd done nothing about saving for retirement, it's not the greatest reward for their diligent savings and hard work.

STEVE'S PLAN: WATCH OUT FOR RISK

Since Steve is 55 and want to retire when he is 65, he's got to decide just how aggressive he's willing to be in both his IRA and his SEP. The worst return Reasonable Runaways ever had over any 10-year period was about 7.5 percent per year. He feels comfortable using this strategy in his IRA, since it's his SEP that contains the bulk of his savings. If Reasonable Runaways earns returns similar to those of the last 45 years, he'll have $325,000 in his IRA when he turns 65, almost three times as much as he would have just investing in bonds. Nevertheless, he worries about the volatility of Reasonable Runaways. By combining Leaders with Luster and Reasonable Runaways in his IRA, Steve could end up with $284,000, while substantially reducing the volatility of his portfolio.

His SEP is a different story. There he wants above-average returns with below-market risk. Since he can decide what investments are available on his SEP, strategy indexes like Reasonable Runaways and Leaders with Luster are available to him. Remember that over the past 45 years a 50–50 split between the two strategies compounded at 16.12 percent after fees. If Steve earns that until he retires, his SEP will be worth $1 million.

But he is still concerned about risk, particularly because he is pretty close to retirement. He'll be happy only when taking less risk than the market. He looks at what would happen if he put 35 percent of his money in Reasonable Runaways, 35 percent in Leaders with Luster, 20 percent in bonds, and 10 percent in cash. Over the last 45 years, the strategy returned 13.51 percent after fees and had an overall risk below the S&P 500. Bingo! Steve has found a great strategy for his SEP—it generates higher returns than the S&P 500 while taking less risk. If he gets returns similar to those of the last 45 years, by the time he reaches 65 his SEP will be worth $831,000. Add the savings in his IRA to that, and Steve will likely have $1.1 million saved when he retires. Not bad for a man who had saved just $54,000 10 years earlier!

Betsy's Plan: Keep Saving

When Steve turns 65, Betsy's IRA invested in Reasonable Runaways will be worth $87,300 and her 401(k) invested in the

S&P 500 will be worth $159,000. If Betsy decided to quit working then, the Johnsons would have $1.3 million saved for their retirement years. But Betsy is really enjoying her work and isn't ready to retire. The fact that Steve accumulated $1.1 million through diligent savings is another incentive for her to keep working and saving. Although she's comfortable using Reasonable Runaways in her IRA, she too thinks she should be somewhat more conservative with her 401(k). If Betsy invests her entire 401(k) in an S&P 500 index fund, it will be worth $350,000 when she is 65. And even if she is more conservative and invests 70 percent of her 401(k) in the S&P and 30 percent in bonds and cash, her account will still be worth over $300,000 when she retires at 65.

What's more, Betsy's extra six years of work really pay off in terms of her net worth. If Betsy continues to work and make contributions to her 401(k) and IRA every year, her IRA mushrooms from $87,300 to $224,000, and her 401(k) grows to over $350,000. Think of it—she can add more than $325,000 to their retirement savings simply by continuing to work for an extra six years—not to mention the extra income they have to live on during that time!

STEVE'S POSTRETIREMENT PORTFOLIO

When Steve turns 65, his portfolio is worth about $1.1 million. While Betsy was making about $70,000 a year selling real estate, he wanted to add another $40,000 to their annual income (after taxes) while still investing some of his savings for growth. He found that pretty easy to do. Florida tax-free municipal bonds were yielding 5 percent at the time. He converted $700,000 of the $1.1 million to these bonds, and they generated a tax-free income of $35,000 a year. He then invested $200,000 in the 10-stock Utility strategy featured in chapter 3. With a yield of 6 percent, Steve earned $8,280 after taxes. Remember that this Utility strategy has the potential to grow through capital appreciation, and historically it has grown about 6 percent a year.

Finally, Steve decided to keep the remaining $200,000 in Reasonable Runaways, even though he had to pay capital gains taxes on his profits.

The Johnsons' Nest Egg When Betsy Retires

Here's what the Johnsons' portfolios look like when Betsy retires at age 65. After taxes, Steve has $403,000 in Reasonable Runaways, $253,000 in the Utility strategy, and $700,000 in Florida municipal bonds, for a total of $1.36 million. Betsy's IRA is worth $224,000, and her 401(k) is worth $350,000, for a total of $574,000. Steve and Betsy have $1.9 million in their retirement accounts, and they can retire in style.

What to Do with an Inheritance

When she was 51, Betsy inherited $100,000 from her mother. Like her, many baby boomers can expect to inherit something from their parents, since economists expect the world's largest-ever intergenerational transfer of wealth—some $7 trillion—to take place in the coming years. Luckily, Betsy had read *How to Retire Rich* before her mother died, so when she received the money she knew she should invest it for the future.

Betsy wanted her inheritance to be extra insurance for their retirement, especially if there were some rough years ahead in the stock market and it didn't perform as well as it had over the last 45 years. So she decided to do some comparison shopping. When she inherited the money, the average AAA-rated tax-free 10-year municipal bond had a yield of 5 percent. If she bought those bonds and reinvested all the proceeds at the same rate, her $100,000 would be worth $208,000 when she turned 65.

But what if Betsy invests her inheritance in Reasonable Runaways? Not wanting to be overly optimistic, she decides to look at the worst return Reasonable Runaways had over any 15-year period. Before taxes, the worst return this strategy ever had over any 15 years was 10.68 percent per year. If Betsy earned a similar return over the next 15 years and paid capital gains taxes of 28 percent, that inheritance would grow to $300,000 when she turns 65, for an annual after-tax return of 7.69 percent. In this instance, she's better off investing in Reasonable Runaways, because even after taxes the worst 15-year period still beats the performance of municipal bonds by a great margin. She wouldn't want to move her inheritance into tax-free bonds unless their yield started to approach 7–7.5 percent.

But then Betsy decided it wasn't fair to use the single-worst 15-year period in Reasonable Runaways' history as her benchmark. She decided to take the average of the five worst 15-year periods and found that it was 13.31 percent, before taxes. Assuming capital gains taxes of 28 percent, her after-tax return becomes 9.58 percent.

Thus, Betsy decides to invest her inheritance in Reasonable Runaways until municipal bonds approach returns of 7.5 percent. If they ever get there, she's going to put half her inheritance in tax-free bonds. Finally, if tax-free bond yields ever exceed 9.58 percent, she's going to remove all the money from Reasonable Runaways and invest it in bonds.

STEVE AND BETSY'S FUTURE

Assuming the yield on tax-free bonds never got high enough for Betsy to shift any money out of Reasonable Runaways and that she got returns similar to the average for the last 45 years, her inheritance from her mother would grow to $672,000 by the time she retires—even after paying $200,000 in taxes. If she used the slightly more conservative blend of Reasonable Runaways and Leaders with Luster, it would be worth $587,000 after taxes.

Thus, because Steve and Betsy maximized their savings and used superior investment strategies, when Betsy turns 65 she and Steve will have $2.6 million! Remember that 16 years ago they had only $54,000 saved—and plenty of worries. Instead of fretting and reproaching themselves for not saving enough, they found simple, easy-to-understand strategies and used them. It would have been easy for Steve to say, "It's too late for me to retire rich. I might as well just live for the day." That attitude might have left him in the same situation as that of Mr. Walters in chapter 1—73 years old and doing heavy, back-breaking labor to support his family. Steve and Betsy's case shows that it's *never too late* to start an intelligent retirement plan—and you can retire richer and happier as a result.

The right plan for you

Throughout this book, we've seen how successful you can be if you're willing to stick with a sensible, disciplined approach to investing. To keep things relatively simple, I've assumed that each couple received returns similar to the 45-year average for these assorted strategies. Obviously, the future is not going to be exactly like the past. During the first 10 years of your investment program, you may earn returns much higher than the average. If that's the case, you may want to invest more money in bonds and cash in subsequent years to preserve your gains. After all, that's what bonds and T-bills are for—keeping you rich! On the other hand, if the first 10 years of your investment program are more like the worst years in the past, you may want to keep a larger portion of your portfolio in the market for a while, delaying the shift to bonds or T-bills.

Use the stories of these four couples as models for your own investment plans. If you're under 40, you should take a long-term view and commit all your money to Reasonable Runaways. With youth and such a powerful strategy on your side, it will be hard for you not to retire rich! But remember that thinking you've got plenty of time is a huge mistake. Every day you delay saving and investing will have a significant effect on your future. Take advantage of your youth today, and tomorrow will be bright. A poem I recall by an author I've forgotten reminds us:

Love and time with reverence use, treat them as a parting
  friend,
Nor the golden gifts refuse, which in youth they send,
For each year, their price is more,
And they less simple than before.

If you're over 40 and haven't started saving for your retirement, *start right now.* Open an IRA account, *today.* You can't
afford to wait any longer—it's your future on the line. By the
time you're 40, you'll know how fast time goes. High school
doesn't seem that long ago, yet it's time to start worrying about
your 25th reunion! It seems like you were just changing diapers,
and now your kids are almost as tall as you are! Believe me, the
next 20 years are going to fly by even faster than the last 20.
Don't be "too soon old, too late smart." Start saving and investing
now, and your retirement will be far richer than it will be if you
continue to delay.

If you're over 50 and still haven't saved much, the worst thing
you can do is throw in the towel. Giving up hope will guarantee
that you'll never have a carefree retirement. By using the strategies in this book you can vastly increase your ability to have a
healthy financial retirement. For example, Steve Johnson is in his
mid-50s. If he thought that it was too late for him, he would
have been turning his back on a plan that allowed him to retire
with over $1 million! Think of the difference that will make in
his quality of life. Instead of having to continue to work into his
70s, he'll be able to retire and play golf, start a new hobby, and
spend many happy days with his grandchildren. Even in your
50s, it's not too late to set up a plan that will materially affect
your future. While it will require more diligence than if you were
in your 30s or 40s, you're probably earning more than you did 10
or 20 years ago as well. The key is that you can reach your retirement goals if you're willing to stretch *now.*

The Broken Record:
Stay in the Market

Once again, remember that if you want to retire rich, you have to use intelligent stock investment strategies. And if you want to retire *really rich,* start investing when you are young. But the most important lesson is that the stock market is not mysterious. The simple strategies in this book will lead you to a rich retirement if you stick with them.

Let's now look at some of the pitfalls and roadblocks that will test your ability to hang in there.

CHAPTER SEVEN

PITFALLS, ROADBLOCKS, AND EXCESS BAGGAGE

One thing I can virtually guarantee is that, on your quest to retire rich, you *will* panic. It is in our nature to panic when confronted with danger. Our adrenaline starts flowing, giving us the boost we need to either start running at top speed or fight with all our strength. In terms of human evolution, this came in very handy when we had lions and tigers and bears pouncing on us all the time, and it still comes in handy when we are in some form of physical danger. But evolution didn't distinguish between physical and mental danger or, more important, real and perceived danger. The modern world is filled with perceived dangers, and they keep our adrenaline flowing—often when we don't need it.

PERILS AND PITFALLS OF INVESTING

On any given day, the stock market presents a host of "dangers" to all investors. Any time the opening bell rings, you face the possibility of losing money in your portfolio. A company you own might go bankrupt, interest rates could skyrocket, or the stock market could tumble. Unfortunately, the adrenaline that protected the caveman—or, nowadays, protects someone walking down a city street at night—works mischievously against us when investing. Each new danger we find in the market helps stoke a fire of anxiety and fear in our hearts. While all these simmer at low boil, something we perceive as particularly dangerous occurs, and we experience full-blown panic.

The Crash of 1987

Imagine that you read this book in 1986 and started Reasonable Runaways in your IRA with a $2,000 contribution. For most of 1987, you'd have been elated as you watched your stocks grow in value. You'd be thinking, "Wow, this stuff really works!" You'd be kicking yourself for not starting your investment program sooner. In just one month's time—between July and August— the Dow Jones Industrial Average alone soars 11 percent.

But small cracks start appearing in your portfolio's performance in late summer. The Dow Jones Industrial Average continues to go up, but your stocks don't, and you start to fret—could it be that this strategy used to work but no longer does? Indeed, the overall market starts to concern you a great deal. That wonderful 11 percent rise is followed by some really erratic behavior in the market. One day, stocks soar, and the next day, they swoon. *Nightline* opens a show devoted to the increasingly wild stock market with a picture of a roller coaster. It has been a nonstop bull market for more than five years, and the Dow seems awfully high at 2,600. You find yourself reading financial publications like *Money* and the *Wall Street Journal* and checking the closing prices of your stocks every day.

Things heat up even more in September. Prices are wildly swinging around, and all of a sudden Reasonable Runaways doesn't look so reasonable. It looks downright rotten—its stocks are falling in price consistently, day in and day out. This grinds on your emotions, and you wish that *How to Retire Rich* included daily historical information, because you're certain that this crazy market is not normal. Yet you vow to stick with the program, since years and years of data have proven that Reasonable Runaways is a great investment strategy, and this is just the sort of day-to-day volatility that *How to Retire Rich* warned you about.

Black Monday

Then comes October 19, 1987—Black Monday. The Dow Jones Industrial Average falls over 500 points, losing more than 22 percent of its value in a single day. Reasonable Runaways is hit hard. *Business Week* runs a cover story with the headline: "How Bad? Will Wall Street Take the Economy Down?" pronouncing that "even if stock prices climb out of the cellar, there is virtually no chance that the violence of the jolt will leave the economy unscathed." A *Newsweek* poll finds that 57 percent of investors think the best place for their money is in cash or equivalents—14 percent say gold, 11 percent say bonds, and just 6 percent say stocks or mutual funds are the best place to put their money!

Panic Spans the Globe

With this ceaseless drumbeat of negative news and fear mongering, and an unprecedented market crash, it might have been virtually impossible for you not to panic and throw in the towel. Thousands did, issuing orders to "sell at any price." The panic wasn't confined to the United States, either. A headline in *Time* magazine screamed: "Panic Grips the Globe." And as the panic spread, untold millions reacted emotionally to the news of the day, without any perspective on how their actions would affect their lives 10 years later.

If you were there and had just started your investment program, what are the chances that you could have avoided panicking? Pretty slim, I'll bet, even with all the long-term data supporting your investment strategy. The short-term violence of the crash would overwhelm your logical side, bringing on a state of full-blown panic. You'd probably be convinced that what used to work no longer did. You'd want to hurl *How to Retire Rich* in the garbage.

More Fuel for the Fire

Every "expert" on TV and in the press was saying that things really were different this time. This crash is unprecedented, they said, and who knows where it might lead. What's more, the short-term evidence reinforced the impulse to panic. Reasonable Runaways, which you had such high hopes for, closed the year down 12 percent, while the S&P 500, despite the crash, was up more than 5 percent. Because the stock market had just crashed and the short-term evidence suggested that Reasonable Runaways was no longer working, your urge to abandon the strategy would have been overwhelming. Your reaction would have been completely natural and understandable, because we are programmed by nature to think like that.

Short-Circuiting Panic

Our emotions take over when we are in a state of panic, leading us to do things that are very bad for us in the long term. But we have an advantage over most animals in the kingdom—big brains. We can short-circuit panic by being prepared for it and understanding what brings it on. Right now, *know that something will happen during your investment program that will make you panic,* and prepare yourself for it. It probably won't be a repeat of the crash of 1987, since things rarely happen exactly as they did in the past. But the same types of events continue to occur. By understanding that panics and sell-offs will occur, just as they have in the past, you can prepare yourself to keep your wits about you. No one can accurately predict when something might bring about the next panic. But by studying history, we can predict things likely to occur after the panic.

Hysteria in the Headlines

Throughout history, people have loved predicting disaster. It looms around every corner and, most important, is easy to sell. Read a selection of predictions from the beginning of the printed word until today, and you'll be amazed that anyone is alive, much less prospering! Take a look at some of these actual forecasts, predictions, and headlines about the stock market from the past:

"DON'T FALL FOR IT WHEN THEY TELL YOU—BUY NOW! PRICES
ARE GOING HIGHER! BECAUSE PRICES ARE HEADING FOR ONE
OF THE WORST PLUNGES YOU'VE EVER SEEN."
(1951, Dow Jones Industrial Average: 262)

"WILL THIS MAJOR SHAKE-UP IN AMERICA'S WEALTH WIPE OUT
YOUR SAVINGS AND CRIPPLE YOUR FUTURE?"
(1954, Dow Jones Industrial Average: 330)

"USSR LAUNCHES SPUTNIK 1, US DOMINANCE IN DOUBT, DOW
OFF ALMOST 10 PERCENT IN UNDER A MONTH."
(1957, Dow Jones Industrial Average: 419)

"CUBAN MISSILE CRISIS JAMS INDEXES SHARPLY LOWER."
(1962, Dow Jones Industrial Average: 590)

"INCREASED VIETNAM BOMBINGS AND TALK OF HIGH TAXES
ROUT MARKETS."
(1966, Dow Jones Industrial Average: 785)

"NIXON RESIGNATION, RUNAWAY INFLATION AND THE CRISIS OF
CONFIDENCE IN THE ECONOMY FOREVER CHANGE THE
MARKET." (1974, Dow Jones Industrial Average: 616)

"JOE GRANVILLE'S 'ABANDON ALL HOPE' MESSAGE SPARKS A
GIANT SELL-OFF ON RECORD VOLUME."
(1981, Dow Jones Industrial Average: 875)

"STOCKS CRASH, DOES A DEPRESSION LOOM?"
(1987, Dow Jones Industrial Average: 1,738)

"IS IT 1929 ALL OVER AGAIN? HUGE BEAR MARKET FEARED."
(1987, Dow Jones Industrial Average: 1,805)

"HIGH INTEREST RATES, THE THREAT OF WAR AND INCREASED
UNEMPLOYMENT ARE MARKET KILLERS."
(1990, Dow Jones Industrial Average: 2,633)

"OUR EXPECTATION IS THAT WE ARE FACING A LONG BEAR
MARKET, PERHAPS AS LONG AS FIVE YEARS, AND THAT A GREAT
PART OF THE ADVANCE OF THE PAST 15 YEARS WILL BE
RETRACED IN THAT TIME."
(1990, Dow Jones Industrial Average: 2,670)

"IF THIS IS NOT A HIGH-VOLUME, CHURNING, DISTRIBUTIONAL,
QUADRUPLE TOP, I'LL EAT MY CHARTS."
(1994, Dow Jones Industrial Average: 3,708)

"IS THIS THE END? THREE SAVVY PROS LOOK AT THE BEAR THAT'S
BEGUN." (1994, Dow Jones Industrial Average: 3,762)

"TWO BEARS FORECAST MARKET MAULING—TAKE PROFITS NOW
RATHER THAN BE PANICKED INTO SELLING LATER AT MUCH
LOWER PRICES."
(1996, Dow Jones Industrial Average: 5,300)

"PROFESSOR'S SOPHISTICATED COMPUTER MODEL FORECASTS
40 PERCENT DECLINE FOR EQUITIES."
(1996, Dow Jones Industrial Average: 5,354)

"VALUE INVESTOR WARNS BEAR IS NO LONGER HIBERNATING."
(1997, Dow Jones Industrial Average: 6,587)

"IF YOU'RE NOT PREPARED FOR THE BEAR, YOU RISK GETTING
MAULED." (1997, Dow Jones Industrial Average: 6,703)

I'll bet that, at the time they ran, these headlines and predictions had their desired effect and scared the bejesus out of people. The best way for you to short-circuit the panic that you will inevitably feel over the course of your investment program is to *focus on all the other panics and their aftermath.* Remember that not even the great crash and depression of the 1930s would have destroyed a long-term investor who stuck with a superior investment strategy.

How to Keep Yourself from Panicking
The best thing to do when you find yourself about to panic is to give today's events some historical perspective. Photocopy these headlines and reread them whenever a new round of doomsday headlines terrifies you. Go to the library and read old newspapers and magazines, and you'll see that many dire predictions never come true. You'll see a pattern in the screaming headlines and talking heads.

If you can focus on history and not let short-term news make you panic, you can successfully overcome your innate impulse to take short-term action that will destroy your future investment success. Pretend that you were investing during those panicky times, and bring it up to the present. Had you panicked and abandoned your long-term investment strategy during the crash of 1987, you would have missed a huge gain in your portfolio. For example, compare the "safety" of keeping your money in cash at the end of 1987 with the "risk" of Reasonable Runaways. Had you panicked and put all your money in cash, like so many investors did back then, at the end of 1996 you would have gained just 61 percent on your money. But if you had kept your money in Reasonable Runaways, you'd be up 456 percent! Does cash seem like such a safe investment now? To me it seems downright reckless.

Other Market Panics Are Just the Same
The same holds true for other stock market panics. Had you let short-term jitters force you out of your strategies at the end of the big 1973–1974 bear market, 10 years later you would have gained only 131 percent from a cash investment but 1,040 percent from an investment in Reasonable Runaways! When you

look at all the panics from the past, remember that a raging bull follows every bear market. Rather than panic, focus on the gains that lay ahead. Let the facts help you see the larger picture.

Bear markets are a fundamental part of life. The problem is that we can't be certain when they will come or how long they will last. Because of this, it's necessary to focus on what comes after a bear market and how well these strategies perform over time. Don't panic—and you'll be far richer than if you do.

What You Should Panic About

Clearly, it's foolish to panic about short-term declines in your portfolio, because stock market declines have always been temporary for long-term investors. But there is something you should panic about—*losing purchasing power* and therefore outliving your money. This is big and scary long-term risk that should keep you up at night and make you break into a cold sweat. If you don't address the issue *now* by saving your money and investing it wisely, you may never have a comfortable retirement.

If short-term fluctuations in the stock market make you panic and keep your savings in cash, you'll never retire, you'll never be financially secure—you may even be bagging groceries when you're 70. Every time you have the impulse to put your savings in cash or tuck it under a mattress, remember that that mattress is going to cost a lot more 25 years from now. Cash alone is not a safe investment, because it will not grow enough to give you the ability to live well and continue to lead an active, interesting life. That costs money—a good deal more money in the future than it does now.

Do you remember what things cost when you were a kid? A lot less than they do today, that's for sure. What's more, today's prices will look ridiculously cheap in the future. In 1972, a median-priced home sold for $26,700 and the monthly mortgage payment on that house was about $150. A postage stamp cost 8 cents, and you could reach out and touch someone for a dime. If you want to be reckless and guarantee a miserable retirement, pull all your money out of the stock market and put it in T-bills. It will never grow fast enough to allow you to retire rich, and each dollar that you have will be worth less and less as time goes by. Keeping your savings in cash may make you feel safe in the short run, but it spells disaster for your future.

Overcoming Emotions and Panic

Believe me, I know how hard it is to overcome the power of emotions and the impulse to panic. I'm not trying to diminish the pain that a bear market causes. Losing money, no matter how temporarily, is painful. Reasonable Runaways lost ground in 12 of the 45 years I studied. In any one of those years, your desire to sell out and abandon the strategy would have been overwhelming. In down years, people all around you—from friends and business colleagues to commentators in the press—will think you are crazy to stick with a losing strategy. Their arguments will sound sensible at the time. And God knows you won't need to be reminded how poorly your portfolio is doing in the short term. They might even say how foolish O'Shaughnessy was in *How to Retire Rich!* Imagine O'Shaughnessy's audacity—telling people to stay in the market when stocks are down 20 percent and cash is the safest bet! When you start to lose your resolve, remember all those panic-inducing headlines from the past, and remember what happened afterwards—the stock market went on to new highs.

Ask anyone who kept their investments in "safe" T-bills over the last 25 years whether they feel safe and secure now. Someone who tucked $10,000 into the so-called safety of T-bills at the start of 1970 has just $14,234 today (1997), after you take inflation into account. That won't even pay for more than a couple years' worth of groceries! The same investment in Reasonable Runaways would be worth $206,000 after inflation.

The More Things Change, the More They Stay the Same

Your experiences in real time are going to frequently overpower your understanding of the long-term successes of strategies like Reasonable Runaways and Leaders with Luster. You'll find yourself saying, "Sure, it all came out for the best in the past, but this time things are different." I can assure you, *things are not different this time*. The underlying laws of economics don't change.

Remember the story about Newton's disastrous investment in the South Sea Trading Company? That was nearly three hundred years ago, yet the same economic laws applied to him then as apply to you now. Newton lost a fortune because he vastly overpaid for a single stock. The same thing could happen to you today if you put all your money in a single, overpriced stock.

If you can stick with these time-tested strategies, you will be rewarded. History will be your weapon against all the short-term thinkers who are incapable of seeing past today's headlines. Just by reading this book, you know more than most investors. Let that give you the confidence to tune out the news of the day that makes everyone else panic. Can you name any of the great investment gurus of yesteryear? Where are they today? Most are forgotten, since their great predictions were anything but great. Yet the urge to listen to these so-called experts is overpowering and ingrained. Most people are unable to retire rich because they are guided by their emotions. They let their human programming get the better of them, focus on the wrong fears, and consign themselves to a future of toil and financial worries.

How to Survive a Long Bear Market

As we've seen time and again, a successful campaign to retire rich is not for the faint of heart or weak of will. The normal gyrations of the market will constantly test your devotion to these strategies. But what will test your will the most is a long-term bear market. With luck, we may not have to face a bear market like the one that tried investors' souls in the early 1970s. But if we do, you'll need to reread every section of this book to hang on and keep the faith. Between 1969 and 1973, Reasonable Runaways lost 5.5 percent a year while the S&P 500 had a slight gain of 2 percent a year. Imagine having to endure that during the first five years of your investment program. The urge to give up on the strategy would be truly overwhelming. The key to your success is to know what can happen and prepare yourself for it—before you begin your investment program.

Knowledge is power. I guarantee that people who jump into the market without an underlying investment plan will run to the "safety" of cash or bonds long before those who understand history. But as any bear market grinds on, every instinct will tell you to sell. Your stocks will be down. All your friends who never owned stocks in the first place (who will never retire rich, by the way) will be amazed at how foolish and reckless you are to be invested in the market. Relatives will try to talk you into more prudent, guaranteed investments. Worse yet, you may be drawn to the idea of market timing and say, "I'll stick with this strategy, but I'll time my purchases so that I can avoid these awful bear markets."

If there were a simple market-timing method with a batting average as successful as that of these strategies, it would be a dream come true, and I would be the first person to recommend it to you. But there isn't one. Many investors believe that they can time their purchases and miss those wrenching bear markets, but no one I know of has effectively demonstrated the ability to do so. Market-timing newsletters scream about all the times you'd be better off on the sidelines, but their actual track records are dismal. Most of them fail to beat even T-bills, and you wind up paying a fortune in commissions as you move in and out of the market. Since no effective market-timing tool has yet been invented, you simply have to gut out those down markets.

Most important, you shouldn't care about the short term. In

the grand scheme of saving and investing for a rich retirement, five years is a short period of time. When a bear market gets you down, revisit the Performance Appendix at the back of this book. You'll see that after suffering through five losing years in the early 1970s, Reasonable Runaways went on to compound at almost 24 percent a year over the next five years, swamping the S&P 500's return of 4.32 percent a year. By focusing on long spans of time and the natural ebb and flow of the market, you'll have a calm and reasonable perspective that all those around you lack.

What If One of My Stocks Tanks?

Even if you don't have to suffer through a long-term bear market, you're going to have to face the fact that over the course of your investment program, you're always going to have a few stocks in your portfolio that are real losers. It's not uncommon for several stocks in Reasonable Runaways to be down by 50 percent or more, and the urge to do something about them will be overwhelming. "Surely I can stick with the basic strategy but avoid these horrible performers," you'll think to yourself. Believe me, I've had exactly the same feeling. But I know from experience that it's foolish to start tinkering around with these strategies. The minute you start to think you can prune your portfolio of just a few bad stocks, you've reopened the door to managing your portfolio in a conventional manner. Most investors think they're capable of singling out the stocks that need to be removed from their portfolios. But, as you know, most investors don't beat the S&P 500 either.

A stock that looks like a real clunker now could easily turn around and surprise you. Goodyear Tire is one example. It was one of the Dogs of the Dow stocks in 1991, and it looked like a real deadbeat as rumors about the company not paying its dividend and firing its chairman popped up frequently in the news. Goodyear did eliminate its dividend—and the stock went up 187 percent that year! Investors who thought they were smart enough to override the strategy probably had already sold the stock and missed the gain.

I used to keep a list of all the stocks that I thought looked like bad investments even though they met my strategies' criteria. I also kept a list of stocks I thought would be great investments but didn't show up in any of my strategies. Well, guess what? The clunkers always outperformed the stocks I thought would do well. Whenever you're compelled to sell a stock that's doing poorly, remember that all the winning strategies we've looked at in this book have contained all sorts of stocks that ended up in the cellar. The 45 years of returns we've looked at include the losing stocks as well as the winners. These strategies are powerful—clunkers and all. Don't try to second-guess them.

WHAT IF I GET ELATED?

Panic and fear have their flip side—greed and elation. Had you started Reasonable Runaways at the end of 1990, you might have become an intolerable boaster by the end of 1993, since you would have gained more than 144 percent in those few years, while the S&P 500 gained just 55 percent. You would feel like a genius, since your portfolio was doing three times as well as the market at a time when the average mutual fund didn't even keep up with the S&P 500.

Elation Has Its Pitfalls Too

Oddly enough, this kind of elation can be even more dangerous than the panic you feel when your portfolio is losing ground. If you've bragged enough, your friends might seek your opinion and ask you for advice about how they should be investing their money. Everyone will think you're absolutely brilliant, and you'll be inclined to agree.

Beware! When the emperors of ancient Rome paraded through the city streets teeming with thousands of admiring citizens, they had slaves at their side whispering in their ears: *Sic transit gloria mundi*—"All worldly glory is fleeting." Since you probably can't afford a full-time whisperer (at least not until you retire rich because of your successful savings and investment program), remember the truth of those words.

Whom the gods destroy, they first make great. The financial industry is littered with famous money managers who did extraordinarily well for a short time but then crashed and burned. Don't let success go to your head and make you think you're smarter than the strategies that made you successful.

Theresa Ramirez recently faced a problem just like this. One of her partners had done particularly well in the stock market last year buying high-flying technology stocks. And even though her portfolio was doing well, Theresa still felt a little cheated—her partner was so elated by his success! Maybe she should trust his advice and buy some of the stocks he was recommending.

But as we've seen over and over, this is the worst thing Theresa could do. When things are going particularly well, just like Theresa we tend to think they could be even better. Theresa compared her portfolio's gain of 25 percent last year with her partner's gain of 40 percent and felt she wasn't doing as well as she should. But the odds are that her partner will soon join the vast majority of investors who get burned when trying to outsmart the market. Her partner currently thinks he's a genius. The market will probably soon teach him otherwise. There's always someone with a portfolio that's up 40 percent, who almost always thinks it's due to his or her brilliant stock picking. More often than not it's just dumb luck. The minute you think that you can outsmart the market, remember the sobering fact that 80 percent of the brilliant, well-connected, and superinformed money managers on Wall Street can't beat the S&P 500 over the long term—primarily because they believe that they can outsmart the market in the short term.

Stay the Course

When you become elated about your portfolio's performance, remind yourself of two things. First, you're once again focusing too much on the short-term performance of your investments. The whole point of strategic investing is to put your long-term investment strategy on automatic pilot and let the time-tested techniques do their stuff. Just like panic, elation is an emotional trap that keeps you from thinking clearly. When the market starts moving against you, you'll probably panic even more than other investors do and want to abandon your strategy even faster.

Second, and on a more positive note, remember that when these strategies outperform the S&P 500, it's the rule, not the exception. The reason you put your money in Reasonable Runaways or Leaders with Luster in the first place is that they do much better than the S&P 500. This is quite normal, not something you deserve to jump up and down about. You're using simple models that have nothing to do with your brilliance and everything to do with empirical research and great batting averages over long periods of time. Stay humble, keep your emotions in check, and you'll be able to stay the course.

WHAT IF SOME OF MY STOCKS SOAR?

Soaring stocks are a problem? You'd be amazed at how big a problem they can be. Once again, your emotions get in the way of your success. When you watch one of your stocks soar, your first impulse will be to lock in your profits by selling it. A 1997 University of California study, cited in the *Wall Street Journal*, found that people tend to hang on to losing stocks longer than they hang on to winners, even though the winning stocks they sell subsequently outperform the stocks they continued to hold.

Let me help you rein in your emotions by showing you the facts. In 1993, Reasonable Runaways gained over 30 percent. If you prematurely sold the five biggest winners in the strategy, your returns would be cut in half. Yet those are exactly the stocks that you'll be most tempted to sell, since most of them were up well over 100 percent in a very short period of time.

Let's say one of your stocks in Reasonable Runaways is up 50 percent for the year. You'll be thinking, "What happens if it turns around and plunges? I'll lose all the money I've just made and maybe end up with less than I started with. I should sell now and lock in my gains—after all, no one ever went broke taking a profit." *Resist the urge*, because it can be just as dangerous to your success as trying to sell stocks that look like losers.

Remember how Goodyear Tire gained 187 percent in 1991? Think of how improbable that is—an old-line tire manufacturer going up almost 200 percent in one year. Had you owned the stock at the time, how would you have felt when it was up 75 percent? You'd never believe that it would go up another 112 percent! Most of the time, stocks that really soar are the ones you simply can't imagine will continue upward. You end up scratching your head in wonder, watching them perform like an Energizer bunny. If you want to retire rich, let these strategies just keep going and going and going.

Remember Your Goals

John Maynard Keynes, one of the most famous economists of the 20th century and a fairly good investor, lamented the short-term focus of investors. He said, "Life is not long enough—human nature desires quick results, there is a peculiar zest in making money quickly, and remoter gains are discounted by the average man at a very high rate."

As you proceed with your quest to retire rich, remember what you're trying to accomplish. You're not after quick results or instant wealth. You're not always going to beat the market or hold the trendiest stocks of the moment. You're not trying to prove that you're smarter than other investors are or have some unique ability to outguess them. You're not trying to time the market, sitting in the safety of cash as a bear market rages, jumping right back before the market starts to pick up. You're not trying to impress your friends with your brilliant stock picks (OK, maybe just a little). *You're trying to avoid the big and scary risk of losing purchasing power.* You are trying to retire with enough money so that you can have the time and freedom to do as you please. Today's events mean nothing as you work toward that goal. Today's hot stocks and scary economic news won't matter 25 years from now. *What matters now is saving your money and investing it wisely so that you don't lose the purchasing power of that money you worked so hard to save.*

THINGS WILL COST MORE WHEN YOU RETIRE

If you're 40, you may not retire for another 25 years. It may seem to go by quickly, but that's still a long time. To put it in perspective, 25 years ago you were 15 years old, maybe sweating out your first date. Do you remember the news when you were in high school? Do you have any idea what the stock market was doing when you were a senior? I'll bet you need to look at a history book to remember most of it. But I'll also bet that you remember how much cheaper everything was back then. I remember working at a gas station selling gas for 50 cents a gallon. I remember that movies cost $1.50—and that was less than 20 years ago.

Whenever you're panicking and have the overwhelming urge to put your savings in cash, remember how much more things are going to cost when you retire. Harness your emotions and avoid letting panic, fear, greed, and elation ruin your investment success. Understanding history gives informed investors a crucial advantage over those who have not studied the past. Informed investors realize that day-to-day gyrations mean almost nothing in the long term. They know that staying in the market is 90 percent of the battle and the only way to retire rich.

ABOVE ALL, STAY IN THE MARKET
When all those around you urge panic or elation, remember this—over the last 35 years, it didn't matter whether you invested

at the top of the market or the bottom, as long as you stayed in the market. In his book *Independently Wealthy,* Robert Goodman looks at three people—one lucky enough to always buy at the exact bottom of every year, one whose horrible luck always found him buying at the exact top for the year, and one who always bought on July 1 of each year, regardless of the state of the stock market. Starting in 1960, each invests $3,000. Here's how they would have done by 1996: the first fellow would have a total of $1,569,519—a compound return of 12.8 percent. The fellow always buying when the market was at a high would have $1,318,300—a compound return of 12.1 percent. The fellow who never timed the market would have $1,486,037—a return of 12.6 percent per year!

Each day brings new events that make us believe things must be different this time. If aliens conquer the earth, things might be different, but until then count on them staying the same. Over the next several decades, we'll have booms and busts, manias and panics, and long drawn-out times when stocks go nowhere, followed by bursts of outstanding performance. *The one constant will be the persistent rise in what it costs to live a good life.* Things could go against us, and we could end up earning returns similar to the worst returns these strategies posted over the last half-century. Or we might get really lucky and invest during a golden age for equities, getting returns like the best we've seen. Feast or famine, these strategies outperform all alternative investments over the long term. No one can tell you whether the next 15 percent change in your portfolio will be up or down. But I'll bet everything I have on which direction the next 100 percent move will be—up.

CHAPTER EIGHT

WHERE TO FIND THE INFORMATION YOU NEED

It's very easy to find all the information you need to invest in the time-tested strategies in this book. If you have a computer with access to the Internet, it's very cheap as well. A lot will depend on how much time and money you're willing to spend to put these strategies together. If you have very little time and don't want to spend much money building your portfolio, you're best off using a mutual fund or a 10-stock strategy like Dogs of the Dow. If you want to put together your portfolio completely on your own, it will take more time but can be quite cost effective, particularly if you have access to the Internet. After reading this chapter you will likely have a very good idea about the best path for you.

ANNUAL REPORTS: TO THE RECYCLE BIN

People frequently ask me, "Do I need to read annual reports?" NO! You're best off avoiding corporate propaganda, letters from the chairman, and CEO reports. The legendary investor Bernard Baruch had 10 rules for successful investing, and he said that if he had to choose just one it was to never pay attention to what the president of a company says. The theme song of most annual reports is "The future's so bright I've got to wear shades!" The

stream of happy talk (or excuses) in annual reports from individual companies has nothing to do with the success of these
strategies. Remember, we're using the Joe Friday school of investing—just the facts, ma'am. The facts will lead you to the
stocks with the characteristics that have proven successful over
long periods of time. Propaganda and stories get you nowhere,
and reading annual reports is a waste of your valuable time.

REASONABLE RUNAWAYS AND LEADERS WITH LUSTER

THE EASY WAY: PICK UP THE PHONE (AND OPEN YOUR CHECKBOOK)

When my son Patrick was an uncooperative three-year-old, I always offered him a choice: the easy way or the hard way. Only
once did he pick the hard way, and that was just because he was
also a very curious three-year-old. Most of us, like my son, want
to do things the easy way. Unfortunately, when it comes to investing in these strategies, the easiest way is sometimes the expensive way as well.

The easiest way to find the current stocks in Reasonable Runaways and Leaders with Luster is to call S&P Compustat (800-
321-6141) or visit its Web site at www.compustat.com, define
the criteria in each strategy, and have Compustat prepare the
lists of stocks for you. In a matter of minutes, you can have a list
of the current stocks sitting on your fax machine or your computer's hard drive.

Although using Compustat is easy, it's also expensive. As of
this writing, Compustat charges $200 per list for the stocks in
Reasonable Runaways and Leaders with Luster. You will, how-
ever, be getting lists from the same database I used for *What
Works on Wall Street* and the one I use at O'Shaughnessy Funds.
Compustat has been around for a long time, and it's always im-

proving its database. You pay a high price for convenience, but don't fret about Compustat's fee just yet. The Internet offers some great databases, and many are free or very reasonably priced.

SURFING THE WEB: THE CHEAP (AND RELATIVELY EASY) WAY

If you're not willing to part with the $200 per list that Compustat charges, the Internet is the place to find the stocks in Reasonable Runaways and Leaders with Luster. If you have a computer and you're not yet on the Internet, *get on it*. The Internet gives you the ability to do research that used to require thousands of man-hours, and it gives you access to information—often free—that you never had before. Strategic investing requires the ability to manipulate huge amounts of information quickly. Nothing does this as well as a computer linked to the World Wide Web.

Excellent Web sites are available to help you find the stocks in Reasonable Runaways, Leaders with Luster, and Dogs of the Dow. The Internet is growing and improving at warp speed, and no doubt between the time this book is written and published there will be even more great sites and on-line databases than those I'll cover here. A good place to start your Web crawl is at www.howtoretirerich.com, where you'll find a current list of the best Web sites to visit when putting together your portfolio.

BIG DATABASE, ITTY-BITTY PRICE

To find the stocks in Reasonable Runaways and Leaders with Luster, I highly recommend visiting www.marketguide.com. It's one of the best values on the Web—a database of more than 8,000 stocks that costs a mere $7.95 per download. Compared with Compustat, that's an incredible value—but you'll have to do some of your own legwork. I never said that free lunch was served on the Internet!

Market Guide was founded in 1983 to provide investors with information on tiny, micro-cap stocks. Since then, it has expanded its coverage and is the source used by such leading information providers as Reuters and the American Association of Individual Investors.

To find the stocks in Reasonable Runaways and Leaders with Luster, download the *StockQuest* program from Market Guide's site. You can choose from two subscription plans. The first costs $7.95, giving you the *StockQuest* program and all the data on more than 8,000 stocks as of the week you download. No data updates are included in this fee. The second plan allows you to update the data weekly, but it costs $19.95 per month. Since you need the data only once a year, don't waste your money— choose the $7.95 plan.

For starters, you'll need a Windows-based 486 machine with 8 MB of memory, 12 MB of free disk space, and a 14.4 BBS modem. Select *Subscribe* and fill out the form either electronically or by fax. Then select *StockQuest* and pick *Download Software and Data Set*. You'll be asked for a user name and password. Downloading takes about 20 minutes. When you exit the Web and double-click on the *Sqinstal.exe* icon, the program will be installed on your hard drive. Enter the program by double-clicking on its icon. This will bring you right to a no-frills Screening page, where you can search for stocks. (The number of stocks currently covered by the database is displayed in the upper right-hand corner of the screen. When I logged on on July 3, 1997, I found 8,294 stocks covered in the database.)

Finding Reasonable Runaways Stocks

Let's start by finding the stocks in Reasonable Runaways. To get the 25 to 50 names you need to implement this strategy successfully, select Screen on the menu toolbar and pick Add Criterion. This brings you to the Criterion Builder Dialog box. Under Screening Variables, double-click on Description. Scroll down to "MktCap" and double-click on it. Market capitalization will appear in the Criterion box (at the bottom of the screen) with the cursor blinking after it. Select the > button and type in "150." After clicking on the Done button, the program will return you to the Screening page and reduce the number of stocks in the database considerably, leaving you with roughly 3,500 stocks with market capitalizations over $150 million.

Select Add Criterion again from the Screen menu, double-click on Description, and scroll to "Pr2sales," the price-to-sales ratio. Double-click and set it to < 1, and push Done. Once again, select Add Criterion, double-click on Description, and select "Pr52w%chg," the percentage change in the stock price over the last 52 weeks. Set this to greater than or equal to ($\geqslant$) 50, and again push Done. When I did this in July 1997, I was left with 151 stocks—more than I wanted. Remember that we're shooting for 25 to 50 stocks in Reasonable Runaways. Through trial and error, I set this final factor (Pr52w%chg) to 91 and got a list of 47 stocks. (You'll always have to experiment with the Pr52w%chg figure, depending on the state of the stock market. In bull markets, you'll need to set this number higher; in bear markets, lower.)

Finally, on the Screening page, you'll see five icons. Click on the fifth—View Results. Up will come your list of Reasonable Runaways stocks, including their ticker symbols, market capitalizations, price-to-sales ratios, and 52-week price appreciation. Choose Export file and export the list to your spreadsheet. You're done!

Finding Leaders with Luster Stocks

You'll find the Leaders with Luster stocks in much the same way as Reasonable Runaways, but with a few differences. Because the database doesn't include a cash flow variable, you must create it. Here's how. Go to Screen on the menu bar and select User-defined Variables and then Add. By pointing and clicking in this Dialog box, create this formula: ({Price}/{Pr2CashFlw})* ShsOuts. This creates a cash flow variable, which is an important element of Leaders with Luster. When prompted, name this formula "cashflow."

Next, set up a screen for Leaders with Luster. The first thing you have to find is the database average for market capitalization (MktCap), common shares outstanding (ShsOuts), cash flow, and sales. List these variables on the Screening page using the same process you used with Reasonable Runaways, but require that each factor be greater than negative 1,000 ($>-1,000$); this ensures that almost every stock in the database is included. On the Screening page, select the View Results icon. Go to the end of the Market cap column, click on the last stock's market capitalization, and then click on the Compute Statistics icon ($\sqrt{\alpha}$). This will give you the database average for market capitalization. Do this for shares outstanding, cash flow, and sales. In July 1997, I found an average market capitalization of $1.2 billion, average shares outstanding of 33 million, average sales of $883 million, and average cash flow of $90 million.

Next, because we don't want utility stocks to dominate the list, you must remove them from consideration. Select Add Criterion from Screen on the menu toolbar. Click on SectorDescr and select Utilities: Is Not a Member. Now, go back to the Screening page and fill in all the averages you found. Finally, use dividend yield as the last variable, reducing the number of stocks in Leaders with Luster to between 25 and 50, depending on your needs.

All in all, www.marketguide.com is an excellent, inexpensive, and reliable place to find the stocks in Reasonable Runaways and Leaders with Luster.

A Big, Free Database for Reasonable Runaways

If you're saving every penny you can to invest for your retirement and don't want to part with the $7.95 that Market Guide costs, check out the free database offered by *Research* magazine at www.researchmag.com. All you need to do to start screening stocks is register. After that, finding stocks—especially those in Reasonable Runaways—is a snap.

Here's what I did when I logged on recently. First, I clicked on the Screens icon and selected Stock Screens. This brought

me to the Screening page. It highlights a variety of criteria, allow-
ing me to select the variables I want by checking a box on the
left-hand side of the screen. First I checked Market cap and said
that it had to be between 150 and 999,999,999 (the upper limit
can be any huge number). Next I checked that Marketvalue/
sales must be less than 1 and Price is at least 100 percent higher
than 12 months ago. (I chose 100 percent because, at the time,
it was a strong bull market. When the market is more bearish,
selecting Price is at least 25 [or 50] percent higher than 12
months ago would be more appropriate.) This reduces the number of stocks you'll end up with, getting you closer to the 25–50
names that you want. Finally, I selected the Submit button.

In a matter of moments, the program found 33 companies
that met the criteria I selected, including a detailed tabulation of
the search. In my search, 3,557 stocks had market capitalizations
greater than $150 million. Of those, 1,092 had price-to-sales ra-
tios lower than 1. Finally, 33 of the remaining stocks had price
increases of 100 percent or more over the last 12 months. (When
I entered Price is at least 75 percent higher than 12 months ago,
I ended up with 73 stocks—that's why I had to choose the 100
percent increase. This final screen will always require you to
tinker with it a bit so that you end up with between 25 and 50
stocks.)

I then scrolled down the list to review the stocks that made
the grade. You'll see each stock's ticker symbol as well as whether
a stock summary, investment report, or Wall Street analysis is
available on it. If you want, you can read a business description
of each company and look at its 52-week high and low share
price, quarterly reports, year-end results, and price charts. And
all this is free! When I ran the Reasonable Runaways model on
www.researchmag.com recently, I found that most—but not
all—of the stocks it came up with were the same ones Compustat generated. You can also create a Watch List at the site,
which will let you check on the current prices of the stocks in
your portfolio.

Unfortunately, www.researchmag.com isn't as effective for building a portfolio of Leaders with Luster stocks, since it doesn't include all the criteria you need. Stick with www.market-guide.com when looking for Leaders stocks—you'll find the right stocks with relative ease, making it worth the small fee.

MORE TO COME ON THE INTERNET

As we'll see in the next chapter, many of the on-line brokers are also adding large databases for their customers, and searching for stocks for our strategies will no doubt get easier and easier as time goes by. E*Trade, Charles Schwab's e.schwab, and Water-house Securities all offer investors the ability to screen large databases of stocks. My guess is that stock-screening capabilities will become commonplace on the Internet, and finding the stocks for these strategies will soon be a very simple endeavor.

IN THE DOGS OF THE DOW HOUSE

The easiest and cheapest way to find the 10 Dogs of the Dow stocks is to buy the *Wall Street Journal.* Once a month, the *Journal* ranks the 30 stocks in the Dow Jones Industrial Average by dividend yield in its "Investment Insight" column, found in the lower left-hand corner of the first page of the "Money & Investing" section. All you need to do is pick the top 10. Or, if you're using the *Value Line Investment Survey for Windows* (which I'll cover in more detail in the next section), you can simply create a universe of the 30 Dow Jones Industrial Average stocks and choose the 10 with the highest dividend yields.

Yet another choice for those who love the easy way is to sub-scribe to *Beating the Dow,* a newsletter devoted to the Dogs of the Dow strategy. Subscriptions are currently $99 a year. Just call the Hirsch Organization at 201-767-4100.

CYBERSPACE CANINES

On the Internet, finding the stocks in the Dogs of the Dow strategy is a snap. Visit www.dogsofthedow.com. In the blink of an eye you'll find the 10 Dow Dogs stocks—they're even updated daily. The site offers a great deal of additional information, from year-to-date performance to a multiyear analysis comparing the performance of the Dogs of the Dow strategy with well-known funds like Fidelity Magellan and the Vanguard Index 500. This is a super site for Dog lovers.

You can also find Dogs of the Dow at the free www. researchmag.com site we used to find Reasonable Runaways. After clicking on the Screens icon, select Portfolio Analysis instead of Stock Screens. This will guide you to a variety of stock groups for analysis, and the Dow 30 is one of them. Click on the Dow 30, scroll down to Types of Portfolio Analysis, click on the Dividend Yield box, scroll down to Select Attribute by Which to Rank Stocks, and pick Dividend Yield. Click on the Perform Analysis button, then scroll down to find the 30 stocks in the Dow ranked by dividend yield.

If you subscribe to America Online, you can also get information on the Dogs of the Dow at the AOL's Motley Fool section. Just enter the keyword "Fool" and you'll be there. The Fools have an ongoing discussion about the Dogs of the Dow strategy (which they refer to as the Dow Dividend Approach). The Motley Fool also has a Web site at www.fool.com, which is very similar to the AOL site.

KEEPING UP WITH NEW SITES

No doubt, given the rate at which the Internet is growing, there will be a huge number of new sites devoted to stock screening by the time this book hits the stores. Microsoft's *Investor* Web site looks extremely promising. It will probably have stock-screening capabilities by the time you read this book, as well as a host of additional investment information. Check it out at www.investor.msn.com. Two other sites to watch for are the Wall

Street Research Net at www.wsrn.com and Wall Street City at www.wallstreetcity.com. Wall Street Research Net has a large search engine, which currently lacks information on price appreciation, a component of Reasonable Runaways. Once it adds that, you'll be able to put together lists of all the Reasonable Runaways and Leaders with Luster stocks free of charge. The Wall Street City site will probably be just as comprehensive.

You can also use one of the many search engines—www.hotbot.com, www.excite.com, www.yahoo.com to name a few—to find the latest and greatest stock search sites. You can also go to a master page like www.indexfund.com/links.com, which lists many of the best stock research sites on the web. You can also check in at www.howtoretirerich.com or www.osfunds.com for information on these strategies.

FINDING CORE VALUE AND UTILITY STRATEGY STOCKS

The easiest way to find the 10 stocks in the Core Value strategy or the Utility strategy is to use the computerized *Value Line Investment Survey for Windows*. Unfortunately, *Value Line* charges $995 for an annual subscription, but for that princely sum you get extremely detailed information—updated weekly—on over 5,000 stocks, including the Safety Ranks, Timeliness Ranks, and Financial Strength ratings that are unique to *Value Line*. You can also get a trial version for just $55 or a 1,700-stock version (which covers all the stocks we are interested in) for $595 per year. I know of very few individual investors willing to spend $600–$1,000 a year for a stock database, so I suggest trying to find a library that offers the computerized *Value Line Investment Survey*. If your library doesn't carry it, beg. Get down on your knees and ask your librarian to order it for the good of the citizenry.

OLD-FASHIONED *VALUE LINE*

In all likelihood, your library will have the paper version of *Value Line*. In it you can find the 10 Utility strategy stocks with relative ease. Simply go to the "Conservative Stocks" section. From the list of 100 or so stocks with safety ranks of 1, choose the 10 with the highest estimated dividend yields.

Unfortunately, finding the 10 stocks in Core Value in the paper version of *Value Line* is nearly impossible, because to find stocks with a financial strength of A++ you have to look through the information on each of the 1,700 stocks covered in the newsletter. This is a thankless, Herculean undertaking, which I do not recommend.

USING THE *VALUE LINE INVESTMENT SURVEY FOR WINDOWS*

If you do get your hands on *Value Line for Windows,* finding the stocks in either Core Value or the Utility strategy is a snap. Click on the Funnel icon (or if you're the menu type, select Tools, Filter) and select the criteria you want. For example, here's how you'd find the 10 stocks in Core Value. First, click on the Funnel icon. That will bring up a menu of criteria. Click on Ratings and select Financial Strength; set that equal to A++. You'll see that only about 40 of the 5,000 stocks in the database have a financial strength of A++. Go to the Statistics section to find the average dividend yield of those approximately 40 stocks. As of this writing, the average was 1.93 percent. Return to the Screening page and add dividend yield and require that it exceed 1.93. When I recently did that, I found just 18 stocks with financial strength ratings of A++ with dividend yields exceeding the average.

Now let's pare the list down to 10 stocks. Go to the Tools menu and select Sort by Projected dividend growth rate. Have those 18 stocks listed in descending order, from highest to lowest projected dividend growth rate. The top 10 stocks are the ones to buy.

You can find the Utility strategy stocks in much the same way. Just select a safety rank of 1, and then sort the stocks by dividend yield in descending order. Again, the top 10 stocks are the ones you want.

Take a minute to look at how the stocks in these 10-stock strategies differ from the market as a whole—after all, it's their unique characteristics that make these stocks good investments. Click on the Summation icon (Σ) or go to the Tools, Statistics menu. When I did this in July 1997, I found that the 10 stocks in the Utility strategy had, on average, yields of 6.45 percent, market capitalizations of $10 billion, price-to-earnings ratios of 14, price-to-sales ratios of 1.16, and price stabilities of 98. These are not average characteristics by a long shot. You can see that the Utility strategy is made up of big, solid, safe stocks, well suited to a 10-stock strategy.

COMPUTERS, OFF-LINE

If you're not yet hooked up to the Internet but do have a computer, there are several affordable databases that you can use to find Reasonable Runaways and Leaders with Luster stocks. The American Association of Individual Investors (AAII) sells a database program called *Stock Investor*. It covers 7,000 stocks and costs $99 a year for members and $150 for nonmembers (membership is $49 a year). It also offers *Stock Investor Pro,* which covers over 8,000 stocks and includes monthly updates. It costs $198 per year for AAII members. Call 800-428-2244 for more information.

Morningstar also offers a comprehensive database, called *StockTools* for Windows. You can get a full trial version for $75 and quarterly updates for $375 per year. Call 800-735-0700 for more information, or visit its Web site at www.morningstar.net.

I'M SCOTTISH—IS THERE HOPE FOR ME?

My maternal grandfather was 100 percent Scottish and as such claimed to be genetically incapable of spendthrift behavior. And even though he kept every one of his employees on the payroll during the Great Depression, he liked to get value for his money. If you don't have a computer and don't want to spend any money on lists or databases, there's still hope for you—your public library. (Another far more famous Scotsman, Andrew Carnegie, devoted the latter part of his life to building libraries for the common man.) The library remains a great resource for those who desire knowledge but may not have (or may not want to spend) the cash.

Stop by your local library. If you're lucky, it will have started expanding its computer capabilities. (Microsoft founder Bill Gates followed in Carnegie's footsteps and donated $200 million to help libraries hook up to the Internet. With luck, your library will benefit from this gift.) Many larger libraries already have some very fancy computer programs and databases. If yours doesn't, ask! Start high and ask your librarian to carry *Compustat PC Plus* or the *Value Line Investment Survey for Windows*. If your librarian is Scottish too, ask him or her to provide an AAII database or access to the Market Guide on the Internet.

CONSIDER A COURSE AT YOUR LOCAL COLLEGE

If your local public library is behind the times, consider taking a course at your local college or university. That will give you access to the school library, which will probably have a good computerized database of stocks. Colleges and universities are also likely to have *Value Line*.

WHAT IF I'M COMPUTER-PHOBIC?

If you want to put your portfolio together yourself but think programming is only for VCRs and surfing is only for waves, you're going to have to either use the Dogs of the Dow strategy or pay Compustat for the Reasonable Runaways or Leaders with Luster lists. And if even that is a turnoff, you can invest in the mutual funds available through many large brokerage firms. Indeed, in a few years, many brokers will probably offer the tools you need to find the stocks that meet all our criteria—both on-line and off-line.

Let's now look at the revolution under way in the brokerage business, which makes strategic investing possible.

CHAPTER NINE

THE BROKERAGE REVOLUTION: YOU WIN

Just a few years ago, it was impossible for individuals to invest in strategies like Reasonable Runaways and Leaders with Luster by themselves. For all but the wealthiest investors, the commission costs incurred when buying 25 to 50 stocks every year were overwhelming, even with a discount broker like Charles Schwab. What's more, placing orders for fewer than 100 shares would have thrown you into an "odd lot" pool—leaving you feeling like a pair of brown shoes in a world of tuxedos. Brokers didn't want that kind of business, and they charged high commissions to buy small numbers of shares.

ON-LINE TRADING EXPLODES

With the dawn of computerized trading over the Internet and programs that link your computer directly to your broker, everything has changed. If computers had declined in price and improved in performance as fast as on-line trading has, we'd have gone from clunky mainframes to Windows-based Pentium machines in just three years! In 1994, almost no on-line trading was possible, and virtually none of it was done on the Internet. It was seen as an extra service that brokers offered their clients, and you paid the same standard commissions as customers placing orders in the traditional manner—usually over the phone.

Fees Plummet

On-line, you can now trade for as little as $8 per trade (about $200 for a 25-stock portfolio) with brokers that have long histories and outstanding institutional sponsorship. In just the last few years, on-line trading has exploded. According to a Forrester Research company report, as of the end of 1996, 1.5 million on-line accounts were available, with assets of over $111 billion. And Forrester projects that 10 million people will be trading on-line by 2001!

This growth has spawned a price war among the dozen or so major Internet brokers so intense that prices are falling and services expanding weekly. For example, when I started writing this book, no major broker had a minimum below $20 per trade. Now the biggest on-line brokers offer low, flat fees for trades up to 5,000 shares. And these aren't fly-by-night companies— Waterhouse Securities (www.waterhouse.com or 800-934-4410) is the fourth-largest discount broker in the United States and has over 700,000 clients and 90 branch offices; and it charges only $12 per trade. Waterhouse recently became a division of Toronto Dominion Bank, one of the largest banks in North America. Lombard Brokerage, soon to be called Discover Brokerage Direct (www.lombard.com or 800-584-6837), is now a division of the Wall Street giant Morgan Stanley, Dean Witter Discover; it charges $14.95 per trade.

Individual investors are the big winners in this revolution, with access to services and information that was reserved for the biggest institutions just a few years ago. And it's all as easy as pointing and clicking.

OPENING AN ACCOUNT

To use any of the on-line brokers, you'll need a computer, a modem, and an Internet browser like Netscape Navigator or Microsoft Internet Explorer. These browsers are important because they encrypt communications between you and your broker, protecting both your privacy and the information that you transmit.

Setting up an account is simple. Download an application from the broker you select, print it, and fill it out and send it back with a check—that's all you need to do. All the on-line brokers I'll cover offer free IRA account setups. A few, like Charles Schwab's e.Schwab (www.schwab.com or 800-435-4000), have an IRA account minimum of $2,000, but many have no minimum at all.

Is It Safe?

On-line brokers have gone to great lengths to make sure that your transactions are secure. First, once you've got your account set up, you will receive a password and a private identifier that you must enter before using your account. Second, in addition to the encryption that Netscape Navigator and Microsoft Explorer offer, on-line brokers have set up a three-tiered security system of firewalls, which prevent hackers and other unwelcome visitors from gaining access to your account; these firewalls allow only certain information to go in and out of an account. Finally, even if some genius hacker managed to break through all the firewalls and data encryption to find your password, he or she still couldn't remove a dime from your account, since these systems don't allow the exchange of money or securities over the Internet.

If you're still worried about someone gaining access to your account, most of these brokers also offer direct dial-up lines that bypass the Internet. You can also opt for Touch-Tone phone service that allows you to trade without a computer. What's more, even the smallest on-line brokers are subject to the same rules, regulations, and capital requirements as are the industries' giants. They all carry at least $500,000 of insurance from the Securities Investor Protection Corporation (SIPC) for every account, and most greatly augment this with additional insurance from private insurance companies.

What to Expect from an On-line Broker

Expect to receive at least the following from the broker you choose:

1. Free IRA setup
2. Free sweeps, which put any spare cash into money market funds
3. Account protection of at least $2 million per account, through SIPC and other insurers
4. Automatic dividend reinvestment programs
5. Free stock quotes
6. The choice to trade by phone—at Internet prices—if online systems are down

These are just the bare bones. Many on-line brokers offer a number of extras. Ceres Securities (www.ceres.com or 800-669-3900) charges $18 a trade whether you trade your account over the Internet or by phone. And if you use this service directly through America Online, the fee is just $8 per trade. Quick & Reilly (www.quick-reilly.com or 800-837-7220) offers free check writing and gives you on-line access to all your recent and previous year's transactions (won't this make your accountant happy!). It provides a host of additional services as well. What's more, as we saw in the last chapter, many on-line brokers are adding databases that allow you to screen for stocks, making it easy and inexpensive to find the stocks in strategies like Reasonable Runaways and Leaders with Luster. PC Financial Network, a division of Donaldson, Lufkin and Jenrette (www.pcfn.com or 800-

825-5723), charges $20 per trade but gives you access to its *Stock Center,* where you can screen 4,500 stocks using a variety of variables. Given the speed of advances in on-line trading, the ability to screen large databases of stocks will probably be commonplace by early 1998.

HOW SHOULD I CHOOSE?

PRICE
Choosing the right broker depends upon your priorities. If price is your main concern, go to the broker with the lowest commisssions. As of this writing, the price champ is Ceres Securities, but only when you link directly through America Online. Ceres will charge you $8 per trade for the first six months you have your account. If you're already an AOL subscriber, this is a very attractive deal. (If you go to Ceres without using AOL, however, the charge is $18 per trade.)

To find the lowest-priced brokers, go to InvestorHome on the Internet (www.investorhome.com) or to Wall Street City (www.wallstreetcity.com) and select the Where to Trade icon and click on Brokerage Houses.

SERVICE
Price shouldn't be your only concern. Most of the big on-line brokers operate in the $12–$20 per trade price range, so you should also consider how easy they are to use and how accessible they are. Request information and see how long it takes to receive it. Ask about how many "hits" the broker's Web site can take before service slows down. Ask how you can get in touch with them if their site is down. Do they engage in "payment for order flow" (a very controversial practice whereby brokers pool stock orders into a large block and then give this block to an exchange to trade)? Brokers often save money by doing this but

then don't pass those savings on to investors. This practice is widely disdained, so make sure the broker you choose fully discloses its trading practices and any other hidden fees.

REPUTATION

Two on-line brokers that have consistently won the best ratings are Waterhouse Securities and Lombard Securities. Both are divisions of huge corporations and offer a wide range of services, including no-fee mutual funds, periodic investments, free IRA accounts, and telephone trading. Per on-line trade, Waterhouse charges $12 and Lombard charges $14.95, and both are constantly improving their sites and services. According to *Barron's*, Lombard is developing its own technology and increasing its bandwidth to handle 2.5 million hits per day on its Web site. *Barron's* also points out that "the Web has changed electronic investing forever." To keep up with all the changes, visit *Barron's* on-line (www.barrons.com) for the most recent survey results and developments in the on-line brokerage business.

SIZE AND CONFIDENCE

Your peace of mind and confidence in the broker that you choose is also important. Although it has one of the higher commissions for on-line trading, Schwab currently has the most on-line assets—over $50 billion in 700,000 accounts. Schwab's size, track record, and huge number of extra services can make its $29.95 per trade fee worth it for many investors.

The key is to find a broker you are comfortable with and get going!

TRADING YOUR ACCOUNT

A 10-STOCK PORTFOLIO

Once you've got an account up and running, you can start your strategy's engines. Let's assume you've got $2,000 to invest and want to buy the 10 stocks in Dogs of the Dow. Remember that you can find the current list at www.dogsofthedow.com. When I got the list recently, I found the 10 stocks listed in Table 1. You want to invest about $200 in each of the 10 stocks, so go through the list and divide $200 by the closing price of each stock to see how many shares to buy of each. In all instances, round your purchases to make sure you don't overspend. Table 1 also lists how many shares of each stock you would buy. You'll have to tinker with the numbers a little to stay within your $2,000 budget. (Note that I left some money on the table because I wanted to stay under $2,000.) If you're trading through Ceres at America Online, you'll need to set aside $80 for commissions. With Waterhouse, budget $120.

Next, log on to your chosen broker's site and enter your stocks

TABLE 1					
TICKER	COMPANY	PRICE	NUMBER OF SHARES	FEE PER TRADE	COST
T	AT&T	36	5	$8	$188
MO	Philip Morris	45.37	4	$8	$189.48
GM	General Motors	56.94	3	$8	$178.82
JPM	J.P. Morgan	110.12	2	$8	$228.24
CHV	Chevron	75.62	2	$8	$159.24
XON	Exxon	64.62	3	$8	$201.86
EK	Eastman Kodak	78.94	2	$8	$165.88
MMM	3M	101.81	2	$8	$211.62
DD	DuPont	63.37	3	$8	$198.11
IP	International Paper	50.62	4	$8	$210.48
					$1,931.73

(by ticker symbol) and the number of shares of each you want to buy. In most cases, you'll receive an e-mail confirmation instantly.

Note that I used a 10-stock strategy and spent around $200 per stock. An account of $2,000 isn't big enough to implement 25- to 50-stock strategies on your own, since it will spread your dollars too thin and leave you with commission costs that are too high. If you are just starting out, I suggest buying a mutual fund with a disciplined investment strategy, until you have saved enough to invest in Reasonable Runaways or Leaders with Luster on your own.

Portfolios with 25 to 50 Stocks

With an account of $10,000 or more, you can implement any of the strategies we've covered. You'll use the same procedure we used with Dogs of the Dow. Set up a spreadsheet with the 10, 25, or 50 stocks you want to buy, budget for the commission you'll pay on each trade, and create a buy list by dividing the amount you'll invest in each stock by its closing price. Again, leave a little room so you don't overspend. If you've saved $25,000 in your IRA and want to buy the 50 stocks in Reasonable Runaways, you'll spend around $500 per stock, before commissions. For instance, if you're buying a $25 stock, subtract the $12 commission from $500 and divide that number by $25 ($488 ÷ $25 = 19.52); then round it off and buy 20 shares. (Again, you'll have to tinker with this number. You may find that you should buy only 19 shares, depending on how the rest of your portfolio comes out.)

Let's look at another example. If you have $25,000 but want to buy only 25 stocks, you would be investing about $1,000 in each stock ($988 per stock, after commissions). Table 2 shows how $25,000 would be distributed in a 25-stock Reasonable Runaways portfolio. To compile the list, I used the *StockQuest* database at www.marketguide.com and exported the results from the Reasonable Runaways strategy to my Excel spreadsheet. In

TABLE 2

TICKER	COMPANY NAME	MARKET CAPITALIZATION	PRICE TO SALES PER SHARE	PRICE % CHANGE (52 WEEKS)	CURRENT PRICE	NUMBER OF SHARES	COMMISSION	TOTAL
AGI	Alpine Group	$195.72	−0.13	133.74	$11.25	88	$12.00	$1,002.00
AMES	Ames Department Stores	$204.15	0.10	255.77	$9.56	103	$12.00	$996.99
CELL	Brightpoint	$651.14	0.96	148.23	$29.12	34	$12.00	$1,002.25
CLST	CellStar	$926.27	0.81	433.33	$32.00	31	$12.00	$1,004.00
CVE	Converse	$320.21	0.79	336.78	$18.56	53	$12.00	$995.84
GDYS	Goody's Family Clothing	$452.30	0.53	159.30	$27.87	35	$12.00	$987.63
GBE	Grubb & Ellis	$321.75	0.97	247.37	$16.50	60	$12.00	$1,002.00

(continued on next page)

TICKER	COMPANY NAME	MARKET CAPITALIZATION	PRICE TO SALES PER SHARE	PRICE % CHANGE (52 WEEKS)	CURRENT PRICE	NUMBER OF SHARES	COMMISSION	TOTAL
ITEQ	ITEQ	$166.59	0.85	196.30	$10.00	99	$12.00	$1,002.00
MWL	Mail-Well	$512.75	0.59	352.17	$26.37	37	$12.00	$987.88
MIKL	Michael Foods	$401.62	0.55	225.82	$18.87	52	$12.00	$993.50
MSTR	Morningstar Group	$423.18	0.94	156.98	$27.62	36	$12.00	$1,006.50
NSS	NS Group	$175.05	0.40	274.07	$12.62	78	$12.00	$996.75
PMRY	Pomeroy Computer Resource	$195.20	0.43	136.36	$26.00	38	$12.00	$1,000.00
QNTM	Quantum	$2,873.27	0.50	206.15	$21.81	45	$12.00	$993.59
SAR	Santa Anita Realty	$354.93	0.14	142.16	$30.87	32	$12.00	$1,000.00
SFD	Smith's Food & Drug	$666.21	0.32	128.72	$55.75	18	$12.00	$1,015.50
SFDS	Smithfield Foods	$1,081.06	0.29	139.00	$59.75	16	$12.00	$968.00

(continued on next page)

TICKER	COMPANY NAME	MARKET CAPITALIZATION	PRICE TO SALES PER SHARE	PRICE % CHANGE (52 WEEKS)	CURRENT PRICE	NUMBER OF SHARES	COMMISSION	TOTAL
SPW	SPX	$948.36	0.86	157.11	$63.31	16	$12.00	$1,025.01
SZA	Suiza Foods	$611.62	0.82	143.18	$40.12	24	$12.00	$975.00
TEX	Terex	$281.69	0.41	135.42	$21.18	47	$12.00	$1,007.84
TWMC	Trans World Entertainment	$171.20	0.35	143.46	$17.50	56	$12.00	$992.00
TUES	Tuesday Morning	$249.26	0.98	128.41	$20.93	47	$12.00	$996.09
XPRSA	U.S. Xpress	$166.29	0.62	140.98	$18.37	54	$12.00	$1,004.25
VIR	Virco Manufacturing	$158.72	0.67	207.14	$26.87	37	$12.00	$1,006.38
WDC	Western Digital	$2,821.18	0.78	163.64	$32.62	30	$12.00	$990.75
	Average	$613.00	0.58	196	$27.00	47		
	Total						$300.00	$24,951.72

Excel, I divided $988 by the share prices to get the number of shares I wanted to buy. After rounding each purchase to the nearest share, I saw that I was spending $51.59 too much. I then looked at each stock and reduced those with the highest dollar investments by one share each. After commissions and all other expenses, that put me just under $25,000. You should always leave some wiggle room, however, just in case some prices jump while you're placing your orders. To be on the safe side, you might allocate $950 (instead of $988) to each stock purchase. You can always buy a few extra shares later.

You may soon be able to e-mail your buy list directly to your broker, bypassing the task of entering each ticker symbol and number of shares by hand. Until then, remember that you only need to do this once a year, and entering this information by hand should take only 10–15 minutes.

OFF-LINE TRADING

TRADITIONAL DISCOUNT BROKERS

If you don't have access to the Internet or aren't comfortable using an on-line broker, you can still sign up with many of these firms and phone in your trades. Ceres Securities charges $18 per trade, regardless of how it's made. This company is an exception, however. Most discount brokers still charge a good deal more per trade if you have a traditional account. Waterhouse, for example, charges $35 per trade if you use its TradeDirect Touch-Tone telephone trading system; it charges $45 per trade if you want to talk to a human being and make your trade through an account officer.

As with on-line brokers, prices are competitive among the traditional discount brokers. You'll get good service from Schwab, Fidelity (www.fidelity.com or 800-544-0003), and Jack White (www.pawws.com/jwc or 800-233-3411). Their minimum commissions are around $35. It really depends which broker offers the right combination of services for you.

It is difficult for me to recommend using a traditional discount broker, however, because the trading fees just add up too fast. If you want to use these strategies but have access only to a traditional broker, you can purchase mutual funds that use these strategies and save yourself a lot of money. The O'Shaughnessy Funds are available on all the major no-transaction-fee networks, like Schwab's OneSource and Fidelity FundsNetwork. You'll have to pay a mutual fund expense fee, but you'll pay no commissions or any other fees.

TRADITIONAL FULL-SERVICE BROKERS

If you don't want to spend the time to do any of this yourself, consider using a full-service broker. Full-service brokers will certainly not win any price wars, but good ones offer clients value for their money. If they can keep you from panicking, help you stay focused on the long term, and make you stick to a good strategy, their fee can be justifiable. What's more, full-service brokers often offer a number of products and services that online brokers do not, such as life insurance, home mortgages, and personal financial advice. Again, your needs and desires will help you choose the right broker for you.

If you want to use a full-service broker, you're again probably best off buying the mutual funds or unit investment trusts that implement these strategies. Niké Securities (www.nikesec.com or 800-621-9533) distributes unit investment trusts that use these strategies through a number of brokers, including Legg Mason (www.leggmason.com or 800-344-5348) and A.G. Edwards (www.agedwards.com or 314-955-3000).

My firm has a relationship with Defined Asset Funds (800-562-2926), a consortium that distributes unit investment trusts through Merrill Lynch (www.merrilllynch.com or 800-637-7455), Smith Barney (www.smithbarney.com or 800-327-6748), Morgan Stanley Dean Witter (www.deanwitter.com or 800-869-

3326), Paine Webber (www.painewebber.com or 800-762-1000), and Prudential (www.prudential.com or 800-843-7625). You might also ask whether they have a no-load mutual fund program as well. For smaller accounts, the fees that you'll pay for unit trusts or mutual funds are actually lower than if you bought and sold the stocks in the strategy yourself.

No Excuses

A few years ago, you had to be quite rich and very dedicated to invest in these strategies. Now, with the information in this book and the low cost of on-line trading, you have no excuse not to invest strategically. It is no longer expensive or difficult to find the right stocks and buy them on-line. It's all just a few mouse clicks away. Even if you're computer-phobic or just plain lazy, you can invest—more and more discount and full-service brokers offer these strategies in the form of mutual funds and unit investment trusts.

There are no more excuses. Start investing in these strategies today and you can retire rich.

CHAPTER TEN

THE SIMPLE WAY

There is a wonderful Zen tale about a fish that was a prince. He kept hearing creatures from the land talk about water, and he wanted to know what they meant by this. He went to his father, the king, and asked: "What is this water I keep hearing about? I don't know what it is and feel that I should understand it." His father replied, "You were born in the water and you will die in the water. You live in it and it flows through you and around you. It is so much a part of you that you are unaware of it."

The same is true of the conventional way we approach investing. Our faith in our innate ability to make superior investment choices based on colorful stories or intuition is like the water to the fish. We are surrounded by it. It is part of human nature to believe that to be successful, we need to dart in and out of the market, buy and sell individual stocks and mutual funds, and try to outsmart and outguess our fellow investors. Unfortunately, it is also part of human nature to be inconsistent and emotional when making investment choices. Yet to question this conventional path is like asking a fish to understand the water. The investor who makes the leap to a new way of investing feels quite like a fish out of water.

The Conventional Way

Almost every aspect of our culture supports and perpetuates the conventional way of investing. Twenty-four hours a day the business news screams about how individual companies are performing now compared with last quarter. All the "experts" pontificate about what's involved in their investment methods, what stocks they like, when investors should sell, and where the market is headed over the next few months. Magazine after magazine lists the hot stocks to own this year. Journals print article after article about why you should sell 30 percent of your stocks now or why the technology sector is the best place to put your money. Everywhere you turn you'll find profiles of the manager du jour, most of them gushing about how smart they are or how many frequent-flyer miles they've racked up because they work so darn hard. (Never mind that all the managers who did poorly probably traveled just as much and spent just as many hours at the office.)

Those Darn Facts

While the conventional way feels so right and fits with the way we think things should be, the facts don't support this way of investing at all. The facts haven't changed much since we started collecting data on the performance of conventionally managed equity funds. Most fail to beat a simple index like the S&P 500 over the long term. But because we're always so focused on today, we forget that this is nothing new. Confronted with all the evidence, conventional managers continue to say, "Just wait until next year!"

What's more, they've been saying that for decades. In 1976, *Fortune* magazine ran a cover story about how poorly money managers performed compared with the S&P 500. It reported that between 1962 and 1975, the S&P 500 beat 87 percent of professional managers. Not much has changed since then. Between 1986 and 1996, the S&P 500 still beat 80 percent of all equity funds tracked by Morningstar, and those money managers were probably working harder than ever.

A NEW, STRATEGIC PATH

Someone who simply stuck to a strategy like Leaders with Luster over the last 45 years would have beaten the S&P 500 97 percent of the time in the long term. What's more, his or her portfolio would now be worth almost four times as much as the S&P 500—all while taking the same amount of risk! It's starting to dawn on people that the conventional model doesn't work. Investing is at a state not unlike that of astronomy right before the Copernican revolution. No one wanted to believe that the Earth wasn't the center of the universe. Every time some new evidence was found contradicting this belief, astronomers would just add some new circles to the orbits of each planet to try to justify their movements.

Explanations of the heavens became more and more complicated—until Copernicus came along. He had the extraordinarily simple idea that the Sun, not the Earth, was the center of the galaxy, and all those old beliefs were swept away.

THE KILLER BROWNIE

Even with reams of evidence showing us that the conventional path doesn't work and that the simple, strategic path does, in the end we are still confronted with that brownie. Tremendously gratifying in the short term, it destroys the best-laid plans of millions of dieters a year. "Surely this one brownie is OK. I'll go right back on my diet tomorrow. Just this once I want to indulge a little. After all, it's such a small sin."

With that tiny surrender, a small, insignificant brownie destroys all the planning of a dieter with the best intentions. The surrender paves the way for future surrenders, and it ends with the poor dieter not only fat but miserable as well.

The same is true with investing. Here the temptation is to react emotionally to short-term news or to tinker with a great strategy "just this once." Investors who succumb find themselves not only poorer but also frustrated with their inability to do better than the market. The road to hell is paved with good intentions, but good intentions alone are meaningless. If you aren't able to consistently act on superior knowledge and rigorously implement these strategies, your chances of retiring rich are slim. Buying hot stocks based on tips and hunches or trying to time the market is every bit as tempting as eating that brownie, and doing so will start you down a slippery slope. If you succumb to temptation and try to second-guess these strategies, you'll be no different than all those professionals who can't even keep up with the S&P 500. Worse yet, you might join the ranks of investors who lose money while the market sets new highs.

Keep the Faith

The reason most people don't retire rich is that it's simply too hard to keep their emotions in check and stay focused on the long term. As much as we might be intellectually swayed by the arguments for strategic investing, it's at odds with our human nature. Ignoring our feelings and discarding the belief that we can pick stocks or time the market is extremely difficult.

Temptations abound. We know that this company will soar. We have personal experience to draw on and are therefore uniquely able to pick a winning stock. Soon, like the dieter, we start to rationalize our behavior. "I like these 45 years of evidence, but I'm going to wait and see how this strategy performs over the next few months. If it continues to do well, I'll go with it." (Even though the next few months—or even years—are meaningless in the long term.)

Or you might think, "Surely it won't hurt me to go with my gut this time. I'm worried about what the Fed might do, so it makes sense to pull my money out of the stock market for the next three months. After all, I'll never go broke taking a profit." And so it goes, until you're firmly in the 80 percent who can't do better than the S&P 500 over the long term.

BET WITH THE HOUSE

How many people entering the Mirage Resort have similar hopes racing through their heads? All of us want to believe in our talents and abilities, yet in the battle between the house and the gamblers, the house always wins. Like the gambler on a winning streak who is willing to bet the house, the urge to tinker—despite the evidence—is strong. "These strategies are a good guide," you'll think, "but I'll pare the list down using my own judgment or move into cash when I think the market has gone too high."

Remember that this is the natural way to approach investment decisions. After all the data, examples, and facts, we're still like the fish that can't understand the concept of water.

STRESS AND THE PROUD WAY

There are two ways to invest—the proud way and the humble way. Most people go with the proud way, because like the fish prince, they know nothing else. Proud investors follow the conventional path, believing they are smarter, faster, and better able to judge an investment's potential than their fellow investors. While these investors believe they can intuitively outsmart others, time and again a simple index like the S&P 500 beats them.

This causes unbelievable stress. Think of yourself, glued to the TV waiting for the latest earnings reports, your pulse racing. You're hoping you made the right pick on stock XYZ. But that's just the start. You might find yourself reading eight different financial magazines and newspapers and still unable to decide whether a stock is a good investment or whether you should be invested in the market at all. Think of all the time you'll spend and the anxiety you'll suffer and what it will do to your life. Instead of spending time with the people you love and doing things that you enjoy, you'll spend it on an endeavor in which the odds are stacked against you from the start.

Peace of Mind and the Humble Way

The other way to invest is the humble way. You accept that you're not smarter, faster, or better than other investors. You're not going to try to outthink or outrun them. All you do is bet with the house and the deep roots of simple, time-tested strategies that have proven themselves over almost half a century of market ups and downs. You then take these strategies and use them.

With the humble way, you embrace a path that many of the world's dominant philosophies have espoused as the best way to live. Ever since the ancient Greeks grappled with finding the best way to lead a good life, the idea of moderation continues to appear. The Greeks called it the golden mean, Buddhists call it the middle path, and Taoists call it the way.

Taoism is one of the three main schools of Chinese philosophy, conceived of by a man named Lao Tzu. While sitting in the woods one snowy afternoon, he watched as the branches of the old, larger trees supported the accumulating snow without bending an inch. But when too much snow accumulated, those old branches snapped and fell to the ground. He contrasted this with the younger trees, whose branches bent with the weight of the snow. As they did, the snow would slip off and the branch would snap back to its original position. He saw that by giving way, the younger branches survived, and by standing firm, the older branches died. The message was clear—those who struggle against life lose, while those who bend with it survive and grow. True strength lay in giving way and going with the flow.

An entire philosophy and way of life sprang from this simple observation, with many stories illustrating its point. One is particularly instructive for investors. A farmer who lived in a small village had only one son and one horse. One day his horse ran away, causing everyone in the town to stop by and offer their condolences. The man simply replied, "We'll see." The next day, the horse returned and brought with it a mighty black stallion. All the townspeople rushed to congratulate him on his good fortune. Again he replied, "We'll see." The next day his son attempted to ride the stallion, but the horse threw him, and the young man broke his leg. Again the man replied to the sympathies of everyone in town, saying, "We'll see." The next day, the emperor's troops came through the town and demanded that all the able-bodied young men join the army, where they were almost certain to meet their deaths. The farmer's son was spared, yet again he smiled and said, "We'll see."

What seems like good or bad news in the short term may prove exactly the opposite when viewed through the fullness of time. Think of your parents. Imagine they possessed this information about strategic investing and had actually used it. Instead of keeping their money in cash or bonds or buying individual stocks based on tips and hunches, let's say they had taken the humble path and kept their savings in the stock market, investing it strategically. Like the farmer in the story, they were able to meet every news item with "We'll see." Inflation is rampant, sell all your stocks—"We'll see." OPEC will destroy the world's economy—"We'll see." The recession of the early 1970s will change the investment arena forever—"We'll see." Stocks are way too high—"We'll see." The market crash of 1987 will usher in a new era—"We'll see."

Had your parents embraced this attitude and stuck with an investment strategy like Reasonable Runaways throughout their working lives, a one-time investment of $10,000 in 1952 would now be worth $20 million!

DON'T IGNORE—ACCEPT

But, you say, it's impossible to ignore the news of the day—to try to do so is just too hard! Indeed it is. So rather than ignore the news about the market and your emotional reactions to it, accept them.

This idea of acceptance really works. I alighted upon it when

I was trying to take a nap one Sunday afternoon in a room near our laundry room. When our dryer finishes a load, it makes a loud buzz, sits still for a few minutes, again spins the clothes and then again announces it's done with that annoyingly loud buzz. I didn't want to get up to turn the dryer off, so I kept trying to ignore the buzzing. But the more I tried to ignore it, the less I could. I can ignore this, I kept insisting to myself. But it kept getting louder and louder in my brain. Then I thought, you know, I can't ignore that buzz, but I can accept it. I can accept that it will continue (and it does at least a half dozen times!), but there is nothing I can do about it unless I get up and turn it off. The minute I accepted that buzz, it became background noise and I drifted off to sleep.

This works with the market as well. Accept that you'll get worried. Accept that there will be times when you feel like an idiot because your portfolio isn't doing as well as the market. Accept that you'll frequently want to override your strategies and follow the panicked or elated crowds of investors. Accept that there will be times when you'll think that people with money stuffed under their mattresses are making a better choice than you are. You won't be able to ignore these feelings, but you can accept them. When you do, it will be much easier to stick with your chosen strategy.

The proud way tempts, because it's also the natural, human way. The proud road is well traveled, and familiar. Many people would rather fail conventionally than succeed unconventionally, and so the humble way can seem difficult. Yet it's the way that works. Contrast the two paths, like Robert Frost did in his poem "The Road Not Taken."

> Two roads diverged in a wood, and I—
> I took the one less traveled by,
> And that has made all the difference.

EVERY DAY, RETIREMENT IS NEARER

The stock market's short-term direction will always be uncertain. What is certain is that each day you are one day closer to retirement. There's nothing you can do to change that. What you can change is what life will be like when you get there, and how much anxiety you will suffer or time you will spend investing your retirement savings. The strategies in this book aren't just buying you a chance at a vastly richer future—they are buying you time, the greatest asset of all.

Think of all the time Bill and Nancy Robinson can devote to their love of music, knowing that their retirement plans are secure. Think of all the time George and Theresa Ramirez can devote to their boys, Robert and Carlo. Think of the great education that awaits them because their parents took action and started sooner rather than later. Imagine the peace of mind Tom and Sarah O'Neil now possess, because they know that they've invested their retirement savings in strategies with a great chance of success. Finally, look at how Steve and Betsy Johnson have removed that huge cloud of uncertainty that had been looming over their lives. Instead of becoming increasingly despondent about their small savings accounts, they know they're doing everything in their power to ensure a rich retirement.

TAKE ACTION AND RETIRE RICH

Action is the key. The worst thing you can do is dither around, saying you'll start saving tomorrow. Think of all the retired people pinching pennies today who said the same thing yesterday. Today is their tomorrow. Scraping by to make ends meet, unable to enjoy their later years to the fullest, many are lamenting what things might have been like had they simply taken action and saved and invested their money earlier.

You have the power to take action *now*. Tomorrow will soon be today. *Act now,* and a rich retirement is within your reach. Delay or falter in your commitment to these strategies, and it never will be. Don't come across this book 30 years from now and ruefully think how things could have been. Remember the words of the poet John Greenleaf Whittier: "For of all sad words of tongue or pen, / The saddest are these: 'It might have been!'"

Your happiness and wealth tomorrow depend on your diligence today. Act now, ensure your future, and retire rich.

PERFORMANCE APPENDIX

THE NUMBERS

The following tables show how the strategies covered in this book have performed historically. When testing Reasonable Runaways and Leaders with Luster, I used the S&P Compustat database. Computstat is the most extensive database of U.S. stock market information currently available, with data on a comprehensive list of stocks going back to 1951. For the period from 1951 to 1994, the data was tested using a rigorous methodology created for *What Works on Wall Street*. The results from 1995 and 1996 represent the actual performance of the strategies.

I gathered the performance data on the Dogs of the Dow strategy from the December 31 issues of the *Wall Street Journal* and the *New York Times*. From 1928 forward, I simply chose the 10 highest yielding stocks from the then current Dow Jones Industrial Average and rebalanced the portfolio annually.

The performance data on the Utility and Core Value strategies is from the *Value Line* database. I selected the 10 stocks that met each strategy's criteria and rebalanced the portfolios annually. Please note that none of the figures reflect any fees, commissions, or taxes.

	TABLE I		
	REASONABLE RUNAWAYS, 50 STOCKS, ANNUAL RETURNS, 1952–1996		
YEAR	REASONABLE RUNAWAYS, 50 STOCKS	S&P 500	DIFFERENCE
1952	7.80%	18.37%	− 10.57%
1953	6.40%	− 0.99%	7.39%
1954	56.90%	52.62%	4.28%
1955	28.80%	31.56%	− 2.76%
1956	30.50%	6.56%	23.94%
1957	− 20.10%	− 10.78%	− 9.32%
1958	67.50%	43.36%	24.14%
1959	32.00%	11.96%	20.04%
1960	2.70%	0.47%	2.23%
1961	49.50%	26.89%	22.61%
1962	− 13.30%	− 8.73%	− 4.57%
1963	31.80%	22.80%	9.00%
1964	26.40%	16.48%	9.92%
1965	55.10%	12.45%	42.65%
1966	− 0.60%	− 10.06%	9.46%
1967	59.90%	23.98%	35.92%
1968	46.30%	11.06%	35.24%
1969	− 33.60%	− 8.50%	− 25.10%
1970	− 5.20%	4.01%	− 9.21%
1971	31.90%	14.31%	17.59%
1972	14.60%	18.98%	− 4.38%
1973	− 20.90%	− 14.66%	− 6.24%
1974	− 23.90%	− 26.47%	2.57%
1975	58.60%	37.20%	21.40%
1976	39.00%	23.84%	15.16%
1977	24.50%	− 7.18%	31.68%
1978	38.40%	6.56%	31.84%
1979	26.30%	18.44%	7.86%
1980	48.50%	32.42%	16.08%
1981	− 7.70%	− 4.91%	− 2.79%
1982	39.50%	21.41%	18.09%

YEAR	REASONABLE RUNAWAYS, 50 STOCKS	S&P 500	DIFFERENCE
1983	35.40%	22.51%	12.89%
1984	− 8.20%	6.27%	− 14.47%
1985	45.20%	32.16%	13.04%
1986	19.30%	18.47%	0.83%
1987	− 12.90%	5.23%	− 18.13%
1988	28.00%	16.81%	11.19%
1989	30.90%	31.49%	− 0.59%
1990	− 12.10%	− 3.17%	− 8.93%
1991	43.70%	30.55%	13.15%
1992	30.70%	7.67%	23.03%
1993	30.40%	9.99%	20.41%
1994	− 6.90%	1.31%	− 8.21%
1995	25.80%	37.43%	− 11.63%
1996	31.50%	23.07%	8.43%
Average	21.74%	13.41%	8.34%
Median	28.80%	14.31%	14.49%
High	67.50%	52.62%	14.88%
Low	− 33.60%	− 26.47%	− 7.13%
$10,000 grows to:	$23,394,653	$1,738,417	$21,656,235

	TABLE 2 REASONABLE RUNAWAYS, 50 STOCKS, ROLLING 5-YEAR COMPOUND RETURNS, 1956–1996		
YEAR	REASONABLE RUNAWAYS, 50 STOCKS	S&P 500	DIFFERENCE
1952			
1953			
1954			
1955			
1956	24.78%	20.18%	4.59%
1957	17.52%	13.58%	3.95%
1958	28.69%	22.30%	6.38%
1959	24.32%	14.96%	9.36%
1960	18.81%	8.92%	9.89%
1961	22.09%	12.79%	9.29%
1962	24.10%	13.31%	10.79%
1963	18.29%	9.85%	8.44%
1964	17.27%	10.73%	6.54%
1965	27.35%	13.25%	14.10%
1966	17.36%	5.72%	11.65%
1967	32.65%	12.39%	20.25%
1968	35.45%	10.16%	25.29%
1969	19.08%	4.97%	14.12%
1970	7.92%	3.34%	4.58%
1971	14.20%	8.42%	5.78%
1972	6.84%	7.53%	−0.69%
1973	−5.53%	2.01%	−7.53%
1974	−2.91%	−2.35%	−0.56%
1975	7.61%	3.21%	4.41%
1976	8.75%	4.87%	3.87%
1977	10.56%	−0.21%	10.77%
1978	23.65%	4.32%	19.33%
1979	36.84%	14.76%	22.08%
1980	35.05%	13.95%	21.10%
1981	24.43%	8.08%	16.35%
1982	27.29%	14.05%	13.25%

YEAR	REASONABLE RUNAWAYS, 50 STOCKS	S&P 500	DIFFERENCE
1983	26.74%	17.27%	9.46%
1984	18.90%	14.76%	4.14%
1985	18.37%	14.71%	3.66%
1986	24.60%	19.87%	4.73%
1987	13.40%	16.49%	−3.09%
1988	12.13%	15.38%	−3.25%
1989	20.38%	20.40%	−0.02%
1990	8.88%	13.14%	−4.26%
1991	13.01%	15.36%	−2.35%
1992	22.57%	15.89%	6.68%
1993	23.02%	14.51%	8.52%
1994	14.92%	8.69%	6.23%
1995	23.46%	16.57%	6.89%
1996	21.29%	15.20%	6.09%
Average	19.13%	11.54%	7.58%
Median	19.08%	13.25%	5.83%
High	36.84%	22.30%	14.53%
Low	−5.53%	−2.35%	−3.17%

	TABLE 3		
	REASONABLE RUNAWAYS, 50 STOCKS, ROLLING 10-YEAR COMPOUND RETURNS, 1961–1996		
YEAR	REASONABLE RUNAWAYS, 50 STOCKS	S&P 500	DIFFERENCE
1952			
1953			
1954			
1955			
1956			
1957			
1958			
1959			
1960			
1961	23.43%	16.43%	7.00%
1962	20.77%	13.44%	7.32%
1963	23.38%	15.91%	7.47%
1964	20.74%	12.82%	7.92%
1965	23.01%	11.06%	11.94%
1966	19.70%	9.20%	10.51%
1967	28.30%	12.85%	15.45%
1968	26.58%	10.01%	16.57%
1969	18.17%	7.81%	10.36%
1970	17.23%	8.18%	9.05%
1971	15.77%	7.06%	8.71%
1972	19.05%	9.93%	9.11%
1973	13.12%	6.01%	7.12%
1974	7.52%	1.24%	6.28%
1975	7.76%	3.27%	4.49%
1976	11.44%	6.63%	4.81%
1977	8.69%	3.59%	5.10%
1978	8.08%	3.16%	4.92%
1979	15.26%	5.86%	9.40%
1980	20.55%	8.44%	12.11%
1981	16.32%	6.47%	9.86%
1982	18.63%	6.68%	11.95%

YEAR	REASONABLE RUNAWAYS, 50 STOCKS	S&P 500	DIFFERENCE
1983	25.19%	10.61%	14.58%
1984	27.56%	14.76%	12.80%
1985	26.43%	14.33%	12.10%
1986	24.52%	13.82%	10.69%
1987	20.15%	15.26%	4.88%
1988	19.21%	16.33%	2.89%
1989	19.64%	17.55%	2.09%
1990	13.53%	13.93%	− 0.40%
1991	18.67%	17.59%	1.07%
1992	17.90%	16.19%	1.71%
1993	17.45%	14.94%	2.51%
1994	17.62%	14.40%	3.22%
1995	15.94%	14.84%	1.10%
1996	17.08%	15.28%	1.79%
Average	18.45%	11.00%	7.46%
Median	18.65%	11.94%	6.71%
High	28.30%	17.59%	10.71%
Low	7.52%	1.24%	6.28%

TABLE 4
REASONABLE RUNAWAYS, 50 STOCKS, HIGH AND LOW RETURNS, 1952–1996

	1-YEAR	5-YEAR	10-YEAR	15-YEAR	20-YEAR	25-YEAR
50 Stock Reasonable Runaways Minimum	−33.60%	−5.53%	7.52%	10.68%	13.51%	15.11%
50 Stock Reasonable Runaways Maximum	67.50%	36.84%	28.30%	27.28%	22.49%	19.87%
S&P 500 Minimum	−26.47%	−2.35%	1.24%	4.31%	6.53%	7.94%
S&P 500 Maximum	52.62%	22.30%	17.59%	16.79%	14.59%	12.55%

	TABLE 5 REASONABLE RUNAWAYS, 50 STOCKS, $10,000 GROWTH	
YEAR	**REASONABLE RUNAWAYS, 50 STOCKS**	**S&P 500**
1951	$10,000.00	$10,000.00
1952	$10,780	$11,837
1953	$11,470	$11,720
1954	$17,996	$17,887
1955	$23,179	$23,532
1956	$30,249	$25,076
1957	$24,169	$22,372
1958	$40,483	$32,073
1959	$53,437	$35,909
1960	$54,880	$36,078
1961	$82,046	$45,779
1962	$71,134	$41,783
1963	$93,754	$51,309
1964	$118,505	$59,765
1965	$183,802	$67,205
1966	$182,699	$60,445
1967	$292,136	$74,939
1968	$427,395	$83,227
1969	$283,790	$76,153
1970	$269,033	$79,207
1971	$354,855	$90,541
1972	$406,664	$107,726
1973	$321,671	$91,933
1974	$244,792	$67,599
1975	$388,239	$92,745
1976	$539,653	$114,856
1977	$671,868	$106,609
1978	$929,865	$113,603
1979	$1,174,419	$134,551
1980	$1,744,013	$178,173
1981	$1,609,724	$169,424
1982	$2,245,564	$205,698

YEAR	REASONABLE RUNAWAYS, 50 STOCKS	S&P 500
1983	$3,040,494	$252,001
1984	$2,791,174	$267,801
1985	$4,052,784	$353,926
1986	$4,834,972	$419,296
1987	$4,211,260	$441,225
1988	$5,390,413	$515,395
1989	$7,056,051	$677,693
1990	$6,202,269	$656,210
1991	$8,912,660	$856,683
1992	$11,648,847	$922,390
1993	$15,190,096	$1,014,537
1994	$14,141,980	$1,027,828
1995	$17,790,610	$1,412,543
1996	$23,394,653	$1,738,417

	TABLE 6 REASONABLE RUNAWAYS, 25 STOCKS, ANNUAL RETURNS, 1952–1996		
YEAR	REASONABLE RUNAWAYS, 25 STOCKS	S&P 500	DIFFERENCE
1952	8.49%	18.37%	− 9.88%
1953	4.75%	− 0.99%	5.74%
1954	73.24%	52.62%	20.62%
1955	32.25%	31.56%	0.69%
1956	27.85%	6.56%	21.29%
1957	− 17.61%	− 10.78%	− 6.83%
1958	81.21%	43.36%	37.85%
1959	37.79%	11.96%	25.83%
1960	6.47%	0.47%	6.00%
1961	61.99%	26.89%	35.10%
1962	− 18.66%	− 8.73%	− 9.93%
1963	35.23%	22.80%	12.43%
1964	24.71%	16.48%	8.23%
1965	61.22%	12.45%	48.77%
1966	− 0.01%	− 10.06%	10.05%
1967	79.94%	23.98%	55.96%
1968	65.94%	11.06%	54.88%
1969	− 31.46%	− 8.50%	− 22.96%
1970	− 5.76%	4.01%	− 9.77%
1971	36.14%	14.31%	21.83%
1972	15.09%	18.98%	− 3.89%
1973	− 27.61%	− 14.66%	− 12.95%
1974	− 25.93%	− 26.47%	0.54%
1975	46.12%	37.20%	8.92%
1976	38.94%	23.84%	15.10%
1977	17.35%	− 7.18%	24.53%
1978	30.30%	6.56%	23.74%
1979	33.94%	18.44%	15.50%
1980	29.36%	32.42%	− 3.06%
1981	− 7.46%	− 4.91%	− 2.55%
1982	39.69%	21.41%	18.28%

YEAR	REASONABLE RUNAWAYS, 25 STOCKS	S&P 500	DIFFERENCE
1983	37.66%	22.51%	15.15%
1984	− 10.12%	6.27%	− 16.39%
1985	40.04%	32.16%	7.88%
1986	22.06%	18.47%	3.59%
1987	− 18.19%	5.23%	− 23.42%
1988	27.57%	16.81%	10.76%
1989	42.34%	31.49%	10.85%
1990	− 3.91%	− 3.17%	− 0.74%
1991	56.79%	30.55%	26.24%
1992	32.12%	7.67%	24.45%
1993	18.96%	9.99%	8.97%
1994	− 19.62%	1.31%	− 20.93%
1995	13.33%	37.43%	− 24.10%
1996	25.64%	23.07%	2.57%
Average	22.63%	13.41%	9.22%
Median	27.57%	14.31%	13.26%
High	81.21%	52.62%	28.59%
Low	− 31.46%	− 26.47%	− 4.99%
$10,000 grows to:	$25,050,243	$1,738,417	$23,311,826

| YEAR | TABLE 7
REASONABLE RUNAWAYS, 25 STOCKS, 5-YEAR
COMPOUND RETURNS, 1956–1996 | | |
	REASONABLE RUNAWAYS, 25 STOCKS	S&P 500	DIFFERENCE
1952			
1953			
1954			
1955			
1956	27.19%	20.18%	7.01%
1957	20.38%	13.58%	6.80%
1958	34.32%	22.30%	12.02%
1959	28.31%	14.96%	13.36%
1960	22.87%	8.92%	13.95%
1961	28.82%	12.79%	16.03%
1962	28.49%	13.31%	15.19%
1963	21.19%	9.85%	11.34%
1964	18.80%	10.73%	8.07%
1965	29.07%	13.25%	15.83%
1966	17.20%	5.72%	11.49%
1967	37.37%	12.39%	24.98%
1968	43.11%	10.16%	32.95%
1969	26.96%	4.97%	21.99%
1970	14.03%	3.34%	10.69%
1971	21.29%	8.42%	12.88%
1972	10.92%	7.53%	3.39%
1973	−6.03%	2.01%	−8.04%
1974	−4.56%	−2.35%	−2.21%
1975	4.19%	3.21%	0.98%
1976	4.61%	4.87%	−0.26%
1977	5.02%	−0.21%	5.23%
1978	18.12%	4.32%	13.80%
1979	32.98%	14.76%	18.22%
1980	29.78%	13.95%	15.83%
1981	19.65%	8.08%	11.56%
1982	23.89%	14.05%	9.84%

YEAR	REASONABLE RUNAWAYS, 25 STOCKS	S&P 500	DIFFERENCE
1983	25.26%	17.27%	7.98%
1984	15.65%	14.76%	0.90%
1985	17.50%	14.71%	2.79%
1986	24.19%	19.87%	4.32%
1987	11.59%	16.49%	− 4.90%
1988	9.90%	15.38%	− 5.48%
1989	20.49%	20.40%	0.08%
1990	11.74%	13.14%	− 1.40%
1991	17.48%	15.36%	2.12%
1992	29.30%	15.89%	13.41%
1993	27.51%	14.51%	13.00%
1994	13.74%	8.69%	5.05%
1995	17.55%	16.57%	0.98%
1996	12.46%	15.20%	− 2.74%
Average	19.81%	11.54%	8.27%
Median	20.38%	13.25%	7.13%
High	43.11%	22.30%	20.80%
Low	− 6.03%	− 2.35%	− 3.68%

YEAR	REASONABLE RUNAWAYS, 25 STOCKS	S&P 500	DIFFERENCE
TABLE 8 REASONABLE RUNAWAYS, 25 STOCKS, 10-YEAR COMPOUND RETURNS, 1961–1996			
1952			
1953			
1954			
1955			
1956			
1957			
1958			
1959			
1960			
1961	28.00%	16.43%	11.57%
1962	24.37%	13.44%	10.93%
1963	27.59%	15.91%	11.68%
1964	23.46%	12.82%	10.64%
1965	25.93%	11.06%	14.87%
1966	22.87%	9.20%	13.68%
1967	32.86%	12.85%	20.01%
1968	31.69%	10.01%	21.69%
1969	22.81%	7.81%	15.00%
1970	21.32%	8.18%	13.14%
1971	19.23%	7.06%	12.17%
1972	23.44%	9.93%	13.51%
1973	15.96%	6.01%	9.96%
1974	10.07%	1.24%	8.84%
1975	9.00%	3.27%	5.72%
1976	12.64%	6.63%	6.01%
1977	7.93%	3.59%	4.34%
1978	5.35%	3.16%	2.19%
1979	12.65%	5.86%	6.80%
1980	16.28%	8.44%	7.38%
1981	11.88%	6.47%	5.41%
1982	14.06%	6.68%	7.38%

YEAR	REASONABLE RUNAWAYS, 25 STOCKS	S&P 500	DIFFERENCE
1983	21.64%	10.61%	11.03%
1984	24.01%	14.76%	9.25%
1985	23.49%	14.33%	9.16%
1986	21.90%	13.82%	8.07%
1987	17.58%	15.26%	2.32%
1988	17.33%	16.33%	1.00%
1989	18.05%	17.55%	0.50%
1990	14.59%	13.93%	0.66%
1991	20.79%	17.59%	3.20%
1992	20.12%	16.19%	3.93%
1993	18.38%	14.94%	3.43%
1994	17.06%	14.40%	2.67%
1995	14.61%	14.84%	− 0.23%
1996	14.94%	15.28%	− 0.34%
Average	19.00%	11.00%	8.00%
Median	18.80%	11.94%	6.86%
High	32.86%	17.59%	15.26%
Low	5.35%	1.24%	4.11%

TABLE 9
REASONABLE RUNAWAYS, 25 STOCKS, HIGH AND LOW RETURNS, 1952–1996

	1-YEAR	5-YEAR	10-YEAR	15-YEAR	20-YEAR	25-YEAR
25 Stock Reasonable Runaways Minimum	− 31.46%	− 6.03%	5.35%	11.61%	11.18%	14.27%
25 Stock Reasonable Runaways Maximum	81.21%	43.11%	32.86%	32.56%	23.90%	20.92%
S&P 500 Minimum	− 26.47%	− 2.35%	1.24%	4.31%	6.53%	7.94%
S&P 500 Maximum	52.62%	22.30%	17.59%	16.79%	14.59%	12.55%

YEAR	REASONABLE RUNAWAYS, 25 STOCKS	S&P 500
	TABLE 10	
	REASONABLE RUNAWAYS, 25 STOCKS,	
	$10,000 GROWTH	
1951	$10,000.00	$10,000.00
1952	$10,849	$11,837
1953	$11,365	$11,720
1954	$19,688	$17,887
1955	$26,036	$23,532
1956	$33,289	$25,076
1957	$27,426	$22,372
1958	$49,698	$32,073
1959	$68,478	$35,909
1960	$72,907	$36,078
1961	$118,100	$45,779
1962	$96,065	$41,783
1963	$129,912	$51,309
1964	$162,013	$59,765
1965	$261,190	$67,205
1966	$261,153	$60,445
1967	$469,911	$74,939
1968	$779,771	$83,227
1969	$534,424	$76,153
1970	$503,615	$79,207
1971	$685,596	$90,541
1972	$789,073	$107,726
1973	$571,232	$91,933
1974	$423,086	$67,599
1975	$618,222	$92,745
1976	$858,951	$114,856
1977	$1,007,988	$106,609
1978	$1,313,457	$113,603
1979	$1,759,252	$134,551
1980	$2,275,775	$178,173
1981	$2,106,114	$169,424
1982	$2,941,982	$205,698

YEAR	REASONABLE RUNAWAYS, 25 STOCKS	S&P 500
1983	$4,049,974	$252,001
1984	$3,640,251	$267,801
1985	$5,097,784	$353,926
1986	$6,222,393	$419,296
1987	$5,090,361	$441,225
1988	$6,493,839	$515,395
1989	$9,243,216	$677,693
1990	$8,881,609	$656,210
1991	$13,925,234	$856,683
1992	$18,398,689	$922,390
1993	$21,886,736	$1,014,537
1994	$17,592,242	$1,027,828
1995	$19,938,111	$1,412,543
1996	$25,050,243	$1,738,417

TABLE II
LEADERS WITH LUSTER, 50 STOCKS, ANNUAL RETURNS, 1952–1996

YEAR	LEADERS WITH LUSTER, 50 STOCKS	S&P 500	DIFFERENCE
1952	14.30%	18.37%	− 4.07%
1953	1.20%	− 0.99%	2.19%
1954	52.50%	52.62%	− 0.12%
1955	28.10%	31.56%	− 3.46%
1956	14.80%	6.56%	8.24%
1957	− 13.50%	− 10.78%	− 2.72%
1958	44.90%	43.36%	1.54%
1959	9.60%	11.96%	− 2.36%
1960	− 0.03%	0.47%	− 0.50%
1961	24.40%	26.89%	− 2.49%
1962	− 2.60%	− 8.73%	6.13%
1963	18.80%	22.80%	− 4.00%
1964	20.30%	16.48%	3.82%
1965	17.60%	12.45%	5.15%
1966	− 10.20%	− 10.06%	− 0.14%
1967	23.70%	23.98%	− 0.28%
1968	26.50%	11.06%	15.44%
1969	− 15.00%	− 8.50%	− 6.50%
1970	11.30%	4.01%	7.29%
1971	15.80%	14.31%	1.49%
1972	14.00%	18.98%	− 4.98%
1973	− 5.90%	− 14.66%	8.76%
1974	− 12.30%	− 26.47%	14.17%
1975	58.20%	37.20%	21.00%
1976	39.20%	23.84%	15.36%
1977	3.30%	− 7.18%	10.48%
1978	3.30%	6.56%	− 3.26%
1979	25.60%	18.44%	7.16%
1980	20.30%	32.42%	− 12.12%
1981	12.80%	− 4.91%	17.71%
1982	19.60%	21.41%	− 1.81%

YEAR	LEADERS WITH LUSTER, 50 STOCKS	S&P 500	DIFFERENCE
1983	38.60%	22.51%	16.09%
1984	4.70%	6.27%	− 1.57%
1985	35.00%	32.16%	2.84%
1986	20.60%	18.47%	2.13%
1987	11.60%	5.23%	6.37%
1988	26.50%	16.81%	9.69%
1989	37.60%	31.49%	6.11%
1990	− 7.00%	− 3.17%	− 3.83%
1991	36.90%	30.55%	6.35%
1992	11.60%	7.67%	3.93%
1993	20.40%	9.99%	10.41%
1994	4.80%	1.31%	3.49%
1995	26.70%	37.43%	− 10.73%
1996	21.90%	23.07%	− 1.17%
Average	16.68%	13.41%	3.27%
Median	17.60%	14.31%	3.29%
High	58.20%	52.62%	5.58%
Low	− 15.00%	− 26.47%	11.47%
$10,000 grows to:	$6,395,862	$1,738,417	$4,657,445

	TABLE 12 LEADERS WITH LUSTER, 50 STOCKS, 5-YEAR COMPOUND RETURNS, 1956–1996		
YEAR	LEADERS WITH LUSTER, 50 STOCKS	S&P 500	DIFFERENCE
1952			
1953			
1954			
1955			
1956	21.00%	20.18%	0.82%
1957	14.44%	13.58%	0.87%
1958	22.96%	22.30%	0.66%
1959	15.10%	14.96%	0.14%
1960	9.53%	8.92%	0.61%
1961	11.31%	12.79%	−1.49%
1962	13.98%	13.31%	0.67%
1963	9.54%	9.85%	−0.31%
1964	11.60%	10.73%	0.87%
1965	15.29%	13.25%	2.04%
1966	8.01%	5.72%	2.29%
1967	13.30%	12.39%	0.91%
1968	14.73%	10.16%	4.57%
1969	7.03%	4.97%	2.07%
1970	5.86%	3.34%	2.52%
1971	11.38%	8.42%	2.97%
1972	9.58%	7.53%	2.05%
1973	3.28%	2.01%	1.27%
1974	3.93%	−2.35%	6.28%
1975	11.50%	3.21%	8.30%
1976	15.68%	4.87%	10.81%
1977	13.42%	−0.21%	13.63%
1978	15.56%	4.32%	11.24%
1979	24.17%	14.76%	9.41%
1980	17.55%	13.95%	3.60%
1981	12.71%	8.08%	4.62%
1982	16.06%	14.05%	2.01%

YEAR	LEADERS WITH LUSTER, 50 STOCKS	S&P 500	DIFFERENCE
1983	23.09%	17.27%	5.81%
1984	18.69%	14.76%	3.93%
1985	21.46%	14.71%	6.74%
1986	23.09%	19.87%	3.22%
1987	21.40%	16.49%	4.91%
1988	19.20%	15.38%	3.82%
1989	25.90%	20.40%	5.49%
1990	16.85%	13.14%	3.71%
1991	19.85%	15.36%	4.49%
1992	19.85%	15.89%	3.96%
1993	18.67%	14.51%	4.17%
1994	12.38%	8.69%	3.70%
1995	19.55%	16.57%	2.98%
1996	16.81%	15.20%	1.61%
Average	15.25%	11.54%	3.71%
Median	15.29%	13.25%	2.04%
High	25.90%	22.30%	3.59%
Low	3.28%	− 2.35%	5.64%

	TABLE 13 LEADERS WITH LUSTER, 50 STOCKS, ROLLING 10-YEAR COMPOUND RETURNS, 1961–1996		
YEAR	LEADERS WITH LUSTER, 50 STOCKS	S&P 500	DIFFERENCE
1952			
1953			
1954			
1955			
1956			
1957			
1958			
1959			
1960			
1961	16.05%	16.43%	− 0.38%
1962	14.21%	13.44%	0.77%
1963	16.06%	15.91%	0.15%
1964	13.34%	12.82%	0.52%
1965	12.37%	11.06%	1.31%
1966	9.65%	9.20%	0.45%
1967	13.64%	12.85%	0.79%
1968	12.11%	10.01%	2.10%
1969	9.29%	7.81%	1.48%
1970	10.47%	8.18%	2.29%
1971	9.68%	7.06%	2.63%
1972	11.42%	9.93%	1.49%
1973	8.86%	6.01%	2.85%
1974	5.47%	1.24%	4.23%
1975	8.64%	3.27%	5.37%
1976	13.51%	6.63%	6.88%
1977	11.48%	3.59%	7.90%
1978	9.25%	3.16%	6.09%
1979	13.60%	5.86%	7.74%
1980	14.49%	8.44%	6.04%
1981	14.19%	6.47%	7.72%
1982	14.73%	6.68%	8.05%

YEAR	LEADERS WITH LUSTER, 50 STOCKS	S&P 500	DIFFERENCE
1983	19.26%	10.61%	8.65%
1984	21.40%	14.76%	6.64%
1985	19.49%	14.33%	5.16%
1986	17.78%	13.82%	3.96%
1987	18.70%	15.26%	3.44%
1988	21.13%	16.33%	4.80%
1989	22.24%	17.55%	4.69%
1990	19.13%	13.93%	5.21%
1991	21.46%	17.59%	3.87%
1992	20.62%	16.19%	4.43%
1993	18.94%	14.94%	3.99%
1994	18.95%	14.40%	4.55%
1995	18.20%	14.84%	3.35%
1996	18.32%	15.28%	3.04%
Average	14.95%	11.00%	3.95%
Median	14.35%	11.94%	2.41%
High	22.24%	17.59%	4.64%
Low	5.47%	1.24%	4.23%

TABLE 14
LEADERS WITH LUSTER, 50 STOCKS, HIGH AND LOW RETURNS, 1952–1996

	1-YEAR	5-YEAR	10-YEAR	15-YEAR	20-YEAR	25-YEAR
50 Stock Leaders with Luster Minimum	−15.00%	3.28%	5.47%	7.47%	9.33%	11.79%
50 Stock Leaders with Luster Maximum	58.20%	25.90%	22.24%	22.88%	20.17%	17.58%
S&P 500 Minimum	−26.47%	−2.35%	1.24%	4.31%	6.53%	7.94%
S&P 500 Maximum	52.62%	22.30%	17.59%	16.79%	14.59%	12.55%

	TABLE 15 LEADERS WITH LUSTER, 50 STOCKS, $10,000 GROWTH	
YEAR	LEADERS WITH LUSTER, 50 STOCKS	S&P 500
1951	$10,000.00	$10,000.00
1952	$11,430	$11,837
1953	$11,567	$11,720
1954	$17,640	$17,887
1955	$22,597	$23,532
1956	$25,941	$25,076
1957	$22,439	$22,372
1958	$32,514	$32,073
1959	$35,635	$35,909
1960	$35,625	$36,078
1961	$44,317	$45,779
1962	$43,165	$41,783
1963	$51,280	$51,309
1964	$61,690	$59,765
1965	$72,547	$67,205
1966	$65,147	$60,445
1967	$80,587	$74,939
1968	$101,943	$83,227
1969	$86,652	$76,153
1970	$96,443	$79,207
1971	$111,681	$90,541
1972	$127,317	$107,726
1973	$119,805	$91,933
1974	$105,069	$67,599
1975	$166,219	$92,745
1976	$231,377	$114,856
1977	$239,012	$106,609
1978	$246,900	$113,603
1979	$310,106	$134,551
1980	$373,058	$178,173
1981	$420,809	$169,424
1982	$503,288	$205,698

YEAR	LEADERS WITH LUSTER, 50 STOCKS	S&P 500
1983	$697,557	$252,001
1984	$730,342	$267,801
1985	$985,961	$353,926
1986	$1,189,070	$419,296
1987	$1,327,002	$441,225
1988	$1,678,657	$515,395
1989	$2,309,832	$677,693
1990	$2,148,144	$656,210
1991	$2,940,809	$856,683
1992	$3,281,943	$922,390
1993	$3,951,459	$1,014,537
1994	$4,141,129	$1,027,828
1995	$5,246,810	$1,412,543
1996	$6,395,862	$1,738,417

TABLE 16			
LEADERS WITH LUSTER, 25 STOCKS, ANNUAL RETURNS, 1952–1996			
YEAR	**LEADERS WITH LUSTER, 25 STOCKS**	**S&P 500**	**DIFFERENCE**
1952	18.80%	18.37%	0.43%
1953	0.70%	− 0.99%	1.69%
1954	54.00%	52.62%	1.38%
1955	28.40%	31.56%	− 3.16%
1956	14.10%	6.56%	7.54%
1957	− 6.20%	− 10.78%	4.58%
1958	40.50%	43.36%	− 2.86%
1959	8.60%	11.96%	− 3.36%
1960	3.60%	0.47%	3.13%
1961	28.10%	26.89%	1.21%
1962	1.00%	− 8.73%	9.73%
1963	21.00%	22.80%	− 1.80%
1964	23.80%	16.48%	7.32%
1965	24.80%	12.45%	12.35%
1966	− 10.20%	− 10.06%	− 0.14%
1967	26.70%	23.98%	2.72%
1968	30.10%	11.06%	19.04%
1969	− 15.70%	− 8.50%	− 7.20%
1970	11.40%	4.01%	7.39%
1971	15.70%	14.31%	1.39%
1972	14.10%	18.98%	− 4.88%
1973	− 8.10%	− 14.66%	6.56%
1974	− 11.10%	− 26.47%	15.37%
1975	75.90%	37.20%	38.70%
1976	39.40%	23.84%	15.56%
1977	12.90%	− 7.18%	20.08%
1978	− 2.10%	6.56%	− 8.66%
1979	14.10%	18.44%	− 4.34%
1980	17.10%	32.42%	− 15.32%
1981	12.30%	− 4.91%	17.21%
1982	22.40%	21.41%	0.99%

YEAR	LEADERS WITH LUSTER, 25 STOCKS	S&P 500	DIFFERENCE
1983	36.40%	22.51%	13.89%
1984	5.90%	6.27%	− 0.37%
1985	34.00%	32.16%	1.84%
1986	20.30%	18.47%	1.83%
1987	14.10%	5.23%	8.87%
1988	23.60%	16.81%	6.79%
1989	34.50%	31.49%	3.01%
1990	− 10.80%	− 3.17%	− 7.63%
1991	44.60%	30.55%	14.05%
1992	5.10%	7.67%	− 2.57%
1993	24.20%	9.99%	14.21%
1994	8.00%	1.31%	6.69%
1995	15.70%	37.43%	− 21.73%
1996	17.21%	23.07%	− 5.86%
Average	17.31%	13.41%	3.90%
Median	15.70%	14.31%	1.39%
High	75.90%	52.62%	23.28%
Low	− 15.70%	− 26.47%	10.77%
$10,000 grows to:	$7,867,772	$1,738,417	$6,129,355

	TABLE 17 LEADERS WITH LUSTER, 25 STOCKS, ROLLING 5-YEAR COMPOUND RETURNS, 1956–1996		
YEAR	LEADERS WITH LUSTER, 25 STOCKS	S&P 500	DIFFERENCE
1952			
1953			
1954			
1955			
1956	21.97%	20.18%	1.78%
1957	16.34%	13.58%	2.76%
1958	24.35%	22.30%	2.05%
1959	15.96%	14.96%	1.00%
1960	11.09%	8.92%	2.17%
1961	13.69%	12.79%	0.90%
1962	15.38%	13.31%	2.08%
1963	11.99%	9.85%	2.13%
1964	14.96%	10.73%	4.23%
1965	19.32%	13.25%	6.07%
1966	11.14%	5.72%	5.42%
1967	16.29%	12.39%	3.90%
1968	17.99%	10.16%	7.83%
1969	9.26%	4.97%	4.30%
1970	6.81%	3.34%	3.47%
1971	12.36%	8.42%	3.95%
1972	10.03%	7.53%	2.50%
1973	2.64%	2.01%	0.63%
1974	3.74%	−2.35%	6.09%
1975	13.66%	3.21%	10.46%
1976	17.98%	4.87%	13.11%
1977	17.73%	−0.21%	17.94%
1978	19.23%	4.32%	14.91%
1979	25.33%	14.76%	10.57%
1980	15.54%	13.95%	1.59%
1981	10.65%	8.08%	2.56%
1982	12.45%	14.05%	−1.60%

YEAR	LEADERS WITH LUSTER, 25 STOCKS	S&P 500	DIFFERENCE
1983	20.16%	17.27%	2.89%
1984	18.38%	14.76%	3.62%
1985	21.62%	14.71%	6.90%
1986	23.30%	19.87%	3.43%
1987	21.58%	16.49%	5.09%
1988	19.21%	15.38%	3.83%
1989	25.05%	20.40%	4.64%
1990	15.27%	13.14%	2.13%
1991	19.59%	15.36%	4.23%
1992	17.65%	15.89%	1.75%
1993	17.76%	14.51%	3.25%
1994	12.70%	8.69%	4.02%
1995	18.72%	16.57%	2.15%
1996	13.84%	15.20%	−1.37%
Average	15.92%	11.54%	4.38%
Median	16.29%	13.25%	3.04%
High	25.33%	22.30%	3.03%
Low	2.64%	−2.35%	5.00%

	TABLE 18		
	LEADERS WITH LUSTER, 25 STOCKS, ROLLING 10-YEAR		
	COMPOUND RETURNS, 1961–1996		
YEAR	LEADERS WITH LUSTER, 25 STOCKS	S&P 500	DIFFERENCE
1952			
1953			
1954			
1955			
1956			
1957			
1958			
1959			
1960			
1961	17.76%	16.43%	1.33%
1962	15.86%	13.44%	2.42%
1963	18.01%	15.91%	2.10%
1964	15.46%	12.82%	2.64%
1965	15.13%	11.06%	4.07%
1966	12.41%	9.20%	3.21%
1967	15.84%	12.85%	2.99%
1968	14.95%	10.01%	4.95%
1969	12.08%	7.81%	4.27%
1970	12.89%	8.18%	4.71%
1971	11.75%	7.06%	4.69%
1972	13.12%	9.93%	3.19%
1973	10.05%	6.01%	4.04%
1974	6.47%	1.24%	5.23%
1975	10.18%	3.27%	6.91%
1976	15.14%	6.63%	8.51%
1977	13.82%	3.59%	10.23%
1978	10.63%	3.16%	7.47%
1979	14.03%	5.86%	8.17%
1980	14.60%	8.44%	6.15%
1981	14.25%	6.47%	7.79%
1982	15.06%	6.68%	8.38%

YEAR	LEADERS WITH LUSTER, 25 STOCKS	S&P 500	DIFFERENCE
1983	19.69%	10.61%	9.08%
1984	21.81%	14.76%	7.05%
1985	18.54%	14.33%	4.21%
1986	16.80%	13.82%	2.98%
1987	16.93%	15.26%	1.67%
1988	19.68%	16.33%	3.36%
1989	21.67%	17.55%	4.12%
1990	18.40%	13.93%	4.48%
1991	21.43%	17.59%	3.84%
1992	19.60%	16.19%	3.41%
1993	18.48%	14.94%	3.54%
1994	18.72%	14.40%	4.32%
1995	16.99%	14.84%	2.14%
1996	16.68%	15.28%	1.40%
Average	15.69%	11.00%	4.69%
Median	15.65%	11.94%	3.71%
High	21.81%	17.59%	4.21%
Low	6.47%	1.24%	5.23%

TABLE 19
LEADERS WITH LUSTER, 25 STOCKS, HIGH AND LOW RETURNS, 1952–1996

	1-YEAR	5-YEAR	10-YEAR	15-YEAR	20-YEAR	25-YEAR
25 Stock Leaders with Luster Minimum	− 15.70%	2.64%	6.47%	9.22%	10.87%	13.13%
25 Stock Leaders with Luster Maximum	75.90%	25.33%	21.81%	22.88%	20.25%	16.99%
S&P 500 Minimum	− 26.47%	− 2.35%	1.24%	4.31%	6.53%	7.94%
S&P 500 Maximum	52.62%	22.30%	17.59%	16.79%	14.59%	12.55%

YEAR	LEADERS WITH LUSTER, 25 STOCKS	S&P 500
	TABLE 20	
	LEADERS WITH LUSTER, 25 STOCKS,	
	$10,000 GROWTH	
1951	$10,000.00	$10,000.00
1952	$11,880	$11,837
1953	$11,963	$11,720
1954	$18,423	$17,887
1955	$23,655	$23,532
1956	$26,991	$25,076
1957	$25,317	$22,372
1958	$35,571	$32,073
1959	$38,630	$35,909
1960	$40,021	$36,078
1961	$51,267	$45,779
1962	$51,779	$41,783
1963	$62,653	$51,309
1964	$77,564	$59,765
1965	$96,800	$67,205
1966	$86,927	$60,445
1967	$110,136	$74,939
1968	$143,287	$83,227
1969	$120,791	$76,153
1970	$134,561	$79,207
1971	$155,687	$90,541
1972	$177,639	$107,726
1973	$163,251	$91,933
1974	$145,130	$67,599
1975	$255,283	$92,745
1976	$355,865	$114,856
1977	$401,771	$106,609
1978	$393,334	$113,603
1979	$448,794	$134,551
1980	$525,538	$178,173
1981	$590,179	$169,424
1982	$722,379	$205,698

YEAR	LEADERS WITH LUSTER, 25 STOCKS	S&P 500
1983	$985,326	$252,001
1984	$1,043,460	$267,801
1985	$1,398,236	$353,926
1986	$1,682,078	$419,296
1987	$1,919,251	$441,225
1988	$2,372,194	$515,395
1989	$3,190,601	$677,693
1990	$2,846,016	$656,210
1991	$4,115,340	$856,683
1992	$4,325,222	$922,390
1993	$5,371,926	$1,014,537
1994	$5,801,680	$1,027,828
1995	$6,712,544	$1,412,543
1996	$7,867,772	$1,738,417

	TABLE 21		
COMBINED PORTFOLIO ANNUAL RETURNS, 1952–1996			
YEAR	COMBINED REASONABLE RUNAWAYS AND LEADERS WITH LUSTER, 50 STOCKS VERSION	S&P 500	DIFFERENCE
1952	11.05%	18.37%	− 7.32%
1953	3.80%	− 0.99%	4.79%
1954	54.70%	52.62%	2.08%
1955	28.45%	31.56%	− 3.11%
1956	22.65%	6.56%	16.09%
1957	− 16.80%	− 10.78%	− 6.02%
1958	56.20%	43.36%	12.84%
1959	20.80%	11.96%	8.84%
1960	1.34%	0.47%	0.86%
1961	36.95%	26.89%	10.06%
1962	− 7.95%	− 8.73%	0.78%
1963	25.30%	22.80%	2.50%
1964	23.35%	16.48%	6.87%
1965	36.35%	12.45%	23.90%
1966	− 5.40%	− 10.06%	4.66%
1967	41.80%	23.98%	17.82%
1968	36.40%	11.06%	25.34%
1969	− 24.30%	− 8.50%	− 15.80%
1970	3.05%	4.01%	− 0.96%
1971	23.85%	14.31%	9.54%
1972	14.30%	18.98%	− 4.68%
1973	− 13.40%	− 14.66%	1.26%
1974	− 18.10%	− 26.47%	8.37%
1975	58.40%	37.20%	21.20%
1976	39.10%	23.84%	15.26%
1977	13.90%	− 7.18%	21.08%
1978	20.85%	6.56%	14.29%
1979	25.95%	18.44%	7.51%
1980	34.40%	32.42%	1.98%
1981	2.55%	− 4.91%	7.46%
1982	29.55%	21.41%	8.14%

YEAR	COMBINED REASONABLE RUNAWAYS AND LEADERS WITH LUSTER, 50 STOCKS VERSION	S&P 500	DIFFERENCE
1983	37.00%	22.51%	14.49%
1984	−1.75%	6.27%	−8.02%
1985	40.10%	32.16%	7.94%
1986	19.95%	18.47%	1.48%
1987	−0.65%	5.23%	−5.88%
1988	27.25%	16.81%	10.44%
1989	34.25%	31.49%	2.76%
1990	−9.55%	−3.17%	−6.38%
1991	40.30%	30.55%	9.75%
1992	21.15%	7.67%	13.48%
1993	25.40%	9.99%	15.41%
1994	−1.05%	1.31%	−2.36%
1995	26.25%	37.43%	−11.18%
1996	26.70%	23.07%	3.63%
Average	19.21%	13.41%	5.80%
Median	23.35%	14.31%	9.04%
High	58.40%	52.62%	5.78%
Low	−24.30%	−26.47%	2.17%
$10,000 grows to:	$13,595,813	$1,738,417	$11,857,396

	TABLE 22 COMBINED PORTFOLIO 5-YEAR ROLLING COMPOUND RETURNS, 1956–1996		
YEAR	COMBINED REASONABLE RUNAWAYS AND LEADERS WITH LUSTER, 50 STOCKS VERSION	S&P 500	DIFFERENCE
1952			
1953			
1954			
1955			
1956	22.95%	20.18%	2.76%
1957	16.05%	13.58%	2.47%
1958	25.93%	22.30%	3.63%
1959	19.85%	14.96%	4.90%
1960	14.30%	8.92%	5.38%
1961	16.85%	12.79%	4.06%
1962	19.24%	13.31%	5.93%
1963	14.10%	9.85%	4.24%
1964	14.57%	10.73%	3.85%
1965	21.58%	13.25%	8.33%
1966	12.91%	5.72%	7.19%
1967	23.10%	12.39%	10.71%
1968	25.21%	10.16%	15.05%
1969	13.56%	4.97%	8.59%
1970	7.38%	3.34%	4.03%
1971	13.32%	8.42%	4.90%
1972	8.54%	7.53%	1.01%
1973	− 0.89%	2.01%	− 2.90%
1974	0.68%	− 2.35%	3.04%
1975	9.72%	3.21%	6.52%
1976	12.30%	4.87%	7.43%
1977	12.22%	− 0.21%	12.43%
1978	19.96%	4.32%	15.63%
1979	30.74%	14.76%	15.98%
1980	26.51%	13.95%	12.57%
1981	19.03%	8.08%	10.95%

YEAR	COMBINED REASONABLE RUNAWAYS AND LEADERS WITH LUSTER, 50 STOCKS VERSION	S&P 500	DIFFERENCE
1982	22.14%	14.05%	8.09%
1983	25.24%	17.27%	7.96%
1984	19.17%	14.76%	4.41%
1985	20.16%	14.71%	5.45%
1986	23.99%	19.87%	4.12%
1987	17.58%	16.49%	1.09%
1988	15.86%	15.38%	0.47%
1989	23.32%	20.40%	2.92%
1990	12.99%	13.14%	−0.16%
1991	16.58%	15.36%	1.22%
1992	21.30%	15.89%	5.41%
1993	20.95%	14.51%	6.44%
1994	13.79%	8.69%	5.10%
1995	21.64%	16.57%	5.07%
1996	19.18%	15.20%	3.98%
Average	17.41%	11.54%	5.86%
Median	19.03%	13.25%	5.78%
High	30.74%	22.30%	8.44%
Low	−0.89%	−2.35%	1.47%

	TABLE 23 COMBINED PORTFOLIO 10-YEAR ROLLING COMPOUND RETURNS, 1961–1996		
YEAR	COMBINED REASONABLE RUNAWAYS AND LEADERS WITH LUSTER, 50 STOCKS VERSION	S&P 500	DIFFERENCE
1952			
1953			
1954			
1955			
1956			
1957			
1958			
1959			
1960			
1961	19.86%	16.43%	3.43%
1962	17.63%	13.44%	4.19%
1963	19.87%	15.91%	3.96%
1964	17.18%	12.82%	4.36%
1965	17.89%	11.06%	6.82%
1966	14.86%	9.20%	5.67%
1967	21.15%	12.85%	8.31%
1968	19.52%	10.01%	9.52%
1969	14.07%	7.81%	6.26%
1970	14.26%	8.18%	6.08%
1971	13.11%	7.06%	6.06%
1972	15.59%	9.93%	5.66%
1973	11.40%	6.01%	5.39%
1974	6.93%	1.24%	5.69%
1975	8.54%	3.27%	5.27%
1976	12.81%	6.63%	6.18%
1977	10.36%	3.59%	6.78%
1978	9.04%	3.16%	5.88%
1979	14.73%	5.86%	8.87%
1980	17.82%	8.44%	9.38%
1981	15.62%	6.47%	9.15%

YEAR	COMBINED REASONABLE RUNAWAYS AND LEADERS WITH LUSTER, 50 STOCKS VERSION	S&P 500	DIFFERENCE
1982	17.07%	6.68%	10.39%
1983	22.57%	10.61%	11.96%
1984	24.82%	14.76%	10.06%
1985	23.30%	14.33%	8.97%
1986	21.49%	13.82%	7.66%
1987	19.84%	15.26%	4.57%
1988	20.46%	16.33%	4.13%
1989	21.23%	17.55%	3.68%
1990	16.52%	13.93%	2.59%
1991	20.23%	17.59%	2.64%
1992	19.43%	16.19%	3.24%
1993	18.37%	14.94%	3.43%
1994	18.46%	14.40%	4.06%
1995	17.23%	14.84%	2.39%
1996	17.88%	15.28%	2.59%
Average	16.98%	11.00%	5.98%
Median	17.73%	11.94%	5.78%
High	24.82%	17.59%	7.23%
Low	6.93%	1.24%	5.69%

TABLE 24
COMBINED PORTFOLIO, 50 STOCKS, HIGH AND LOW RETURNS, 1952–1996

	1-YEAR	5-YEAR	10-YEAR	15-YEAR	20-YEAR	25-YEAR
Combined RR plus Leaders 50 Stock Minimum	−24.30%	−0.89%	6.93%	9.42%	11.94%	14.85%
Combined RR plus Leaders 50 Stock Maximum	58.40%	30.78%	24.82%	24.32%	21.60%	18.16%
S&P 500 Minimum	−26.47%	−2.35%	1.24%	4.31%	6.53%	7.94%
S&P 500 Maximum	52.62%	22.30%	17.59%	16.79%	14.59%	12.55%

	TABLE 25 COMBINED PORTFOLIO $10,000 GROWTH	
YEAR	COMBINED REASONABLE RUNAWAYS AND LEADERS WITH LUSTER, 50 STOCKS VERSION	S&P 500
1951	$10,000.00	$10,000.00
1952	$11,105	$11,837
1953	$11,527	$11,720
1954	$17,832	$17,887
1955	$22,906	$23,532
1956	$28,094	$25,076
1957	$23,374	$22,372
1958	$36,510	$32,073
1959	$44,104	$35,909
1960	$44,693	$36,078
1961	$61,207	$45,779
1962	$56,341	$41,783
1963	$70,595	$51,309
1964	$87,079	$59,765
1965	$118,733	$67,205
1966	$112,321	$60,445
1967	$159,271	$74,939
1968	$217,246	$83,227
1969	$164,455	$76,153
1970	$169,471	$79,207
1971	$209,890	$90,541
1972	$239,904	$107,726
1973	$207,757	$91,933
1974	$170,153	$67,599
1975	$269,522	$92,745
1976	$374,905	$114,856
1977	$427,017	$106,609
1978	$516,050	$113,603
1979	$649,966	$134,551
1980	$873,554	$178,173
1981	$895,829	$169,424
1982	$1,160,547	$205,698

YEAR	COMBINED REASONABLE RUNAWAYS AND LEADERS WITH LUSTER, 50 STOCKS VERSION	S&P 500
1983	$1,589,949	$252,001
1984	$1,562,125	$267,801
1985	$2,188,537	$353,926
1986	$2,625,151	$419,296
1987	$2,608,087	$441,225
1988	$3,318,791	$515,395
1989	$4,455,477	$677,693
1990	$4,029,979	$656,210
1991	$5,654,060	$856,683
1992	$6,849,894	$922,390
1993	$8,589,767	$1,014,537
1994	$8,499,574	$1,027,828
1995	$10,730,713	$1,412,543
1996	$13,595,813	$1,738,417

TABLE 26
COMBINED PORTFOLIO, 25 STOCKS, ANNUAL RETURNS, 1952–1996

YEAR	COMBINED REASONABLE RUNAWAYS AND LEADERS WITH LUSTER, 25 STOCKS VERSION	S&P 500	DIFFERENCE
1952	13.65%	18.37%	− 4.72%
1953	2.72%	− 0.99%	3.71%
1954	63.62%	52.62%	11.00%
1955	30.32%	31.56%	− 1.24%
1956	20.98%	6.56%	14.42%
1957	− 11.91%	− 10.78%	− 1.13%
1958	60.85%	43.36%	17.49%
1959	23.19%	11.96%	11.23%
1960	5.03%	0.47%	4.56%
1961	45.04%	26.89%	18.15%
1962	− 8.83%	− 8.73%	− 0.10%
1963	28.12%	22.80%	5.32%
1964	24.25%	16.48%	7.77%
1965	43.01%	12.45%	30.56%
1966	− 5.11%	− 10.06%	4.95%
1967	53.32%	23.98%	29.34%
1968	48.02%	11.06%	36.96%
1969	− 23.58%	− 8.50%	− 15.08%
1970	2.82%	4.01%	− 1.19%
1971	25.92%	14.31%	11.61%
1972	14.60%	18.98%	− 4.38%
1973	− 17.85%	− 14.66%	− 3.19%
1974	− 18.52%	− 26.47%	7.95%
1975	61.01%	37.20%	23.81%
1976	39.17%	23.84%	15.33%
1977	15.13%	− 7.18%	22.31%
1978	14.10%	6.56%	7.54%
1979	24.02%	18.44%	5.58%
1980	23.23%	32.42%	− 9.19%
1981	2.42%	− 4.91%	7.33%

YEAR	COMBINED REASONABLE RUNAWAYS AND LEADERS WITH LUSTER, 25 STOCKS VERSION	S&P 500	DIFFERENCE
1982	31.04%	21.41%	9.63%
1983	37.03%	22.51%	14.52%
1984	−2.11%	6.27%	−8.38%
1985	37.02%	32.16%	4.86%
1986	21.18%	18.47%	2.71%
1987	−2.05%	5.23%	−7.28%
1988	25.59%	16.81%	8.78%
1989	38.42%	31.49%	6.93%
1990	−7.36%	−3.17%	−4.19%
1991	50.69%	30.55%	20.14%
1992	18.61%	7.67%	10.94%
1993	21.58%	9.99%	11.59%
1994	−5.81%	1.31%	−7.12%
1995	14.52%	37.43%	−22.91%
1996	21.43%	23.07%	−1.65%
Average	19.97%	13.41%	6.56%
Median	21.43%	14.31%	7.11%
High	63.62%	52.62%	11.00%
Low	−23.58%	−26.47%	2.89%
$10,000 grows to:	$16,404,008	$1,738,417	$14,665,591

	TABLE 27 COMBINED PORTFOLIO, 25 STOCKS, ROLLING 5-YEAR COMPOUND RETURNS, 1956–1996		
YEAR	COMBINED REASONABLE RUNAWAYS AND LEADERS WITH LUSTER, 25 STOCKS VERSION	S&P 500	DIFFERENCE
1952			
1953			
1954			
1955			
1956	24.67%	20.18%	4.48%
1957	18.48%	13.58%	4.90%
1958	29.59%	22.30%	7.29%
1959	22.44%	14.96%	7.49%
1960	17.27%	8.92%	8.35%
1961	21.61%	12.79%	8.81%
1962	22.44%	13.31%	9.14%
1963	17.00%	9.85%	7.14%
1964	17.20%	10.73%	6.47%
1965	24.66%	13.25%	11.41%
1966	14.52%	5.72%	8.80%
1967	27.06%	12.39%	14.67%
1968	30.79%	10.16%	20.63%
1969	18.67%	4.97%	13.70%
1970	11.09%	3.34%	7.75%
1971	17.56%	8.42%	9.14%
1972	10.91%	7.53%	3.38%
1973	−1.41%	2.01%	−3.42%
1974	−0.14%	−2.35%	2.22%
1975	9.23%	3.21%	6.03%
1976	11.44%	4.87%	6.57%
1977	11.54%	−0.21%	11.75%
1978	19.12%	4.32%	14.80%
1979	29.56%	14.76%	14.80%
1980	22.81%	13.95%	8.86%
1981	15.51%	8.08%	7.42%

YEAR	COMBINED REASONABLE RUNAWAYS AND LEADERS WITH LUSTER, 25 STOCKS VERSION	S&P 500	DIFFERENCE
1982	18.54%	14.05%	4.49%
1983	22.96%	17.27%	5.69%
1984	17.28%	14.76%	2.52%
1985	19.79%	14.71%	5.08%
1986	23.89%	19.87%	4.02%
1987	16.89%	16.49%	0.40%
1988	14.86%	15.38%	− 0.52%
1989	23.10%	20.40%	2.70%
1990	13.84%	13.14%	0.69%
1991	18.91%	15.36%	3.55%
1992	23.55%	15.89%	7.66%
1993	22.75%	14.51%	8.24%
1994	13.65%	8.69%	4.97%
1995	18.57%	16.57%	2.00%
1996	13.56%	15.20%	− 1.64%
Average	18.19%	11.54%	6.64%
Median	18.54%	13.25%	5.29%
High	30.79%	22.30%	8.48%
Low	− 1.41%	− 2.35%	0.94%

	TABLE 28 COMBINED PORTFOLIO, 25 STOCKS, ROLLING 10-YEAR RETURNS, 1961–1996		
YEAR	COMBINED REASONABLE RUNAWAYS AND LEADERS WITH LUSTER, 25 STOCKS VERSION	S&P 500	DIFFERENCE
1952			
1953			
1954			
1955			
1956			
1957			
1958			
1959			
1960			
1961	23.13%	16.43%	6.70%
1962	20.44%	13.44%	7.00%
1963	23.14%	15.91%	7.22%
1964	19.79%	12.82%	6.97%
1965	20.91%	11.06%	9.85%
1966	18.01%	9.20%	8.81%
1967	24.73%	12.85%	11.88%
1968	23.70%	10.01%	13.70%
1969	17.93%	7.81%	10.12%
1970	17.68%	8.18%	9.50%
1971	16.03%	7.06%	8.97%
1972	18.71%	9.93%	8.78%
1973	13.55%	6.01%	7.55%
1974	8.86%	1.24%	7.62%
1975	10.16%	3.27%	6.89%
1976	14.46%	6.63%	7.83%
1977	11.23%	3.59%	7.64%
1978	8.37%	3.16%	5.21%
1979	13.75%	5.86%	7.89%
1980	15.82%	8.44%	7.38%
1981	13.46%	6.47%	6.99%
1982	14.99%	6.68%	8.31%

YEAR	COMBINED REASONABLE RUNAWAYS AND LEADERS WITH LUSTER, 25 STOCKS VERSION	S&P 500	DIFFERENCE
1983	21.03%	10.61%	10.42%
1984	23.27%	14.76%	8.51%
1985	21.29%	14.33%	6.96%
1986	19.63%	13.82%	5.80%
1987	17.71%	15.26%	2.45%
1988	18.84%	16.33%	2.52%
1989	20.16%	17.55%	2.61%
1990	16.78%	13.93%	2.85%
1991	21.37%	17.59%	3.78%
1992	20.17%	16.19%	3.98%
1993	18.74%	14.94%	3.80%
1994	18.28%	14.40%	3.89%
1995	16.18%	14.84%	1.34%
1996	16.20%	15.28%	0.92%
Average	17.74%	11.00%	6.74%
Median	18.15%	11.94%	6.20%
High	24.73%	17.59%	7.14%
Low	8.37%	1.24%	7.13%

TABLE 29
COMBINED PORTFOLIO, 25 STOCKS, HIGH AND LOW RETURNS, 1952–1996

	1-YEAR	5-YEAR	10-YEAR	15-YEAR	20-YEAR	25-YEAR
Combined RR plus Leaders 25 Stock Minimum	−23.48%	−1.41%	8.37%	11.57%	13.49%	15.24%
Combined RR plus Leaders 25 Stock Maximum	63.62%	30.79%	24.73%	25.63%	20.75%	18.42%
S&P 500 Minimum	−26.47%	−2.35%	1.24%	4.31%	6.53%	7.94%
S&P 500 Maximum	52.62%	22.30%	17.59%	16.79%	14.59%	12.55%

	COMBINED REASONABLE RUNAWAYS AND LEADERS WITH LUSTER, 25 STOCKS	
YEAR	VERSION	S&P 500
1951	$10,000.00	$10,000.00
1952	$11,365	$11,837
1953	$11,674	$11,720
1954	$19,101	$17,887
1955	$24,894	$23,532
1956	$30,115	$25,076
1957	$26,530	$22,372
1958	$42,674	$32,073
1959	$52,572	$35,909
1960	$55,219	$36,078
1961	$80,091	$45,779
1962	$73,020	$41,783
1963	$93,551	$51,309
1964	$116,242	$59,765
1965	$166,235	$67,205
1966	$157,745	$60,445
1967	$241,852	$74,939
1968	$357,990	$83,227
1969	$273,569	$76,153
1970	$281,277	$79,207
1971	$354,177	$90,541
1972	$405,874	$107,726
1973	$333,411	$91,933
1974	$271,672	$67,599
1975	$437,422	$92,745
1976	$608,759	$114,856
1977	$700,836	$106,609
1978	$799,671	$113,603
1979	$991,755	$134,551
1980	$1,222,141	$178,173
1981	$1,251,747	$169,424

TABLE 30
COMBINED PORTFOLIO, 25 STOCKS, $10,000 GROWTH

YEAR	COMBINED REASONABLE RUNAWAYS AND LEADERS WITH LUSTER, 25 STOCKS VERSION	S&P 500
1982	$1,640,337	$205,698
1983	$2,247,766	$252,001
1984	$2,200,375	$267,801
1985	$3,014,947	$353,926
1986	$3,653,524	$419,296
1987	$3,578,757	$441,225
1988	$4,494,405	$515,395
1989	$6,221,116	$677,693
1990	$5,763,487	$656,210
1991	$8,685,208	$856,683
1992	$10,301,734	$922,390
1993	$12,524,752	$1,014,537
1994	$11,796,974	$1,027,828
1995	$13,509,580	$1,412,543
1996	$16,404,008	$1,738,417

TABLE 31 DOGS OF THE DOW ANNUAL RETURNS, 1952–1996			
YEAR	DOGS OF THE DOW	S&P 500	DIFFERENCE
1952	13.77%	18.37%	− 4.60%
1953	− 7.21%	− 0.99%	− 6.22%
1954	66.73%	52.62%	14.11%
1955	34.90%	31.56%	3.34%
1956	10.53%	6.56%	3.97%
1957	− 8.07%	− 10.78%	2.71%
1958	43.84%	43.36%	0.48%
1959	9.52%	11.96%	− 2.44%
1960	− 0.10%	0.47%	− 0.57%
1961	24.16%	26.89%	− 2.73%
1962	− 0.15%	− 8.73%	8.58%
1963	22.73%	22.80%	− 0.07%
1964	23.07%	16.48%	6.59%
1965	20.42%	12.45%	7.97%
1966	− 15.66%	− 10.06%	− 5.60%
1967	26.86%	23.98%	2.88%
1968	11.19%	11.06%	0.13%
1969	− 12.78%	− 8.50%	− 4.28%
1970	3.48%	4.01%	− 0.53%
1971	5.75%	14.31%	− 8.56%
1972	23.85%	18.98%	4.87%
1973	3.88%	− 14.66%	18.54%
1974	1.02%	− 26.47%	27.49%
1975	58.79%	37.20%	21.59%
1976	34.47%	23.84%	10.63%
1977	− 2.66%	− 7.18%	4.52%
1978	2.40%	6.56%	− 4.16%
1979	9.67%	18.44%	− 8.77%
1980	27.53%	32.42%	− 4.89%
1981	2.68%	− 4.91%	7.59%
1982	20.68%	21.41%	− 0.73%
1983	39.22%	22.51%	16.71%

YEAR	DOGS OF THE DOW	S&P 500	DIFFERENCE
1984	6.27%	6.27%	0.00%
1985	31.20%	32.16%	−0.96%
1986	28.12%	18.47%	9.65%
1987	6.89%	5.23%	1.66%
1988	22.00%	16.81%	5.19%
1989	27.37%	31.49%	−4.12%
1990	−7.90%	−3.17%	−4.73%
1991	39.00%	30.55%	8.45%
1992	15.40%	7.67%	7.73%
1993	28.20%	9.99%	18.21%
1994	4.00%	1.31%	2.69%
1995	37.70%	37.43%	0.27%
1996	26.40%	23.07%	3.33%
Average	16.87%	13.41%	3.46%
Median	15.40%	14.31%	1.09%
High	66.73%	52.62%	14.11%
Low	−15.66%	−26.47%	10.81%
$10,000 grows to:	$6,600,019	$1,738,417	$4,861,602

TABLE 32
DOGS OF THE DOW ROLLING 5-YEAR RETURNS, 1952–1996

YEAR	DOGS OF THE DOW	S&P 500	DIFFERENCE
1952			
1953			
1954			
1955			
1956	21.28%	20.18%	1.10%
1957	16.22%	13.58%	2.65%
1958	26.87%	22.30%	4.57%
1959	16.64%	14.96%	1.69%
1960	9.84%	8.92%	0.92%
1961	12.43%	12.79%	− 0.37%
1962	14.30%	13.31%	1.00%
1963	10.73%	9.85%	0.88%
1964	13.34%	10.73%	2.62%
1965	17.66%	13.25%	4.41%
1966	8.90%	5.72%	3.19%
1967	14.24%	12.39%	1.85%
1968	12.01%	10.16%	1.85%
1969	4.56%	4.97%	− 0.41%
1970	1.43%	3.34%	− 1.91%
1971	6.13%	8.42%	− 2.29%
1972	5.62%	7.53%	− 1.91%
1973	4.19%	2.01%	2.18%
1974	7.30%	− 2.35%	9.65%
1975	16.89%	3.21%	13.69%
1976	22.65%	4.87%	17.77%
1977	16.88%	− 0.21%	17.09%
1978	16.54%	4.32%	12.22%
1979	18.47%	14.76%	3.71%
1980	13.39%	13.95%	− 0.56%
1981	7.44%	8.08%	− 0.65%
1982	12.16%	14.05%	− 1.89%
1983	19.26%	17.27%	1.99%

YEAR	DOGS OF THE DOW	S&P 500	DIFFERENCE
1984	18.51%	14.76%	3.76%
1985	19.19%	14.71%	4.47%
1986	24.58%	19.87%	4.71%
1987	21.60%	16.49%	5.11%
1988	18.43%	15.38%	3.04%
1989	22.80%	20.40%	2.39%
1990	14.41%	13.14%	1.26%
1991	16.29%	15.36%	0.92%
1992	18.08%	15.89%	2.19%
1993	19.26%	14.51%	4.75%
1994	14.52%	8.69%	5.83%
1995	24.11%	16.57%	7.54%
1996	21.78%	15.20%	6.57%
Average	15.15%	11.54%	3.60%
Median	16.29%	13.25%	3.04%
High	26.87%	22.30%	4.57%
Low	1.43%	−2.35%	3.79%

	TABLE 33 DOGS OF THE DOW ROLLING 10-YEAR COMPOUND RETURNS, 1961–1996		
YEAR	DOGS OF THE DOW	S&P 500	DIFFERENCE
1952			
1953			
1954			
1955			
1956			
1957			
1958			
1959			
1960			
1961	16.77%	16.43%	0.34%
1962	15.26%	13.44%	1.82%
1963	18.53%	15.91%	2.62%
1964	14.98%	12.82%	2.16%
1965	13.68%	11.06%	2.62%
1966	10.65%	9.20%	1.45%
1967	14.27%	12.85%	1.42%
1968	11.37%	10.01%	1.36%
1969	8.86%	7.81%	1.05%
1970	9.25%	8.18%	1.06%
1971	7.51%	7.06%	0.45%
1972	9.85%	9.93%	−0.09%
1973	8.03%	6.01%	2.02%
1974	5.92%	1.24%	4.68%
1975	8.89%	3.27%	5.62%
1976	14.09%	6.63%	7.46%
1977	11.11%	3.59%	7.52%
1978	10.20%	3.16%	7.04%
1979	12.75%	5.86%	6.89%
1980	15.13%	8.44%	6.68%
1981	14.79%	6.47%	8.32%
1982	14.49%	6.68%	7.81%
1983	17.90%	10.61%	7.29%

YEAR	DOGS OF THE DOW	S&P 500	DIFFERENCE
1984	18.49%	14.76%	3.74%
1985	16.25%	14.33%	1.92%
1986	15.69%	13.82%	1.87%
1987	16.78%	15.26%	1.52%
1988	18.84%	16.33%	2.52%
1989	20.64%	17.55%	3.09%
1990	16.77%	13.93%	2.85%
1991	20.36%	17.59%	2.77%
1992	19.83%	16.19%	3.64%
1993	18.84%	14.94%	3.90%
1994	18.59%	14.40%	4.19%
1995	19.16%	14.84%	4.32%
1996	19.00%	15.28%	3.72%
Average	14.54%	11.00%	3.55%
Median	15.06%	11.94%	3.11%
High	20.64%	17.59%	3.04%
Low	5.92%	1.24%	4.68%

TABLE 34
DOGS OF THE DOW HIGH AND LOW RETURNS, 1952–1996

FOR ANY	1-YEAR	5-YEAR	10-YEAR	15-YEAR	20-YEAR	25-YEAR
Dogs of the Dow minimum compound return was	−15.66%	1.43%	5.92%	8.34%	10.36%	11.36%
Dogs of the Dow maximum compound return was	66.73%	26.87%	20.64%	20.83%	18.54%	18.38%
S&P 500 minimum compound return was	−26.47%	−2.35%	1.24%	4.31%	6.53%	7.94%
S&P 500 maximum compound return was	52.62%	22.30%	17.59%	16.79%	14.59%	12.55%

	TABLE 35 DOGS OF THE DOW $10,000 GROWTH	
YEAR	DOGS OF THE DOW	S&P 500
1951	$10,000.00	$10,000.00
1952	$11,377	$11,837
1953	$10,557	$11,720
1954	$17,601	$17,887
1955	$23,744	$23,532
1956	$26,244	$25,076
1957	$24,126	$22,372
1958	$34,703	$32,073
1959	$38,007	$35,909
1960	$37,969	$36,078
1961	$47,142	$45,779
1962	$47,072	$41,783
1963	$57,771	$51,309
1964	$71,099	$59,765
1965	$85,617	$67,205
1966	$72,210	$60,445
1967	$91,605	$74,939
1968	$101,856	$83,227
1969	$88,839	$76,153
1970	$91,930	$79,207
1971	$97,216	$90,541
1972	$120,402	$107,726
1973	$125,074	$91,933
1974	$126,350	$67,599
1975	$200,631	$92,745
1976	$269,788	$114,856
1977	$262,612	$106,609
1978	$268,914	$113,603
1979	$294,918	$134,551
1980	$376,109	$178,173
1981	$386,189	$169,424
1982	$466,053	$205,698
1983	$648,839	$252,001

YEAR	DOGS OF THE DOW	S&P 500
1984	$689,521	$267,801
1985	$904,652	$353,926
1986	$1,159,040	$419,296
1987	$1,238,898	$441,225
1988	$1,511,456	$515,395
1989	$1,925,141	$677,693
1990	$1,773,055	$656,210
1991	$2,464,546	$856,683
1992	$2,844,087	$922,390
1993	$3,646,119	$1,014,537
1994	$3,791,964	$1,027,828
1995	$5,221,534	$1,412,543
1996	$6,600,019	$1,738,417

YEAR	DOGS OF THE DOW	S&P 500	DIFFERENCE
1929	− 15.76%	− 8.42%	− 7.34%
1930	− 26.10%	− 24.90%	− 1.20%
1931	− 48.88%	− 43.34%	− 5.54%
1932	4.64%	− 8.19%	12.83%
1933	64.08%	53.99%	10.09%
1934	17.53%	− 1.44%	18.97%
1935	32.10%	47.67%	− 15.57%
1936	22.17%	33.92%	− 11.75%
1937	− 31.77%	− 35.03%	3.26%
1938	53.97%	31.12%	22.85%
1939	1.57%	− 0.41%	1.98%
1940	− 9.50%	− 9.78%	0.28%
1941	− 10.61%	− 11.59%	0.98%
1942	33.60%	20.34%	13.26%
1943	15.98%	25.90%	− 9.92%
1944	20.90%	19.75%	1.15%
1945	44.27%	36.44%	7.83%
1946	− 5.50%	− 8.07%	2.57%
1947	10.04%	5.71%	4.33%
1948	− 0.52%	5.50%	− 6.02%
1949	24.52%	18.79%	5.73%
1950	33.05%	31.71%	1.34%
1951	24.16%	24.02%	0.14%
1952	13.77%	18.37%	− 4.60%
1953	− 7.21%	− 0.99%	− 6.22%
1954	66.73%	52.62%	14.11%
1955	34.90%	31.56%	3.34%
1956	10.53%	6.56%	3.97%
1957	− 8.07%	− 10.78%	2.71%
1958	43.84%	43.36%	0.48%
1959	9.52%	11.96%	− 2.44%
1960	− 0.10%	0.47%	− 0.57%
1961	24.16%	26.89%	− 2.73%

BONUS TABLE 36
DOGS OF THE DOW ANNUAL RETURNS, 1929–1996

YEAR	DOGS OF THE DOW	S&P 500	DIFFERENCE
1962	− 0.15%	− 8.73%	8.58%
1963	22.73%	22.80%	− 0.07%
1964	23.07%	16.48%	6.59%
1965	20.42%	12.45%	7.97%
1966	− 15.66%	− 10.06%	− 5.60%
1967	26.86%	23.98%	2.88%
1968	11.19%	11.06%	0.13%
1969	− 12.78%	− 8.50%	− 4.28%
1970	3.48%	4.01%	− 0.53%
1971	5.75%	14.31%	− 8.56%
1972	23.85%	18.98%	4.87%
1973	3.88%	− 14.66%	18.54%
1974	1.02%	− 26.47%	27.49%
1975	58.79%	37.20%	21.59%
1976	34.47%	23.84%	10.63%
1977	− 2.66%	− 7.18%	4.52%
1978	2.40%	6.56%	− 4.16%
1979	9.67%	18.44%	− 8.77%
1980	27.53%	32.42%	− 4.89%
1981	2.68%	− 4.91%	7.59%
1982	20.68%	21.41%	− 0.73%
1983	39.22%	22.51%	16.71%
1984	6.27%	6.27%	0.00%
1985	31.20%	32.16%	− 0.96%
1986	28.12%	18.47%	9.65%
1987	6.89%	5.23%	1.66%
1988	22.00%	16.81%	5.19%
1989	27.37%	31.49%	− 4.12%
1990	− 7.90%	− 3.17%	− 4.73%
1991	39.00%	30.55%	8.45%
1992	15.40%	7.67%	7.73%
1993	28.20%	9.99%	18.21%
1994	4.00%	1.31%	2.69%
1995	37.70%	37.43%	0.27%
1996	26.40%	22.20%	4.20%

YEAR	DOGS OF THE DOW	S&P 500	DIFFERENCE
Average	14.90%	11.85%	3.04%
Median	15.69%	13.38%	2.31%
High	66.73%	53.99%	12.74%
Low	−48.88%	−43.34%	−5.54%
$10,000 grows to:	$33.956,939	$6,177,062	$27,779,878

TABLE 37 UTILITY STRATEGY ANNUAL RETURNS, 1985–1996			
YEAR	UTILITY STRATEGY	S&P 500	DIFFERENCE
1985	28.84%	32.16%	−3.32%
1986	36.99%	18.47%	18.52%
1987	−5.12%	5.23%	−10.35%
1988	14.70%	16.81%	−2.11%
1989	26.22%	31.49%	−5.27%
1990	3.97%	−3.17%	7.14%
1991	27.01%	30.55%	−3.54%
1992	13.10%	7.67%	5.43%
1993	12.33%	9.99%	2.34%
1994	−10.45%	1.31%	−11.76%
1995	33.90%	37.43%	−3.53%
1996	8.30%	23.07%	−14.77%
Average	15.82%	17.58%	−1.77%
Median	13.90%	17.64%	−3.74%
High	36.99%	37.43%	−0.44%
Low	−10.45%	−3.17%	−7.28%
$10,000 grows to:	$52,818	$64,914	−$12,096

TABLE 38
UTILITY STRATEGY $10,000 GROWTH

YEAR	UTILITY STRATEGY	S&P 500
1984	$10,000.00	$10,000.00
1985	$12,884.00	$13,216.00
1986	$17,649.79	$15,657.00
1987	$16,746.12	$16,475.86
1988	$19,207.80	$19,245.45
1989	$24,244.09	$25,305.84
1990	$25,206.58	$24,503.64
1991	$32,014.88	$31,989.51
1992	$36,208.82	$34,443.10
1993	$40,673.37	$37,883.97
1994	$36,423.00	$38,380.25
1995	$48,770.40	$52,745.97
1996	$52,818.35	$64,914.47

TABLE 39 CORE VALUE STRATEGY ANNUAL RETURNS, 1985–1996			
YEAR	CORE VALUE STRATEGY	S&P 500	DIFFERENCE
1985	45.15%	32.16%	12.99%
1986	31.24%	18.47%	12.77%
1987	10.55%	5.23%	5.32%
1988	22.84%	16.81%	6.03%
1989	30.15%	31.49%	− 1.34%
1990	8.76%	− 3.17%	11.93%
1991	19.66%	30.55%	− 10.89%
1992	15.91%	7.67%	8.24%
1993	15.85%	9.99%	5.86%
1994	4.80%	1.31%	3.49%
1995	43.18%	37.43%	5.75%
1996	13.50%	23.07%	− 9.57%
Average	21.80%	17.58%	4.22%
Median	17.79%	17.64%	0.15%
High	45.15%	37.43%	7.72%
Low	4.80%	− 3.17%	7.97%
$10,000 grows to:	$100,208	$64,914	$35,293

YEAR	CORE VALUE STRATEGY	S&P 500
TABLE 40		
CORE VALUE STRATEGY $10,000 GROWTH		
	$10,000.00	$10,000.00
1985	$14,515.00	$13,216.00
1986	$19,049.49	$15,657.00
1987	$21,059.21	$16,475.86
1988	$25,869.13	$19,245.45
1989	$33,668.67	$25,305.84
1990	$36,618.05	$24,503.64
1991	$43,817.16	$31,989.51
1992	$50,788.47	$34,443.10
1993	$58,838.44	$37,883.97
1994	$61,662.68	$38,380.25
1995	$88,288.63	$52,745.97
1996	$100,207.59	$64,914.47

INDEX